W9-BSA-095

FROM THE
OTHER SIDE *of*
THE WORLD

FROM THE
OTHER SIDE *of*
THE WORLD

EXTRAORDINARY
ENTREPRENEURS,
UNLIKELY PLACES

ELMIRA BAYRASLI

PublicAffairs
New York

Copyright © 2015 by Elmira Bayrasli.

Published in the United States by PublicAffairs™, a Member of the Perseus Books Group

All rights reserved.
Printed in the United States of America.

No part of this book may be reproduced in any manner whatsoever without written permission except in the case of brief quotations embodied in critical articles and reviews. For information, address PublicAffairs, 250 West 57th Street, 15th Floor, New York, NY 10107.

PublicAffairs books are available at special discounts for bulk purchases in the U.S. by corporations, institutions, and other organizations. For more information, please contact the Special Markets Department at the Perseus Books Group, 2300 Chestnut Street, Suite 200, Philadelphia, PA 19103, call (800) 810-4145, ext. 5000, or e-mail special.markets@perseusbooks.com.

Library of Congress Cataloging-in-Publication Data

Bayrasli, Elmira.
   From the other side of the world : extraordinary entrepreneurs, unlikely places / Elmira Bayrasli.—First Edition.
      pages cm
   Includes bibliographical references and index.
   ISBN 978-1-61039-303-4 (hardback)—ISBN 978-1-61039-304-1 (e-book)
1. New business enterprises. 2. Creative ability in business. 3. Success in business. I. Title.

HD62.5.B397 2015
338'.04—dc23
                                                                   2015015169

First Edition

10 9 8 7 6 5 4 3 2 1

$$A + B = E^3 + L + R,$$
with infinite love

Contents

Beyond Silicon Valley

> Sometimes it is the people who no one imagines anything of who do the things that no one can imagine.
>
> —*THE IMITATION GAME* (2014)

Just before I turned eight years old, my family and I traveled to my parents' hometown in central Turkey. Having made the long trip several times before, I braced myself for a summer of dirt roads and diarrhea, which the hole-in-the-ground toilet made abundantly more dreadful. This was a poor and underdeveloped country that had missed the Industrial Revolution and most of the advances that came along with it. There was electricity, but only intermittently. Telephones could only be found at the post office. On that trip I learned, much to my horror, that Turks did not even have—ketchup.

"Why can't I have ketchup?" I cried to my grandmother when she made me a plate of French fries.

"This isn't America," she consoled. In America, anything and everything was possible. Not in Turkey.

"Why doesn't someone just make some?" I asked indignantly.

Paved roads, clean water, proper plumbing, reliable electricity, and working phones require organized civil society and government. Having heard my parents complain about Turkey's inept leaders, I understood that the country my parents had left could not enjoy those things. Prosperity was something to be had in another language.

Ketchup, on the other hand, as only an eight-year-old mind can deduce, requires little more than tomatoes, which are plentiful in Turkey. Why, I asked my grandmother, had no Turk started a ketchup factory?

"Oh, hoh," my grandmother exclaimed, "it's so much trouble to start a business in Turkey."

Too young to understand what she meant, I took my grandmother's response as some sort of explanation for why Turkey was poor—and why my parents had made the difficult decision to emigrate to the United States. That realization stayed with me, along with the struggles my family faced in letting go of Turkey and adapting to America. Straddled between these two worlds, I became, at an early age, captivated with the idea of "saving the world": helping those who lived in places like Turkey, where little seemed to work.

Saving the world, I naïvely assumed in later years, could only be done by government, by the people in charge. Business to me was synonymous with Wall Street greed. Having held a summer job over several years at the white-shoe law firm Sullivan & Cromwell, where brothers Allen and John Foster Dulles—the former director of the CIA and secretary of state under President Eisenhower, respectively—once served as senior partners, I had witnessed the private sector's ugliness, its relentlessness and ruthlessness. There was just one way to look at business, and that was dog-eat-dog. That experience led me to believe that prosperity could only come from the public sector, through bureaucrats who were not caught up in the world of money.

Armed with degrees in political science and Middle Eastern studies, I joined the State Department in 1993, working as an assistant to Madeleine K. Albright, first when she was the US ambassador to the United Nations and then when she was secretary of state. At the State Department I grappled with the pressing and often heart-wrenching challenges of Rwanda, Bosnia, and Iraq, to which the only credible answer seemed to be government action.

During a four-year stint in Bosnia-Herzegovina, where I had signed on to a mission to help Bosnians recover from a brutal series of wars, I realized that I had overestimated the government's ability to resolve global challenges of economic development. I spent the majority of my time writing reports and navigating a bureaucratic maze, not contributing to the rehabilitation of a country and a people who had just survived war and genocide. While the government intended to "do good," it couldn't get out of the procedural straitjacket it had created for itself.

Procedure trumped people. Process trumped action. My work was confined to milestones that I was expected to achieve rather than being contingent upon improving the circumstances for Bosnians: rebuilding their homes, improving their education, and creating jobs.

"We need jobs," an older Bosnian woman told me during a visit to the country's east. "We need work to rebuild our country. But we don't have work. Our men go to Europe to find work." Bosnians needed businesses that would help the economy grow and bring jobs that would enable people to earn a decent living.

Job creation hadn't yet factored into diplomacy or aid work. Aid was squarely focused on human rights and democracy, which, as the same Bosnian woman pointed out to me, meant nothing when they couldn't make a living. By the time I left Bosnia in 2006, I was disillusioned with the State Department as well as outside intervention and handouts. Diplomacy alone could not improve lives. More than roundtables, confidence-building measures, and platitudes, places like Bosnia needed jobs, markets, trade, and commerce. They needed to develop their economies. They needed entrepreneurship.

By the start of the new millennium entrepreneurship had become all the rage. It seized the imagination of businesspeople, celebrities, and politicians and became a buzzword that could be heard everywhere: a better way of making a living than an office career, a better way of creating jobs and wealth, a better way of solving problems, and especially, a better way of saving the world. After joining the New York–based nonprofit Endeavor, which supports emerging market entrepreneurs, in 2006, I came to understand what all those things meant—and what they didn't mean.

Many consider entrepreneurship to be the culmination of an idea or a dream. But this conventional wisdom barely skims the surface of what actually happens. In coming face to face with individuals around the world who had started businesses and scaled them up to be million-dollar-plus enterprises, I came to understand that there was much more.

While entrepreneurship does start with an idea or dream, it is in fact the ability to overcome obstacles and embrace, as economist and godfather of innovation Joseph Schumpeter noted, "creative destruction." Creative destruction is the elimination of old methods and activities, replacing them with new approaches, new markets, and new paradigms. That is what makes entrepreneurship different from a small business such as a dry cleaner, a diner, or a repair shop. Whereas a small business provides a good or a service and employs a handful of people, entrepreneurs are the manifestation of an opportunity that not only generates wealth and produces prosperity, but also remakes the socioeconomic landscape. Entrepreneurs create new business models and give rise to new industries, which enable new possibilities. In the wake of globalization, individuals everywhere—in Africa, Asia, Latin America, and the Middle East—were enabled with those new possibilities.

Globalization in the post–Cold War era had made it easier to communicate and travel across borders. That stimulated tremendous economic activity. High-tech companies in Silicon Valley outsourced production to countries such as China, India, and Israel. In doing so they created jobs and, more significantly, transferred knowledge and inspiration.

Today the next Steve Jobs lives in the likeliest of places: in Turkey, Nigeria, Pakistan, Mexico, Russia, India, China, and beyond. It is only a matter of time before we see his or her big idea, an idea that will no doubt change our lives, and if we're lucky, maybe it will be an idea that saves the world.

It's the Obstacles, Stupid

Obstacles are those frightful things you see when you take your eyes off your goal.

—HENRY FORD

Invincible—that's the only way to describe eBay at the start of the new millennium. The Internet company not only survived the dot-com bust that wiped out thousands of Silicon Valley startups in 2000. By 2004 it netted over $3 billion in revenues. Hundreds of millions of people in nearly two dozen countries were buying and selling on eBay's platform. It was well on its way to becoming, as its slogan boasted, "The World's Online Marketplace."

In 2004 eBay decided to conquer new customers in new territory. China stood high on its list. With a billion plus people and a rising economy in which millions had moved into the middle class and were eager to spend their newly found wealth, China would make eBay the most valuable company in the world. The company didn't think twice about expanding into the country—and the approach it would take to do so.

Perhaps it should have. When eBay entered China in 2004, it encountered a rapidly evolving and ambitious market, filled with rapidly expanding and determined—even relentless— entrepreneurs, entrepreneurs like those in Silicon Valley, with big dreams and unconventional methods of operation. Jack Ma, a former English teacher in southern China, was one such entrepreneur. He stood ready to foil eBay's plans.

Following a visit to the United States in the mid-1990s, where he discovered the Internet, Ma brought this technology back to China. While he, like many others at the time, had no real idea of the Internet's true potential and impact, he saw it, much as others did, as a new tool to advance business. Advancing business was something everyone in China, particularly its heavy-handed government, took an interest in.

Ma launched China Pages, a searchable listing of Chinese companies, in 1995. It flopped. Yet instead of retreating to teaching, Ma soldiered on. The Internet, he suspected, would only increase in importance. Therefore he not only kept his hand in the tech space, he followed Web trends with a religious fervor. He even agreed to spend some time running a state-owned information technology company, the China International Electronic Commerce Center.

A few years later the Internet did explode. It had entered the mainstream, especially for business. More and more companies used it as a resource to improve their operations as well as their bottom line. More and more online startups sprouted. The future of business lay in the digital realm. Honing in on this development, Jack Ma rolled out Alibaba, a site that connected China's businesses to one another— the Google of supply chains.

Alibaba took off. It had become a hit with businesses and those wanting to start a business in China, which made it one of China's fastest-growing websites.

Jack Ma felt, however, that he could not stop there. In order to survive in and eventually win the tech space in China—let alone emerge as a contender on the world stage—Alibaba needed to move beyond being a site for business. The site had to offer value to individuals and convince them to use it.

The tech startups in Silicon Valley that had survived the dot-com bust—Amazon, eBay, and Priceline—had done just that. Each in its own way had become an integral tool for those who used its site. As time passed, these companies—especially eBay—looked abroad to persuade others to see them the same way.

"Someday, eBay would come in our direction," Jack Ma once told a reporter. Ma was prepared to stop it—and to do more. He wanted to prove that China could also innovate. Given its history and political circumstances—China was a communist state—Chinese talent had not been given an opportunity to do anything beyond laboring in factories. Throughout the twentieth century, China not only lagged behind the West, it suffocated under dire poverty and underdevelopment. This impeded Chinese potential.

"Chinese brains are just as good as theirs," Ma told seventeen people who had gathered in his apartment in 1999 to work on what became Alibaba. The "theirs" he referred to were the engineers and techies in Silicon Valley and Seattle who had pioneered the tech and Internet revolution.

"If we're a good team and we know what we want to do, then one of us can defeat ten of them," Ma said.

This was not just mere trash talk. As the Internet grew, Jack Ma saw the potential for it to emancipate China from its assembly-line economy, which merely put together Western products. This new technology could make it possible for Chinese minds to come up with their own products and services—for China as well as the world. The Internet transformed customers into participants: critics, inventors, and troubleshooters. The Internet gave people a voice to share their concerns, ideas, and stories. And that started to turn progress into a two-way street. Though China, along with many other countries outside the West, still had many obstacles to overcome—a lack of skilled labor, poor infrastructure, a lack of capital, insecurity, monopolies, corruption, a weak rule of law, and the status quo—it finally could compete with advanced economies such as those of the United States, Europe, and Japan. China even had a shot at beating them.

Committed to competing with the likes of eBay, Ma launched an eBay-like consumer-to-consumer marketplace in 2004, Taobao. He did so just as eBay landed in China and stood ready to capture the market. eBay had acquired Each-Net, a Chinese e-commerce site. Because the Internet and, in particular the e-commerce industry, had not reached any type of tipping point in China, Ma aimed to influence and shape both and thus thwart eBay's efforts. China, Ma felt, no longer had to import from the West. On the Internet, China could make its own mark.

The strength Jack Ma built into Taobao was the very thing that had underpinned eBay's success, but that the company had lost sight of: customer satisfaction. Ma made sure that Taobao, which translates into "hunt for treasures," resonated with Chinese consumers, who were different from those in the West. Chinese customers valued social interaction with sellers—they wanted to know them. Taobao's instant messaging and chat feature met that need. Taobao was also free. Though eBay's management criticized Jack Ma, noting that "free is not a business model," and continued to charge both buyers and sellers for transactions, Ma remained steadfast. He chose customers over profit.

Within two years, Alibaba and its subsidiary, Taobao, had captured 95 percent of the Chinese online marketplace share. eBay had put up a fierce fight, pouring hundreds of millions of dollars into its efforts in China. It even offered to acquire Alibaba and Taobao. eBay's chief executive officer (CEO) at the time, Meg Whitman, famously invited Jack Ma to Silicon Valley for a visit to eBay's headquarters. It was not, however, enough to persuade Jack Ma to sell or to beat his company. Ma had brokered an agreement with the search engine Yahoo, which invested $1 billion in Alibaba. That deal, along with Jack Ma's persistent efforts to build a world-class company, forced eBay to fold. Alibaba had won. And that win was a warning to Silicon Valley: global entrepreneurs have arrived.

Entrepreneurs like Jack Ma—not only from China but from many other places outside the West—are building high-growth companies that are challenging established businesses in the West and the newer Silicon Valley tech titans. These individuals are shifting the axis of global innovation and entrepreneurship. As they do so, they offer important reminders about entrepreneurship and the entrepreneurial process. Entrepreneurship isn't about a place.

Regardless of locale, entrepreneurship is about community, fortitude, persistence, resilience, trust, and values—and using those qualities to overcome obstacles.

• • •

THE ASTONISHING ascent of former "developing" countries such as China in recent years supports the excitement surrounding entrepreneurship. Their transition from aid dependence to economic growth has come not at the hands of corporations and conglomerates, but through startups. Indeed, entrepreneurs have catalyzed progress in previously downtrodden and hopeless places.

Yet it is a mistake to see Jack Ma and other entrepreneurs around the world as a new phenomenon. The developing world has long been filled with entrepreneurs who have brought few results or benefits to greater society. Lacking alternative educational or employment opportunities, people's very survival has depended on their launching their own endeavors. Because of a lack of support systems, these microenterprises haven't grown into roaring businesses that generate jobs or revenue or stimulate investment. To paraphrase economist and historian Ranil Dissanayake, what distinguishes techies in Silicon Valley from a roadside seller or a shopkeeper isn't their sophistication, but simply the presence of conditions that are necessary to sustain and scale a business idea. This is a key reason that rich countries are rich and poor ones are not. *It's the obstacles, stupid.*

Obstacles are the bane of every entrepreneur. Anyone who has started a business, anywhere in the world, has confronted some barrier that has made running that business difficult, if not impossible. In weak and underdeveloped societies, these barriers are so numerous and entrenched that they represent a profound impediment to economic growth and national development.

In my work with entrepreneurs around the world, I found seven recurring obstacles: lack of skilled labor and management, poor infrastructure, lack of collaborative space, monopolies, corruption, weak rule of law, and the resistance of the status quo.

From the Other Side of the World examines these obstacles and how seven entrepreneurs from seven countries are battling them. They are bright, creative, and ambitious people determined to realize their respective visions, in their own countries. Undeterred by the roadblocks in their way, they have focused on building culture, leveraging networks, creating collaborative spaces, collaborating with the competition, leading with values, harnessing talent, and simply using technology. Their approaches bypass barriers, create jobs, generate revenue, and draw in investments—ultimately aiding in their respective countries' development. And that is redefining entrepreneurship globally.

This book contains eyewitness accounts that open a window on new kinds of entrepreneurs who are disrupting markets and forcing a universal shift in business, investment, economics, politics, and society. Their work, as well as their approaches, offer business and leadership lessons to entrepreneurs and everyone looking to lead—everywhere:

- In İstanbul, Turkey, Bülent Çelebi, an experienced engineer, struggles to find the right talent to roll out his cutting-edge wireless technology across his country as well as in Europe and the United States, where his company has expanded.

- In Lagos, Nigeria, Tayo Oviosu, a former Silicon Valley executive, grapples with poor infrastructure to bring financial services to Nigerians and all Africans—and thereby jumpstart African growth.

- As CNN displays images of the latest bombing in Pakistan, Monis Rahman, a computer engineer, uses his Internet business to reframe the world's perceptions of his people.

- In Monterrey, Mexico, Enrique Junco Gomez, an entrepreneur running an energy-efficiency business, battles his country's monopolies.

- In Mumbai, India, Shaffi Mather, an activist, tries to tackle his country's endemic corruption through a for-profit ambulance service.

- Yana Yakovleva, the founder of a chemical company in Moscow, Russia, who had been unjustly jailed, stands up to the Kremlin and refuses to be defeated by her country's weak rule of law.

- Finally, in Beijing, Lei Jun, the so-called Steve Jobs of China, develops cutting-edge smartphones and software applications in an environment hungry to unleash Chinese innovation but resistant to social and political change.

These entrepreneurs' stories offer important insights into and important lessons about building enterprises under impossible conditions—and succeeding. They are lessons not only for entrepreneurs but also for companies and investors eager to move beyond global markets and supply chains and step into, understand, and collaborate on global innovation. As Turkey, Nigeria, Pakistan, Mexico, India, Russia, and China grow in wealth, so too do their capacity and capability for developing groundbreaking inventions. Apple, Facebook, and Google may have come out of Silicon Valley, but with the rapid pace of globalization, it is almost certain that the next "big thing" will hail from another corner of the world.

The greatest dynamism in the business world today is no longer confined to Silicon Valley. Entrepreneurship and innovation—along with the lessons they beget—now thrive overseas. Entrepreneurs around the world are changing the Silicon Valley startup story into a universal one.

ONE

The Green Light:
Attracting Talent and Nurturing Culture

It's not a faith in technology. It's faith in people.

—STEVE JOBS

Kars and İstanbul

A piercing green light caught my eye. It blinked at the end of the hallway of a shabby hotel in an isolated town in a remote corner of Turkey. I had traveled to Kars, once a battleground of empires—Armenian, Georgian, Ottoman, Russian—but now a forgotten outpost on the rocky plain where eastern Anatolia touches the Caucasus Mountains.

Mount Ararat, the fabled resting place of Noah's ark, is nearby. The Christian tour groups that use it as a rendezvous and resting point are one of the few contacts Kars has with the world outside. A recent excavation of the ancient Armenian city of Ani had begun to attract archaeologists and history buffs from all over. Curious about what had brought me, a Turkish-American woman traveling alone, to this whistle-stop, the desk clerk who greeted me upon my late-night arrival quizzed me, "What are your plans in Kars?" The handful of mustachioed men with leathery skin sitting in the lobby's creaking chairs momentarily put down their Marlboros and worry beads to listen to my response. I shrugged my shoulders and, in Turkish, asked for a room.

With my key in hand, I rode up in the cramped, unsteady elevator and stepped out into the hall. That's when I saw the green light. What a strange place for a security camera, I thought. Or was it an alarm system? Though poor and primitive, Kars didn't feel dangerous. It felt monotonous and resigned. Aside from a handful of tourists who passed through it, little had changed over the centuries. People farmed, milked their cows, went to the mosque, and went to bed early. Until the late 1990s the local newspaper had still published day-old news on a nineteenth-century Baumann woodblock press. I felt my way down the dark corridor and into my room.

I tried to sleep, but the couple next door made dozing off impossible. Turning up the volume on the television did not help. In desperation, I reached for my laptop to write or do some work, even though I had come to Kars to escape both.

Inspired by Orhan Pamuk's novel *Snow*, which was set in Kars, I had traveled there in 2007 to undertake a self-guided literary tour. It was my getaway from the daily grind of a job focused on supporting entrepreneurs around the world through startup challenges and making introductions to mentors and investors. It was a great job—one that had opened my eyes to the talent and ideas that existed abroad, but a job in which I only grappled with data about the wealth and jobs these entrepreneurs created. I had not more than a vague idea, much less appreciation, for what that meant. These entrepreneurs only existed to me on a piece of paper. I was not yet aware of their accomplishments and true significance, not yet aware of how they were breaking barriers and the status quo, changing what was economically possible in their countries, laying the foundations for an entrepreneurial ecosystem similar to that of Silicon Valley, and thereby turning entrepreneurship into a global phenomenon.

After grabbing my MacBook out of the bottom of my bag and running my fingers over the keyboard, however, I stumbled upon something that made me take notice of one particular entrepreneur.

I began to type a diary entry about the long day's travel. As is my habit, I started at the end, with the most recent event: *Got to Kars near midnight; streets completely empty . . .* when midsentence a pop-up box appeared: *Choose the WiFi network you want to join from the list below.* WiFi?! I didn't expect that. From its paper-thin walls that bled yellow stains at the edges to its cheap wooden bed slats, this was a fleabag hotel in the middle of nowhere.

My head jerked left and right as my eyes scanned the room for a router. *Wait, the green light that was flickering down the hall; could that be a? . . .* Before I could finish the thought I had run out into the hall. Sure enough, the light that I had noticed upon my arrival came from a wireless router. Still not convinced, I stepped closer to it for further confirmation. As I did, I noticed that it wasn't a router with labels I was familiar with in the United States: D-Link,

Linksys, or Netgear. It had the logo of a Turkish company on it: AirTies.

I knew AirTies, a company that develops and manufactures wireless devices in Turkey. Its CEO, Bülent Çelebi, was one of the entrepreneurs whom the nonprofit I worked for, Endeavor, assisted. Until that moment, however, I had only read about his products. I had never seen or used them. Since this was a wireless router—hardly an innovation— I hadn't thought much about it. Standing before it, however, and watching its blinking green light, I started to get excited. *Technology by a Turk!*

In all the years I had traveled to and from Turkey, the country where my parents grew up, Turks hadn't managed to deliver and receive reliable water, electricity, or phone service. A Turkish wireless router represented a significant leap forward—a fact that only resonated with me as I stood in front of it. It filled me with pride and the urge to run back downstairs and tell the room full of men, "The WiFi is Turkish!"—a revelation that would surely shock them as it did me, a revelation possibly more shocking than my solitary midnight arrival.

"The wireless Internet," I said to the desk clerk upon entering the deserted lobby the next morning, "I'm so impressed you have it." But before I could say anything about it being Turkish, the clerk leapt to life. "*Abla*," he leaned in, engaging me as his "sister." "It is made by a Turk." Taken aback, I didn't know how to respond. I couldn't imagine that someone in Kars would know about AirTies and its Turkish founder.

"Yes," he said, nodding his head. "It is someone who started a company in İstanbul. He came from the United States to start a technology business here, in Turkey, can you believe that, *abla*?"

In 2004 Bülent, the forty-nine-year old CEO of Ubicom, a microchip company, relocated his family—a wife and two sons—from Silicon Valley to İstanbul to develop a new wireless router that would connect the Internet not only to a computer but to other electronic devices such as a music player, a game console, or a television set. Bülent even talked about connecting a washing machine to the World Wide Web. As a seasoned engineer, Bülent saw the direction technology was headed. In the future, every device and gadget—air conditioners, cars, dishwashers, doors, televisions, and thermostats—would connect to the Internet—what technologist Kevin Ashton in 1999 called "the Internet of things."

Indeed, launching a tech startup in Turkey did seem unbelievable. Turks were not businesspeople or entrepreneurs. They were the heirs of rulers and fighters—sons and daughters of the Ottoman Empire. Turks conquered. They left trade, commerce, and business to other ethnic groups: Armenians, Greeks, and Jews.

Neither were Turks "techies," the slang term for computer and gadget geeks. For decades, Turks acquired their technology from abroad, investing little to no resources in developing their own. Even then the technology was limited, targeted primarily for defense or used by the upper class. Throughout the twentieth century the majority of Turks had little access to innovations, nor would they until well into the second decade of the twenty-first century. Their country was a politically unstable backwater. Moreover, Turkish leaders commanded a closed market, cluttering the economy with unproductive, state-run enterprises. That, along with a handful of family monopolies, stifled competition and thereby entrepreneurship.

A series of military coups from 1960 to 1980 further worsened economic conditions and the country's already inadequate infrastructure. The government in Ankara lacked funds for roads, bridges, and electrical networks. It was one of the reasons landline telephones only became mainstream in Turkey in the mid-1980s, and cable television didn't appear in the country until the 1990s. Unleashing any type of technology under such conditions seemed naïve, as did building an innovation-based business. Turkey didn't have the framework, let alone the ecosystem to nurture startups. Startups in Turkey, regardless of the industry, faced the same obstacles I had seen elsewhere: poor infrastructure, lack of collaborative space, monopolies, corruption, weak rule of law, and resistance to changing the status quo. That is why so many of its talented citizens left. In fact, it was this lack of talent—another pressing obstacle—that made it hard to believe that Bülent Çelebi could actually make a go of AirTies.

Yet he did.

Curious to learn how, I dived deep into understanding AirTies and Bülent's journey to build it. What I found opened my eyes and made me see entrepreneurs and entrepreneurship in a new light: It's no longer just about Silicon Valley.

Individuals around the world are overcoming obstacles and building scalable businesses. Some, like AirTies, are becoming globally competitive. As they do they are transforming what is possible in their communities. At the same time, they are expanding the scope and depth of entrepreneurship itself.

• • •

MAJESTICALLY SITUATED between Europe and Asia, İstanbul is known as the "city of seven hills." It should be seventy. The former seat of the Roman, Byzantine, and Ottoman Empires, this ancient metropolis is up and down at every corner, with nothing on a straight plane. The city has no grid. Its only constant reference point is the Bosporus strait. İstanbul's streets flow like the strait: they are winding and random. Its buildings are the same, locking together without rationale, but naturally, like Lego blocks on top of one another.

The older of these buildings are made of dense and impenetrable concrete. Sound does not carry easily between or within their thick walls. Nor do the continuous wavelength signals that American-designed wireless routers emit.

The average wireless router is a device that transfers data from a phone line or fiber optic cable to a computer. The router transfers the data through radio waves, which often have a limited range and require manual intervention in the case of interruption. When radio waves are cut off the user has to reset the router. Amid İstanbul's dense and impenetrable buildings, routers cut off regularly.

"That impenetrability was an opportunity," Bülent Çelebi told me as we sat in his large, spacious office. "We wanted to build a wireless router that could stream without interruption, *okay?*" Bülent added "okay" at the end of just about every point he made—a nervous tick.

His office is headquartered in Mecidiyeköy, the part of the city that has become İstanbul's financial district. It is a massive headquarters. AirTies takes up several sleek-styled buildings on an entire block in what is otherwise a crowded and traffic-choked neighborhood. It is reminiscent of the jumbo campuses in Silicon Valley, where Cisco, Google, Yahoo, and other high-tech companies occupy miles of ground. This is highly unusual in İstanbul, where offices and people are crammed into a single, or even half of, a floor.

Even the interior of the AirTies office, with an open work plan and a college-like cafeteria, pays homage to Silicon Valley's innovation giants. Yet for the first several years of operation, Bülent struggled to find Silicon Valley–like talent to fill this space and execute his idea for a wireless router that could stream without interruption, through an already existing technology called mesh.

Mesh technology doesn't receive data from a central access point such as a router. Instead, it picks it up through any wired device. It does so through pulses and bursts rather than a single stream. These continued pulses and bursts, already broken, make it hard for a signal to weaken or break down.

In a mesh network every device is a recipient and provider at the same time. Mesh does not rely on a single or dedicated source to connect to the Internet, but rather multiple ones. Since the device is constantly renewing, it doesn't require the user to reset anything. That, Bülent recognized in 2003, would benefit Turks and possibly hundreds of millions of users in places beset by poor infrastructure and who have no access to phone lines or fiber optic cables; where architecture interrupts radio waves, such as a subway tunnel; where natural disasters cut off phone lines and cables; or where there is a crowd. Mesh technology does not slow down when there is an increase in the number of users or devices being used. Mesh was used in Haiti after that country's devastating earthquake in 2010. A group of Egyptians launched the Open Mesh Project in 2011 after their government shut off the Internet during the Tahrir Square protests. In Red Hook, Brooklyn—a neighborhood hit hard during Hurricane Sandy in 2012—mesh networks are keeping a community, largely isolated from subways and vulnerable to floods, connected.

What mesh technology does require, however, is a lot of sophisticated and savvy engineers to make it work. Talent is among the most important factors for a startup—or any company. More than an idea, it is the ability to execute that idea that makes the difference. The best startups depend on capable and driven individuals. Attracting such individuals—and then retaining them—is among a startup's top challenges.

Turkey had plenty of smart and well-educated engineers, but few had the initiative and the drive to innovate. They could assemble a technology under direction, but could not design and develop one from scratch. No one had taught them how.

"Turkey didn't have the experience base to tap into Silicon Valley–type talent," Bülent told me. What it did have was "a bunch of bright kids that needed the right management and leadership to do that type of a thing," with that "thing" being exceptional results. Compared to some of the other hurdles Bülent had to overcome to get AirTies going in İstanbul, namely Turkish red tape and a lack of capital, nurturing Turkey's kids *seemed* easy. Dust off the Silicon Valley rule book, Bülent presumed, and zoom in on the one rule the best startups swore by: culture.

Culture, the organizational values and principles of a company, is not limited to Fortune 500 companies. It has brought out the ingenuity of and, more important, motivated, American twenty-somethings throughout Silicon Valley. Bülent believed it could work in Turkey, too.

The values Bülent outlined for AirTies, which are prominently displayed in the company's lobby, seem familiar to most Americans:

- Customer satisfaction
- Engaged employees
- Customer-driven innovation
- Fun and dynamism
- Excellence and execution
- Ethics and sustainability

But for Turks, they changed the game. They had a dissonant ring to them and stood in contrast to what they knew and what they had experienced in the workplace. What they knew had little to do with satisfying customers, innovating, or having fun. For decades, the government had run the majority of workplaces in Turkey. And it did so much as it did the state: from the top-down, with a heavy hand, and, as a result, with little regard for public opinion. The majority of Turkish bosses demanded deference from subordinates, with little consideration for anything else, including output. To achieve that, they exploited Turkey's culture of *ayıp*— shame, wherein speaking up or out of place is unaccept-able. Indeed, the Turkish language uses formal and familiar forms of address, like the French "vous" and "tu"—with the formal trumping the familiar. This contributes to the chain-of-command, know-your-place atmosphere that in most places still persists today.

Cast against this pervasive and entrenched culture, the one Bülent proposed had a hard time gaining traction. Still, he remained steadfast, if only for himself. Every startup has to have guiding principles, he told himself. Parameters safe-guard vision. They serve as a map that keeps companies focused. Though Bülent struggled to tap into and unleash Turkish talent through culture, culture did manage to push forward his idea to integrate mesh technology into the wire-less router. Culture kept his startup alive.

• • •

BÜLENT ÇELEBİ, tall, with thick, dark hair and thick, dark, knitted eyebrows to match, learned about mesh technol-ogy during his time as an engineer in Silicon Valley. Though born in Ankara, Turkey's capital, he considered himself a son of the Valley. He had moved to the United States as a young boy when his father, a special education teacher, won a Fulbright Scholarship to spend a year in San Fran-cisco. The family eventually went back to Turkey. But after a couple of years back in Turkey, Bülent's father decided his two sons would have more opportunity in America and permanently relocated the family to the Bay Area.

The family's back-and-forth life had made it difficult for the already shy Bülent to maintain any one language and any friendships. As a result, he retreated into math and science—and earned a degree in engineering and computer science at the University of California at Berkley.

While at Berkley he held a part-time job at a small technology company. After marrying a vivacious Greek-American he had met in the Bay Area, Bülent was hired by National Semiconductor, a major company in that field, in 1987 to work in its office in Hong Kong. There, Bülent worked on connectivity, first through local area networks (LANs), followed by multi-controller units (MCUs), and eventually WiFi.

In the late 1990s WiFi was relatively new. While everyone relished its novelty, Bülent thought about what this technology could unlock. He had by this time returned to Silicon Valley, worked at Analog Devices as its general manager, and become the CEO of Ubicom, a microchip manufacturer in the Valley.

Mesh had been deployed for radio. At the start of the new millennium, a number of engineers who worked on wireless routers, including Bülent, experimented to see if mesh could work over WiFi. If it did, it could transfer data without interruption. That, Bülent knew, could make a real difference in places like İstanbul, a historic city whose architecture hampered regular wireless signals. It would also be invaluable in remote outposts, such as Kars, with poor infrastructure.

Excited by this prospect, Bülent approached several American wireless companies with a proposal to integrate mesh technology into a router—especially those routers that they eventually planned to export abroad. They were not interested, Bülent said. In 2003 the Silicon Valley region had just started to recover from the dot-com crash three years earlier. Companies and investors hesitated to take risks. Moreover, wireless technology in the United States was still new. The most basic WiFi modems were being used to connect to the Internet, which was largely being used for basic transactions: e-mail, e-commerce, and news consumption. In those early days the Internet was a broadcast and information platform, not the everything platform—the data storage, accountant, virtual office, entertainment medium, and design and building tool—that it is today. For that, regular routers performed sufficiently. Adding mesh technology seemed unnecessary at that point, as did thinking about exporting routers to foreign markets.

A mesh-enabled router also conflicted with the business model wireless companies had hatched. In partnership with broadband or mobile phone operators, wireless companies made money from selling single-use devices for a monthly subscription. A mesh network would enable a single device to provide wireless to multiple users. In that scenario, mobile phone operators would not be able to make money.

Bülent saw beyond the bottom line. He saw what mesh technology could enable, how it could change lives, just as the Internet had begun to do at the start of the new millennium. Mesh technology, Bülent believed, could facilitate that process and solve WiFi range issues as well as the failure of WiFi during a crisis. That, he thought, was where the value—and profit—of mesh technology lay. And so he quit his job as Ubicom's CEO, drafted a business plan, raised $300,000 among friends and family, and convinced a handful of people he knew in Silicon Valley to join him—in İstanbul.

Leaving Silicon Valley in 2003 to launch a startup in İstanbul sounded ridiculous. Silicon Valley was the unquestionable capital of innovation and the mecca for tech talent. Turkey was a tech wasteland. Yet it is precisely because the best flocked to Silicon Valley and venture capitalists poured billions in investments into startups located there that Bülent left. Silicon Valley was too expensive.

Bülent's idea to build mesh-enabled routers and possibly other gadgets required hardware—physical material and parts. His idea also required design, testing, research and development (R&D), and a lot of manpower, all of which depended on talent. Hardware and talent cost money. To see that his idea got off the ground, Bülent needed considerable capital. The cost of living in Silicon Valley ranked among the highest in the United States. Bülent needed a place with lower rents and lower labor costs. Turkey had both.

Turkey also had something that had slowly been dissipating in Silicon Valley: perspective. Turkey lacked Silicon Valley's hubris.

Deluged by success stories such as the founding of Fairchild Semiconductor, Intel, Apple, Google, and Facebook, Silicon Valley couldn't see beyond itself. Though the region was (and remains) unrivaled in terms of the number of companies producing technological breakthroughs, it ignored developments for and in the rest of the world. For one thing, the Valley had amassed such a volume of talent and ideas that its entrepreneurs and venture capitalists snubbed advances made elsewhere, dismissing them as too local or too small. They regarded cities abroad as locations of manufacturing subcontractors, not hubs in which to build and leverage innovative enterprises.

Second, many in Silicon Valley in the early years of the new millennium didn't consider adapting their products and services for foreign markets. What worked in the United States or in the West, they believed at the time, would work everywhere. One size would fit all. In fact, the irony of Silicon Valley was that while it embraced foreigners—openly welcoming engineers from China, India, and Israel—it intentionally cut itself off from the rest of the world. The outside did not matter to Silicon Valley. For those in Silicon Valley, Silicon Valley was the only thing that mattered.

Bülent rejected this attitude. Perhaps no place rivaled Silicon Valley—or could rival it—but to disregard anything outside of the region was shortsighted. Silicon Valley may have been having its moment. But if its own ethos about "creative destruction"—the process of destroying the status quo and replacing it with fresh ideas—held true, then at some point, some other region would reign supreme. Having lived in Hong Kong, Bülent certainly saw a lot of potential in Asia. With the advent of the mobile phone there was lots of talk, even in 2003, about Africa's rise.

Convinced that the next tech success story could come from abroad—possibly from his own Turkey—Bülent Çelebi boarded a flight for İstanbul just a few days after the New Year in 2004.

· · ·

LANDING ALONGSIDE Bülent was another Turkish expat engineer, Metin İsmail Taşkın. Short, with salt-and-pepper hair and blue eyes, Metin had spent nearly a decade in the United States, first in Boston and then working in Silicon Valley, at the technology firm Cisco. He had never planned on staying permanently. His time in America was about gaining experience before heading back to Turkey, where he might start his own company.

Turkey had made considerable advances since Metin had left it in the 1990s. The country, eager to become a member of the European Union, had flung open its markets after 1980. Foreign investment poured in. Infrastructure began to improve. By 2003, the Turkish economy had steady average growth. This hardly made Turkey an ideal nation—the country still suffered (and sadly still does) from political gridlock and weak institutions. This opening did, however, pave a path for entrepreneurs. Small businesses had replaced government factories in the Anatolian countryside. A few even prospered.

A handful of Turkish cotton farmers successfully brokered deals with American brands such as Levi's and Tommy

Hilfiger. An Anatolian furniture manufacturer agreed to supply European conglomerates. Turkey's once sleepy cities in the Anatolian heartland became roaring economic powerhouses that created jobs, generated wealth, and fostered a positive brand for Turkey. Known as the Anatolian Tigers, they slowly improved Turkey's image. They also produced a middle class.

Turkey's rising middle class started to snap up the luxury consumer goods they had seen on American television programs: couture, cars, and cutting-edge devices such as high-definition television sets, smartphones, and computers.

By the end of 2003, Turkey had twenty-eight million mobile phone subscribers, 40 percent of its population. According to the Turkish Statistical Institute, household consumption in Turkey had grown 10 percent from the prior year. Also in 2003, the Turkish government opened up the country's telecommunications industry to allow private sector companies to operate landline, mobile, and Internet platforms. That presented a huge opportunity for AirTies. Among European countries, Turkey had the highest rate of credit card penetration, with over 50 percent of the population purchasing goods with plastic. That finally made the country an ideal place to launch a startup—even one that set out to develop and test a mesh-enabled wireless router.

When Bülent approached Metin with his idea to improve, develop, and test a mesh-enabled wireless router in Turkey—with an eye to transforming home electronics altogether—Metin immediately signed on. He became AirTies's chief technology officer.

In the first few months after they arrived in Turkey, Bülent and Metin worked out of a cramped apartment in

İstanbul that they shared like a pair of college students. They spent those first months grappling with Turkey's serpentine bureaucracy. They had been plunged into a vortex of paperwork, which could have disappeared if they had paid the requisite bribes. Fearing that there would be no end to the proverbial extended palm, they opted for the longer, more time-consuming road. Shortcuts, they felt, would lead them down the wrong path. It went against the culture the two had vowed to cultivate. AirTies had to be a place of ethics. Integrity mattered.

So did customers. Without the benefit of a marketing and sales team, Bülent and Metin approached electronic resellers in İstanbul with their mesh-enabled modems. They had produced several prototypes in the few months they had been working in the city. These helped them sign a handful of agreements. By October 2004, eight months after launching the company, AirTies modems began to populate Turkish homes. They became a big hit among high net worth individuals who lived in big houses, where the mesh-enabled wireless signals did not give out (and who loved to boast about having the latest in technology).

By 2006 the company had garnered a considerable reputation. Its mesh-enabled modems sold well. Customers were particularly satisfied with the company's localized manuals and twenty-four-hour call number for questions and concerns. No Turkish company had ever provided such support. Few provided any customer service at all. AirTies started receiving special orders from various individuals and businesses. That caught the attention of Türk Telekom, the country's largest communication firm. Türk Telekom invited

AirTies to submit a bid on a tender, something it had not done in the past. The company had strict limitations on who could participate in a tender. Once allowed to participate, AirTies eventually won a contract to supply Türk Telekom with several hundred thousand wireless routers.

More than ticking off a milestone, the Türk Telekom deal put AirTies to the test. The company had invested in developing a startup culture that would encourage and motivate employees, which few, if any, Turkish institutions did. As the company signed partnerships with the likes of Türk Telekom and grew, the enormity of that effort became evident. The entry- and midlevel engineers Bülent hired had the technological smarts but couldn't design and set their own work plans, much less iron out glitches independently. Though Bülent and Metin had brought a cadre of senior engineers from abroad who could push forward their company culture and methodology, they still had to lay out step-by-step instructions for their largely Turkish workforce.

A lack of initiative emerged as another problem. Certain team members needed constant handholding and approval. Few were flexible, knew how to adapt to changes, could take responsibility, or could work on teams. Office politics poisoned the environment, drained resources, and led to mistakes. AirTies's engineers, in one notable instance, had misjudged Turkey's electric infrastructure. They built what they believed to be a world-class modem that could be used in Silicon Valley. But their modem would be used in Turkey, where voltage fluctuated to such lows that it entirely stopped the devices, even the best designed ones, from working.

Turkish engineers took orders, when Bülent needed them to take risks, just like the engineers in Silicon Valley, who are in a perpetual race to put out the latest, cutting-edge gadgets and innovations.

Bülent poured more effort into bolstering the company's culture. He encouraged participation, soliciting ideas from his staff. Against the advice of some, he promoted transparency, openly sharing the company's financials with everyone. He provided feedback and listened to employees. These efforts would take years to yield the results he expected. Turkish talent could be cultivated—just not by re-creating what he called "a Silicon Valley-type of atmosphere." Turkish talent had to be built on its own terms. At the time Bülent started AirTies, Turkey had ceased to be what most people dismissively called a "third world nation." It would take time, however, for it to become a member of the so-called first.

"İstanbul isn't Silicon Valley because it lacks a Stanford or because there aren't venture capitalists. It's because there isn't a culture that combines risk taking and 'it doesn't matter'," he told me. "In Silicon Valley, it doesn't matter if you're Chinese or Indian or Turkish or American. If you are good at what you're doing, you're going to go up in the ranks and you're going to be appreciated, *okay*."

Duplicating that environment, Bülent found, was extremely difficult. While he could try to build culture, Bülent could not single-handedly replicate Silicon Valley's disregard for rank, race, economic background, and labels—things that mattered in Turkey. Those changes required critical mass and time.

For the time being, Bülent chose to forge ahead despite his ongoing personnel issues. Technology, he knew, did not wait for perfection. He had managed to market AirTies modems in the region surrounding Turkey. Buyers in Greece, Russia, and Ukraine showed interest in AirTies's personalized modems and its localized services. He made sure that AirTies continued to deliver its routers. Though revenues rose and the AirTies brand strengthened, there was a disconnect between the products it developed and the approach it took to marketing them. As Bülent described, this was a "high-end" product catering to emerging markets rather than "high-end" Western ones. Even though emerging markets were on the ascent and each displayed increased confidence, pride, and solidarity with one another, their citizens continued to turn to Western brands or else resort to cheap imitations. Because Turkish technology had no track record or validation, these markets expected a Turkish product to be cheap. It was not. In order to convince customers in emerging markets to buy AirTies products, AirTies had to gain legitimacy—some sort of "seal of approval." Bülent decided it would do so in the West, which is where the company turned its attention in 2008.

• • •

JUST AS AIRTIES turned its attention to expanding into Europe, the 2008 global economic crisis hit. And it hit AirTies hard. Orders for the company's modems plummeted. The company's earnings fell from $45 million in 2008 to $40 million in 2009 and $30 million in 2010. Its angel investors and board members advised Bülent to diversify his offerings.

Bülent had talked about building other wireless products, including set-top boxes. Now was the time.

What wireless routers are to computers, set-top boxes are to television sets. A set-top box allows TV to stream programming from the "cloud" or the Internet rather than a cable or satellite dish. It is specifically designed to deliver high-performance video. YouTube had demonstrated the importance of Web video as a market segment. The popularity of digital video recorders and TiVo had revealed consumer demand for content. Internet television was the next frontier. Bülent's vision for what he called a "connected home," in which every electronic device connects to the Internet and to each other through one source, came into sharper view. Set-top boxes were a natural progression from modems.

To build set-top boxes, AirTies required a significant cash infusion, more than what a single angel investor could put up. At the time, venture capital was an elusive concept in Turkey. In 2010 there were only a handful of venture capital–like funds in Turkey, largely started at the government's behest. Those in Silicon Valley had yet to show interest in the Turkish market. As far as the Turks were concerned, venture capital happened in the West.

AirTies turned to the private equity firm Invus. Unlike venture capital, which takes a risk on an entrepreneur and idea in the hopes of finding the next Facebook or Google, private equity investors are focused on turning companies around and improving financial performance. That is what Invus wanted for AirTies: solid returns. The firm provided AirTies the necessary funds, on certain conditions. Bülent had to cut staff and expand the business faster.

This should have further exacerbated AirTies's talent challenges. Yet the culture AirTies had cultivated when it started a few years before did two important things that allowed the company not only to weather through startup challenges but also to scale up. First, the six bullet-pointed values Bülent outlined gave the company direction. More than just empty words or feel-good rhetoric, AirTies's corporate values kept the company focused on customers and excellence, not on problems. Problems, Bülent noted to me, are always a "dime a dozen": "too easy and cheap to get caught up in, with no upside at the end." Bülent had come to Turkey for the opportunity to create something. Culture enabled him to do exactly that.

Second, the culture AirTies had adopted cracked open a new way of doing business in Turkey. While it did not single-handedly transform Turkish business, the six bullet points snowballed to inspire other Turkish companies to formulate their own guiding principles and abandon old, corrupt practices. This was the ripple that helped start the slow erosion of Turkey's paternalistic method of operation. In turn, that has made İstanbul more appealing to foreign businesses, particularly multinationals. Technology titans such as Dell, Google, and Microsoft have set up headquarters or satellite offices in İstanbul. International banking and finance use İstanbul as a hub. The changing culture has also helped to transform Turkey's talent base.

Foreigners began to relocate to the country. Turks abroad moved back home. Eren Soyak, a Turkish engineer working in Chicago, was one who did. Eren had gone to the United States to study at Northwestern University. He graduated with a PhD in engineering and then joined a tech startup in downtown Chicago. He had thought about moving back to Turkey, but concern about what he would do there troubled him. He did not want to work for a multinational or, especially, a Turkish company. He didn't know if he wanted to be an entrepreneur but knew that he wanted to experience startup life.

"Coming to Turkey as an engineer is like walking out into the desert," Eren told me as we sat in AirTies's cafeteria. "There is nothing here. Whatever you want to find you have to build from the ground up. Good engineers here have learned to do just that. Instead of making incremental improvements to something that's already really cool, you have to create something from complete scratch."

Bülent was one of the "good" engineers who had created something that Eren saw he could improve upon. That is significant. Not every engineer wants to be—or can be—an entrepreneur. In fact, the majority of people in Silicon Valley aren't entrepreneurs. According to a study conducted by the Global Entrepreneurship Monitor in 2013, fewer than 13 percent of Americans run their own businesses. The rest are in search of a stable job and a regular paycheck.

Eren had met Bülent in Chicago and was impressed by the risks Bülent had taken in returning to Turkey at a time when there was a great deal of uncertainty about succeeding. Moreover, Eren appreciated that Bülent had worked to replicate a Silicon Valley culture that inspired people to challenge themselves and take risks. AirTies not only welcomed ideas, it rewarded them.

Eren was not alone. A handful of twenty-something Turkish expats who had good jobs in the United States and Europe—at places like Microsoft—moved back to Turkey to work at AirTies, just at the moment when AirTies started to roll out its new product line, set-top boxes.

In 2010 Bülent oversaw the development of an initial product that his staff had been marketing in India, Dubai, and Russia with mixed success. His investors advised him to turn to Europe. However, persuading Europeans to trust Turkish technology would require tremendous effort. Few Turkish brands outside of fashion had managed to penetrate the Continent. Hüseyin Çağalayan, Arzu Kaprol, and Rıfat Özbek had become recognized fashion designers, and Mavi Jeans had become a very popular clothing retailer.

Eren Soyak, along with a number of other Turkish "millennial" engineers who came of age and joined AirTies that same year, helped AirTies gain recognition. Bülent had just won his first European Internet protocol television (IPTV) contract, with a Danish firm. That caught the attention of Andreas Martschitsch, a senior official at Swisscom, an aptly named telecom provider in Switzerland. Andreas headed Swisscom's "digital home" department. It was his job to find new products and services. As an engineer and innovator himself, Andreas believed the most radical ideas and experiments came out of small companies. Increasingly, as the success of Skype, the Estonian communications startup had shown, those small companies were in the unlikeliest places.

Martschitsch discovered AirTies and its exclusively produced customized wireless products. Swisscom wanted products that could differentiate it from competitors. AirTies's mesh technology did exactly that, as did the company's commitment to customer satisfaction. Andreas reached out to the company. What they did impressed him. Andreas put AirTies on a trajectory to become a Swisscom vendor.

People within Swisscom found Andreas's selection of AirTies, as he put it, "puzzling."

"They wondered why we now had to suddenly get wireless devices from Turkey. Turks are famous for their exquisite food; they are the 'kings of kebab,' but high tech? It required a lot of willpower not only on AirTies's side but also on mine to get past preconceived ideas and stereotypes," he told me. They didn't believe that Turks had the talent to execute on such a huge concept: set-top boxes and next generation software. The majority of Swiss had only known the migrant workers who came to their country to take up blue-collar jobs. Those Turks were largely uneducated and unwilling to abandon their conservative and traditional beliefs. Few learned how to speak German, French, or Italian. AirTies had to work hard to convince Swisscom that the company did possess the talent to deliver high-quality and high-tech set-top boxes. And it did. "You could clearly see that they wanted to fulfill all our requirements, no matter what," said Andreas. AirTies listened to the feedback Swisscom provided. The company iterated on its technology, testing it under every possible condition until it was right. AirTies found top-of-the-line material—the quality that has made Apple products coveted items—and put a lot of effort into design. This persuaded Andreas's colleagues.

Three years after their first meeting, in 2013, Swisscom picked AirTies to deliver set-top boxes to Swiss households under a ten-year contract. The people who had perfected watchmaking and valued precision would have Turkish-made technology in their homes. In a press release the company noted that it had selected AirTies because of its "smart, adaptable wireless technology capable of delivering the best streaming experience possible." When I talked to Andreas, he noted that it was AirTies's entrepreneurial business model and culture that appealed to Swisscom. Because the company customizes its products, it was able to deliver to Swisscom set-top boxes with particular specifications. Those specifications have made Swisscom the number one player in that country's digital TV market.

The Swisscom deal was a breakthrough for AirTies, setting off a domino effect. Internet or "connected" television had grown as a market. In 2013 a little over 300 million television sets streamed programming from the World Wide Web. In the United States, they have done so through providers including Apple TV and Roku and through services such as Hulu and Netflix. That number is expected to increase to 759 million worldwide by 2018, with one in four television sets connected to the Internet.

Soon after the Swisscom deal, AirTies signed agreements with British media giant SkyTV and France Telecom Orange, and has most recently done so with companies in Iceland, Italy—and the United States. In 2014 AirTies signed a deal to provide its technology to AT&T and DirectTV. From a shabby hotel in a remote corner of Turkey, Turkish technology has made it to America.

• • •

IT IS PERHAPS ironic that as Bülent Çelebi fixated on fostering talent—hiring the best people for AirTies—his investors at Invus called into question his own capabilities. Though Bülent had built and scaled up the company, the investors at Invus did not feel he was doing so at the pace they wanted. AirTies, they felt, should have been further along in its product development and expansion. As a result, in 2012 Bülent's investors at Invus asked him to step aside. They brought in an industry veteran who had experience in digital media and the telecommunications space—a former executive at the French-based Phillips Corporation—to lead AirTies. Bülent still retains his seat as executive chairman of the board and is involved in the development of products.

"In order to be able to grow the company in this particular space," Bülent told me when I asked him about the change, "we needed to bring on board additional talent that actually had dealt with different products." He explained that he was a "chip and tech guy," who didn't have the background necessary to sell a variety of different products, products that Bülent had imagined a decade earlier.

"You need talent in the area that you are trying to operate. Tech is a fast-moving market. We don't have the time and luxury to go through a learning curve," he said.

In recent years, tech has rapidly moved into a rapidly growing Turkey. Nearly half of the country's seventy-eight million people are online. Turkey has the fifth-largest Internet audience in Europe and is among the top twenty in the world.

The Turkish economy, which by 2010 had become the sixteenth largest in the world, had grown so fast that the average Turk in 2013 earned twice as much as he or she did in 2003. As a result, startups have proliferated across İstanbul and the rest of Turkey. Today, universities in İstanbul offer courses on entrepreneurship and organizational management specifically for technology ventures. A number of these schools have launched incubators and set up seed funds for young entrepreneurs to tap into. eTohum and Girişim Fabrikası are the two most notable. Investments, particularly from the United States, have started to pour into Turkey.

In 2011 venture capital godfather Kleiner Perkins, along with Tiger Global—another investment firm—put a combined $26 million into Trendyol, a Turkish version of Gilt Group, an online flash sales site. That same year South Africa's Naspers—a firm that has invested in China's Tencent—invested in Markafoni, another online flash retailer. Not long after these deals, Amazon, eBay, and Intel Capital injected optimism into the Turkish startup scene by taking positions in online flower and chocolate marketer Çiçeksepeti, online auction clone GittiGidiyor, and daily deals namesake Gruponya, respectively. In 2012 New York private equity firm General Atlantic announced a $44 million stake in Turkish online food order platform Yemeksepeti. In one of Turkey's largest deals to date, the German-based Delivery Hero, an online food delivery and service platform acquired Yemeksepeti for $589 million in May 2015.

Turks have also started their own venture capital investment funds. In 2000 Access Turkey Capital Group, a financing house, established a venture arm, iLabs. The government-led İstanbul Venture Capital Initiative (IVCI) launched in 2007 with a €160 million fund. In 2012 an İstanbul-based venture investment firm, 212, rolled out its first fund raised among Turks and foreigners, totaling $30 million, to invest in early stage startups. In 2014 the firm started to raise its second fund. In 2015 Diffusion Capital Partners launched a €30 million technology transfer seed fund.

AirTies has become a multimillion-dollar technology enterprise, with the majority of its revenues coming from international sales such as the one made to Swisscom. The company has filed for patents in the United States. AirTies also has plans to eventually go public on a global stock market such as the New York Stock Exchange (NYSE). That would make it one of the most significant "exits"—its investors would earn a return. That would solidify the role of high-growth startups in Turkey and Turkey's place on the entrepreneurial/innovation spectrum.

That matters. As *New Yorker* economics and business writer James Surowiecki noted in "What Microloans Miss," businesses that can grow, generate jobs for others, and exploit economies of scale are the best hope for any country to "put a serious dent in its poverty rate." "In any successful economy," he wrote, "most people aren't entrepreneurs—they make money by working for someone else."

In building AirTies, Bülent Çelebi unlocked the doors of the Turkish mind, which didn't think it was possible for a Turk to triumph, and not only as an entrepreneur in Turkey. He proved that while obstacles certainly make doing most things in Turkey, namely running a business, difficult—especially the one that plagued him, a lack of skilled talent—they didn't make it impossible. Bülent showed that the startup dream didn't exist in Silicon Valley alone. It could exist in Turkey, too.

AirTies stands as an example—a beacon for others in Turkey—in the same way Sir Roger Bannister did in 1954 when he became the first person to run a mile under four minutes. Sir Roger, as Fadi Ghandour, a Jordanian entrepreneur and founder of the logistics company Aramex, said at a meeting of entrepreneurs convened by the White House in 2010, broke a record and, more important, people's perceptions. No one had ever run a mile in less than four minutes, so few people could imagine that it could be done. Sir Roger threw open an entirely new realm of possibilities. Forty-six days after Sir Roger's run, another person broke his record. Two others broke those by the end of that year. Today, lots of people run a mile in under four minutes.

In Turkey, a significant number of people are endeavoring to become entrepreneurs. More important, however, are the numerous people who want to return to the country and many more potential entrepreneurs who want to stay in Turkey and make a go of it. Bülent Çelebi's significance isn't just that he has built a tech firm that is innovating the "Internet of things" and expanding the use of mesh technology. It is also in his creating a space for bright and driven people—through culture, principles, and values. Entrepreneurial ecosystems sprout where there is talent and energy—where there is a critical mass of people eager to experiment and take risks, a point explored in chapter 3.

That is exactly what I found when traveling around the globe meeting entrepreneurs like Bülent, who are tackling obstacles that have otherwise prevented prosperity and, therein, innovation, from being something to be had outside the United States. There may be entrepreneurs everywhere, but there is only entrepreneurship—real Silicon Valley–like innovation—going on in those places where there are individuals willing to break down barriers and replace them with community, trust, values, and vision. That is what I found in Turkey. It is also what I discovered in Nigeria in the remarkable story of Tayo Oviosu, a man who had to overcome obstacles many times more difficult than those Bülent faced.

TWO

Moving Money:
Improving Infrastructure

If opportunity doesn't knock, build a door.
—MILTON BERLE

Lagos

As the workday drew to a close, Tayo Oviosu swayed in his chair. Pulsating rhythms by the Nigerian techno star P-Squared spilled from his flat-panel Apple desktop. The computer was the only high-end item in his threadbare office on the top floor of a four-story, brightly painted building in Lagos, Nigeria's largest city and commercial capital.

A few of Tayo's employees were drifting out the door toward home. Outside, rush hour was in full swing. Cars and motorcycles vied with the decrepit and rusting yellow minivans, *dankos*, that function as makeshift public transport. Street peddlers snaked between vehicles, hawking goods they miraculously balanced atop their heads.

I, too, had been gathering my things and preparing to head back to my hotel, when suddenly the music stopped. I looked up expectantly. Tayo no longer looked like the laid-back, thirty-six-year-old hipster, unshaven and sporting dark-framed glasses, who had spent the day enthusiastically telling me about his startup, Paga Tech, a digital payments company. He looked worried as he stared at the e-mail message he had just received.

"Our connection to GLO has gone out," it read.

An important piece of Nigeria's infrastructure was buckling again. GLO is Globocom, a Lagos-based telecom operator that runs one of the mobile networks on which Paga Tech relies. The fiber optic connection between Paga and GLO had been inexplicably lost and would take several hours to repair. Tayo scrambled to deploy a backup, as he had done many times before. Assuring regular, continuous service—of any kind—to this vast, crowded, and increasingly important nation on Africa's west coast is one of Tayo's biggest challenges. A lack of proper infrastructure stalls everything in Nigeria and keeps the country from realizing its full potential.

Poor infrastructure—bad roads, corroding bridges, insufficient plumbing and electricity, improper sanitation, dilapidated public transportation, and neglected ports, waterways, and airports—hampers mobility. At best, it slows down physical movement, adding days and weeks to the transport of goods and people that should only take hours. At its worst, poor infrastructure prevents access to and the distribution of services: education, health care, and, as Tayo realized is the case in Nigeria, finance. Despite being Africa's largest economy and having an abundance of wealth due to oil, Nigeria's inability to distribute and extend services such as banking has been one of the country's greatest challenges.

More than just bad roads or the lack of electricity, the inability to provide financial services—to move money and save—has been a key obstacle to growth and commerce. This situation exists not just in Nigeria, but throughout Africa, Asia, Latin America, and the Middle East.

Until his backup connection kicked in, thousands of Tayo's customers on the GLO network would not be able to access Paga Tech's services, which enable people to work around the problems resulting from Nigeria's poor infrastructure. What Tayo provides to Nigerians is a facility and mechanism for handling everyday financial transactions.

Despite Nigeria's being Africa's largest economy and having the largest population of any country on the continent, 136 million of its 170 million people—80 percent—do not have access to a bank. Because its people lack access to banks, Nigeria is one of the world's richest cash-based societies. Almost all transactions are handled in hard currency. Few stores or businesses accept credit cards. Hotels require prepayment from everyone, including visitors from abroad. Consequently, even those with bank accounts and credit cards must carry large sums of money. It is not unusual to see people hauling sacks of cash—or at least clutching plastic or paper bags—through the streets. This is especially true of the poor, who are forced to carry whatever currency they have or store it in jars or literally under the mattress. Nigeria's currency, the naira, starts with a twenty naira note, which is worth a little more than ten cents, then goes up in various denominations to one thousand naira, which equals about six dollars and some change.

Some bypass this risky system altogether and hold their wealth in the form of gold or in the more illiquid form of livestock. Others put their money in notoriously unreliable, ad hoc community savings schemes. Money in Nigeria drifts and evaporates, never staying long enough to become an asset or investment.

In 2009 Tayo launched Paga Tech as a way to solve this problem. Paga Tech is the closest thing to a one-stop shop for financial services one can imagine, like a Western Union, PayPal, and bill payment center rolled into one. One aspect of its business is person-to-person money transfers, for which it charges a small transaction fee. This supplements other services, which are the lion's share of its growth. These include bill payments, the purchase of additional airtime for a mobile phone, and the ability to make deposits into a rudimentary savings account. Paga also provides retailers—or anyone who wants to sell goods—with a PayPal-like mechanism for processing payments online or through a mobile phone. Tayo has integrated Paga—its name is taken from the Spanish word "to pay" (because, according to Tayo, it is easy to say and remember)—on a number of point of sales (POS) devices—cash registers—at retail shops and chain stores in Nigeria as well as on a number of Nigerian e-commerce sites that have grown in popularity.

Moving money over a mobile phone or, as Tayo has also proposed, over the Web, has the potential to be, as economist Philip Auerswald has noted, as powerful as the transcontinental railroad in the United States in the late nineteenth century. The transcontinental railroad joined different rail lines between the East and West Coasts. That combination not only connected people and places, it expanded economic activity.

Similarly, connecting people and businesses to mechanisms that move money has the potential to help jumpstart Nigeria's growth. Where the lack of physical infrastructure slows down and obstructs daily life in the country, the lack of a financial one has choked it. Mobile money and a mobile payments system have the potential to solve a major challenge in Nigeria and propel the country forward—and up.

• • •

A NUMBER OF African countries, particularly Kenya, already had started to use mobile phones to transfer money long before Tayo Oviosu hit upon the idea. In 2007 the Kenyan telecom giant Safaricom, a Vodafone holding, enabled anyone with a handset to send and receive money through short message service, or SMS. That service, M-Pesa, took off. Today, nearly half of Kenya's population uses M-Pesa to wire cash as well as pay bills. The company has franchised its model to other countries beset by infrastructure problems, including Afghanistan, India, Tanzania, Romania, and South Africa.

M-Pesa has not penetrated Nigeria. Nigeria lagged behind other African nations in setting up the framework to allow for mobile money. When it finally established that framework a few years later, it banned Vodafone—and in fact all telecom providers—from operating independently in the mobile money space. Nigeria's leaders required mobile money providers to work through the country's central bank, where they could then regulate them. Nigeria's central bank has no authority to regulate telecom companies and therefore could not force telecoms to comply with rigorous financial reporting requirements. Nigeria already suffered from, and still does, the negative consequences of online scams—"419 scams" as they are known in the country, denoting the section of the criminal code related to such activity. The potential for further abuse—money laundering or Ponzi schemes—through an unregulated telecom operator was too great. As a result, Nigeria's leaders made it a point to only allow banks and third-party vendors that would work through banks to offer mobile money services in Nigeria.

Tayo seized the opportunity to fill the space that he believed banks would not, and had not. Banks in Nigeria had online and mobile banking services for existing customers. They had not ventured, however, into mobile payments: moving money between merchants and customers, including customers who may or may not have a bank account. Banks make money on money. As a result, they have hesitated to extend services to the unbanked, namely the poor. The poor simply do not have enough money and therefore do not bring in the transactional volume necessary for a bank to offset operational expenses. That view, Tayo believed, was shortsighted. One reason the poor didn't have enough money was that they didn't have access to the mechanisms that would protect and leverage their money. Mobile money, he recognized, could solve that problem. It is an industry he believed holds enormous potential—not just in Africa, but also worldwide.

Digital has already revolutionized the global economy. Nearly every industry has a cyber component. This phenomenon has prompted a demand for alternatives to traditional financial mechanisms of cash, credit cards, and banks. Mobile phone and Internet users want tools that complement and integrate seamlessly into their digital experience. Hence the success of PayPal, the Silicon Valley online payment system that launched in 1998. Today, alternative financial mechanisms—"financial tech"—are one of the most coveted tech and startup pursuits, inside and outside Silicon Valley.

Dozens of companies have rolled out their own digital payment platforms: Amazon with Amazon Payments, Apple with Apple Pay, Google with Google Wallet, and Master-Card with MasterPass. The social media platform Facebook has also dipped its hand into the mobile payment space.

The US-based telecom companies AT&T, T-Mobile, and Verizon have banded together to form a technology that allows users of all three networks to use a smartphone for purchases. Similarly, big retailers in the United States, including Best Buy, CVS, Shell, Target, Walmart, and 7-11, have created the Merchant Customer Exchange (MCX), another mobile app that customers can use through a smartphone. Stripe has helped companies and services integrate mobile or electronic payments into their business models. Starbucks, for example, has its own payment system, as does Uber, the mobile app taxi service.

The startup space is crowded with mobile money, mobile wallet, or digital wallet applications—everywhere. In the United States, Square, the brainchild of Twitter cofounder

Jack Dorsey, is the most well-known. Clinkle, Loop, and Venmo are three other mobile payment platforms that are trying to penetrate the US market. The Lemon Wallet, now LifeLock, is a fully integrated wallet that can incorporate all one's credit cards.

Dwolla, Gyft (a gift card service), LevelUp, Remitly (a remittance service), Wrapp, and Znap are others. There are thousands more around the world. Pozitron, a Turkish startup acquired by the UK-based Monetise, is one. Alipay, the financial payment system of the Chinese Internet giant Alibaba, is the best known in China. In 2013 Alipay recorded more than 100 million users and 2.78 billion transactions, valued at $148 billion.

The mobile phone market is enormous. As Benedict Evans, a partner at the venture capital firm Andreesen Horowitz who specializes in the mobile space, has noted, "We're going from 1.5 billion PCs (personal computers) on earth . . . to perhaps 3 billion smartphones." On their own—not counting mobile advertising (which in 2013 was valued at $17.96 billion), hardware sales (1.8 billion units sold in 2013), and app downloads (a $26 billion market in 2013)— mobile payments are already a nearly $250 billion industry worldwide, with 245.2 million users. Gartner, an information technology research and advisory firm, projects that by 2017 the mobile payment market will grow to $721 billion, with over 450 million people making purchases, transferring money, and paying bills. In Africa, mobile payments are forecast to be $160 billion.

As Tayo Oviosu started to put together his plans for that service, he saw that he could do more. Technology provided the basis for reaching millions of Nigerians, especially those unable to access a bank, as well as business owners and entrepreneurs, and provide them with a means not only to move but also to *secure* and *save* money. It could do for Nigeria and beyond what the microchip did for computing, what the iPod did for music, and what Facebook did for social connections: transform an industry, in this case banking and finance.

Tayo saw that it was time to lay the foundations for a financial system that would serve a broad range of people—both poor and rich. He has gambled that the mobile financial system he has crafted—one that has different features and far-reaching access, across multiple mobile networks and with a connection to the Internet—can help establish that framework.

In order to do that, however, Tayo knew that he could not rely on technology alone.

First, because Nigeria operated as a cash-based society, its citizens still required a physical place to deposit and withdraw their cash—a bank or repository of some sort. Tayo created an "agent" network out of existing storefronts throughout the country. These storefronts, spread across Nigeria, act as "cash-in" and "cash-out" points for people using mobile phones to transfer money.

Second, Tayo had to grapple with Nigeria's poor infrastructure. Despite the promise that technology would "leapfrog" this obstacle—and economically boost countries like Nigeria—poor infrastructure also stymies technology. It complicates, and thereby drives up the costs of, the installation, distribution, and upkeep of things like fiber optic lines as well as broadband signals that connect phones and computers to a digital network. Using data throughout much of the world is expensive. That is true not just in Nigeria, but also in the United States, where aging and often neglected infrastructure is a creeping problem. According to the World Economic Forum's Global Competitiveness Index for 2012–2013, the United States ranks twenty-fifth in infrastructure quality—a drop of twenty spots since 2002, when it ranked fifth. Finland, France, Hong Kong, Singapore, and even Saudi Arabia and the United Arab Emirates ranked, and still rank, higher.

It goes without saying that whether in Nigeria or the United States, businesses, including tech startups, require infrastructure. Infrastructure investments directly correspond to economic growth. According to the World Bank, a 10 percent increase in infrastructure investments expands GDP growth by 1 percent. China's growth over the past two decades is in large part the result of the Chinese government's enormous investments in infrastructure. Yet China is an exception. Most countries in Africa lack the funds, and increasingly the United States lacks the political will, to invest in infrastructure. Instead, they are turning to the private sector to bankroll and finance projects. Launching an enterprise—whether in Nigeria or the United States— has required startups and businesses to invest in the mobile and WiFi networks that power digital devices. It also has required startups—whether in Nigeria or the United States— to invest in the backup mechanisms for those networks, as I witnessed in Lagos one June afternoon.

• • •

IN 2014 NIGERIA overtook South Africa to become Africa's largest economy, with $510 billion GDP. About 14 percent of that GDP is generated from oil. Nigeria is Africa's number one and the world's fourth-largest oil producer, with exports valued at $143 billion.

While the spoils of these oil exports have not reached the majority of people in Nigeria—60 percent of Nigerians live at or below the poverty line—it is one factor drawing investors and other business interests to the country. Another is Nigeria's potential as a lucrative consumer market, with 170 million people and growing. A number of South African businessmen have set up a presence in the country. Western brands, mainly in the food and beverage industry, have turned their attention to Nigeria. Every other billboard across Lagos seems to boast an advertisement for consumer products such as Hennessy, Budweiser, or Domino's Pizza.

Convinced that Nigeria is Africa's—and the world's—next big story, Tayo returned from the United States to Nigeria in 2008 to be a part of his country's ascent. That was not something he had thought he would do when he left Lagos fourteen years earlier to be a college freshman in California. America—not Nigeria—was a place that celebrated and rewarded hard-working people, as he explained to me as we had breakfast on a balcony without much of a view. It overlooked a row of houses in one of Lagos's few upscale neighborhoods. Tayo was dressed in a crisp pink shirt with the sleeves rolled up. He was ready to tackle the day's challenges.

Hard work defined everything about Tayo's life. His single mother provided for him and his three older stepbrothers from her salary as an administrator for the military-controlled government. That set them above most in Nigeria, but nowhere near the opulent life the elite in the country seemed to have, particularly the generals who ruled.

Until 1999, when a civilian government replaced military rule, Nigeria's soldiers loomed over the daily life in the country—controlling the government and operating key sectors of the economy, namely oil. Due to the dearth of opportunities, like most young men in Nigeria, Tayo considered going into the armed forces after high school. His godfather was an admiral in the Nigerian navy. After some thought, he opted for engineering.

Nigeria's oil industry prompted many young people to study engineering. The ability to design and build structures and machines for the oil industry seemed perhaps the best way to climb the economic ladder. Other than being a soldier, it was the only opportunity in a militarily dominated country with few manufacturing or business opportunities. Many of these young people enrolled in engineering programs in the United Kingdom, Nigeria's former colonial overseer from 1900 to 1960. Tayo, however, wanted to go to the United States to study. A few of Tayo's friends had traveled there and had come back with stories about the country: its massiveness, its fast pace, its abundance. American universities offered a wide range of scholarships and tuition assistance. That appealed to Tayo. While he had the desire, Tayo lacked the means to attend university abroad.

Tayo aimed high. He first tried but failed to gain admission to the Massachusetts Institute of Technology. A family friend suggested that he might have better luck at Bakersfield College, a small, obscure college in the suburbs of Los Angeles where she lived. He applied there, not knowing much about the school or what might be there for him. Bakersfield offered the engineering courses Tayo hoped to enroll in. It also offered generous scholarships based on financial need and for those who showed particular promise. Tayo applied for all of them—and with that he headed West.

. . .

FIREWORKS EXPLODED over the city as Tayo Oviosu's flight touched down in America's entertainment capital on July 4, 1994. Knowing little about his new home, Tayo assumed the spectacle was for him and other arrivals in Los Angeles. That overwhelmed him. Hurray, indeed, for Hollywood. Yet even after he realized that the fireworks marked Independence Day, Tayo still felt enormous inspiration during his next decade and a half in the United States. This was a place that celebrated and rewarded hard-working people.

Settling into Bakersfield came relatively easily for Tayo. Coming from an underdeveloped society, however, there were a few things that surprised him. For one thing, the phones worked. He could pick up the receiver and hear an instant dial tone. That, he said, never happened in Nigeria. "I didn't think that [having a dial tone] was possible. What I was used to is, you pick up the phone and press the thing [switch hook] multiple times until you get a tone and then you dialed. Realizing that this was normal in the US was a bit of a shock," he said, elongating the "i" of bit to sound like "ee."

This pronunciation is one of the few traces of Tayo's Nigerian roots. He otherwise has a perfect American accent and rhythm. While his fellow compatriots speak with an up-and-down syncopation, Tayo's tone rarely fluctuates.

His intonation, however, is merely a surface manifestation of his experience in America. Deeper is his embrace of the American anticipation of and excitement about advancements and inventions. He enjoyed being an early adopter, the first to try the latest gadget. When the mobile phone burst onto the mainstream in the late 1990s, he purchased a clunky and heavy device that operated on a 2G network. By then he had transferred from Bakersfield to the University of Southern California, where he majored in electrical engineering. The mobile phone became critical for him as he juggled coursework and several part-time jobs. In between classes, Tayo worked as a janitor for the school. After earning his undergraduate degree he spent time at two startups in LA. He passed up the chance at working for a third one based in Silicon Valley for a "proper job" at the consulting giant Deloitte. "You'll never guess what that startup was," he said and paused. "Google," he continued, smiling and shaking his head.

In 2003 Tayo enrolled at Stanford Business School, where he earned a master of business administration(MBA). After graduation, he joined the acquisition and ventures team at global technology titan Cisco Systems. In that role he searched for innovative startups that the company could invest in, partner with, or acquire. The job excited him. It gave him the chance to work with ebullient and energized people who had started their own companies and then sought his guidance about incorporating technology and scaling up their enterprises. He found his calling in venture capital. These investors are the startup world's kingmakers, venerated for their ability to spot and, in many cases nurture, a winning idea. That is what Tayo wanted to do.

A childhood friend from Lagos suggested he might want to try investing back home. He told Tayo, "Nigeria felt like India and China fifteen years ago."

In the early 1990s a handful of individuals from India and China had launched tech enterprises that have since grown into globally competitive conglomerates and have served as a basis for each country's growth and transformation. Some, like Sunil Bharti Mittal from India, had even penetrated the African market in telecommunications—the very industry that Tayo eventually found himself in. In 1992 Mittal won a license to operate a mobile phone network in India, a nation also plagued—then and now—by poor infrastructure, such as rolling blackouts and unpaved roads. He called the company AirTel. AirTel is now one of the top three mobile network providers in Nigeria.

Since the start of the millennium, China has become a global phenomenon and the second-largest economy in the world, after the United States. The Chinese have poured investments in the billions into Nigeria, helping the country build oil refineries, roads, bridges, and other infrastructure staples. Chinese hotel chains, shops, and restaurants are now commonplace in Lagos.

Planeloads of Nigerian expats already had been making their way back to the country between 2006 and 2007, just before the global financial meltdown. Worldwide people were looking for opportunities to invest. Nigeria seemed to be a place to do that. Even if a technology startup wasn't possible in Nigeria at that moment and poor infrastructure crippled business, the critical mass of returnees, along with a growing Nigerian economy, signaled the promise of opportunities to come.

Following a vacation that took him to Bhutan and Nepal, including climbing Mount Everest, Tayo decided to move back to Nigeria. Meeting the challenges of climbing Everest had dispelled any doubts he may have had about his homeland. If his plans didn't work out, he thought, he could always leave. With that mind-set, Tayo said good-bye to California in August 2008.

• • •

WHEN TAYO returned to Nigeria, he took up a position with a local private equity firm, making decisions about which companies the firm should invest in. It gave him a unique vantage point for observing Nigeria's market and the businesses that operated in it—all with an eye to starting his own. While his eventual goal was to be a venture capitalist, he wanted to be able to say that he too had muddled through the startup trenches. "The best investors are always those who started their own businesses," he said.

Yet life at the private equity firm did not pan out as Tayo had hoped. He clashed with the firm's management. After one particularly frustrating week at work, just three months after he had arrived back in Lagos, Tayo found himself writing out a list of startup ideas. They spanned a wide range—from those that could cater to Nigeria's elite to businesses that targeted the country's poor.

In a black journal, he jotted down the number 1 and next to it wrote "poker house." On four more sheets, Tayo poured out every thought that came to mind: build toilets, operate a helipad, systematize payroll, work in agriculture, deliver food, become the Dell of Nigeria, and import hair extensions.

"If you take a look," Tayo observed "you'll see many women not wearing their own hair." They paid premium prices for locks from India, Malaysia, Peru, and even Russia. Tayo had the idea of sourcing, importing, and then distributing the product for reduced costs.

At the end of several hours he had listed twenty ideas. Over the next several days he looked over each one. Two jumped out at him. As numbers 10 and 11 he had written down "financial inclusion" and "mobile money," respectively. Mobile money hit home especially when he went out on that Saturday night for an evening of music and dancing. After fourteen years in Silicon Valley, Tayo considered carrying cash around, especially at a nightclub, an inconvenience.

It wasn't until the start of the next work week, as he commuted from his serene home in Leikki, an upper-middle-class neighborhood in Lagos, past the gray ghettos at the edge of the city that blend into the dark-colored waters upon which they sit, that he realized that financial inclusion also mattered. While he found carrying cash an inconvenience, the majority in Nigeria had no choice but to do so. Tayo had a bank account. Most people in Nigeria didn't.

Not being able to keep money in a safe place and either save or invest it is one factor that impacts the opportunity for steady employment and thereby income and stability. It is one of the root causes of Nigeria's poverty. That spurred Tayo to start researching the issues of financial inclusion and mobile money. The more he found out, the more he knew he had put his finger on a combination that had potential for a business. And this was an opportunity to do more than just start a business, since Tayo had come back to Nigeria not just to make money. He had returned to make a difference.

The lack of financial services in Nigeria strangled commerce. Manufacturing has struggled to take hold. The country has few brick and mortar retailers. There is no Nigerian equivalent to Walmart, even on a much smaller scale. Multinationals and foreign businesses have been slow to set up operations in the country. Coca-Cola has a manufacturing facility in Lagos, as does Indomie, an Indonesian brand of instant noodles that is wildly popular. It is not, however, possible to find a McDonald's or Starbucks franchise in Nigeria. The cost of moving supplies and distributing products is high. It requires a lot of up-front capital. Some big retail chains have decided to make the investment. A representative from Domino's Pizza told the *Wall Street Journal* in April 2014 that the company, which also draws and purifies its own tap water from custom-built wells, is able to bear the costs because it has "lots of volume." A representative from the South African chain Shoprite noted in 2014 that Nigeria's poor infrastructure results in shipping delays of up to 117 days.

Poor infrastructure is one of the reasons business in Nigeria is catch-as-catch-can. Instead of big retailers or a major Nigerian brand, peddlers fill Nigeria's roadsides and street corners, hawking every item imaginable. During my time in Lagos—a city comprised of islands—I saw people selling the usual newspapers, refreshments, and peanuts, but also socks, underwear, and extension cords. I watched one man take bids for an iron.

The more Tayo thought about this challenge, the more he thought about how mobile payments and, indeed, an entire digital financial framework could work around it—and lay the foundations for a robust financial system in Nigeria. Mobile payments could do what PayPal in the United States and Alipay in China had done: empower hundreds and thousands to become individual proprietors, small business owners, or even entrepreneurs. And it would be these people, with a vested interest in protecting their earnings and striving to gain more, who would repair and strengthen Nigeria.

Tayo had witnessed the impact PayPal had when it rolled out its services in 1998. People made livelihoods through PayPal. "If you brought Peter Thiel and his other cofounders to Nigeria at the time they started PayPal, they would come up with Paga today," Tayo told me. Nigeria lacked financial mechanisms. It needed something to help people move money as well as something that could ignite its markets and help retailers. Reviewing his list, he circled financial inclusion and mobile money together. "They were naturally connected."

• • •

ONCE A SYMBOL of luxury, the mobile phone is now a necessity—especially in Nigeria. It has proliferated to the country's most remote and rural parts in record time, as is the case throughout Africa. For the past decade the number of handsets across the continent has grown fortyfold, with nearly eight hundred million Africans possessing a device. It has an 80 percent penetration rate and is growing at 4.2 percent annually. Africa's mobile phone market is bigger than that of either the United States or the European Union. The continent has more mobile handsets than the United States and Europe combined. Analysts predict that there will be one billion mobile phone subscribers in Africa by 2016. A report by the international consulting firm McKinsey notes that between now and 2025 the number of Internet-enabled smartphones in all of Africa will increase from 67 million to 360 million.

With the mobile phone and now smartphones, huge distances and impassable roads are no longer insurmountable impediments. Farmers and fishermen coordinate trades and sales with various marketplaces. The sick seek medical attention from doctors located far away. Laborers send money more quickly and safely to families back in villages. Those in trouble call for help. In each circumstance, the mobile phone has provided a way for the individual to climb beyond his or her circumstances—to trade, to heal, and especially significant, to seek help.

Mobile phone signals can determine the location of a user. That has helped refugees, victims of famine, floods, wars, or other crises. At the same time, it has handed millions across Africa a sort of identity.

The majority of Africans have been invisible, since they have been unaccounted for on government rolls. In Nigeria, slightly over 40 percent of the population has a birth certificate—a remarkable 102 million people do not. Even more lack any form of identification. Without papers, these people can't receive benefits, rights, or protections, and worse, are subject to all forms of abuse, such as bribes and extortion. They remain on the sidelines and underground, economically and socially—unable to fully participate in everyday life. That reality has been another reason for Africa's underdevelopment.

The mobile phone has for the very first time given undocumented individuals—predominantly the poor—a way to be counted. Mobile money—and the process of opening up an account, which requires someone to confirm that the applicant not only has the funds to utilize it but also is not a criminal—has given them a way to be identified. That, far more than the mobile phone or any technology itself, Tayo believed, presented a huge opportunity to finally move his country forward. Nigeria would finally have a critical mass of people participating in its economic activities in a way that could be measured and tracked. Nigerians could save enough to open up a bank account and finally establish a credit history, which provided a lens for investors to gauge the health of a given market.

Key people at major development agencies and influential economists and academics believe that the mobile phone has already moved Nigeria forward, along with other countries in Africa. The World Bank, the African Development Bank, the International Finance Corporation, the

International Telecommunications Union, and a number of economists, including Jeffrey Sachs, the author of *The End of Poverty*, have noted that the device has "leapfrogged" the twentieth-century landline directly into twenty-first-century innovation—at lower cost and to greater effect. Yet as Tayo scrambled to deploy a backup server to keep the GLO lines in operation on that day in 2013 when I was visiting him in his office, the issue of infrastructure popped up again. For the mobile phone to prove truly revolutionary, it has to do the most basic thing: stay connected.

Though there are about 110 million active mobile subscribers in Nigeria, the actual number of users is estimated to be half that, only one-third of Nigeria's population. The majority of these users possess at least two and up to four handsets. These multiple handsets compensate for the poor quality of service. The majority of mobile connections, 62.7 percent, are over 2G. Dropped calls are common. In addition, Nigeria's mobile network lacks adequate coverage, particularly from urban to rural areas. Some parts of rural Nigeria, particularly in the north, where there is an ongoing and violent Islamic insurgency, have no mobile network coverage at all.

Part of the problem is that the number of base transceiver stations (BTS), the mechanism that carries wireless signals, falls short of the minimum requirement. There are only 20,000 BTS points throughout Nigeria, when there need to be 70,000. Telecom operators in Nigeria have been slow to assume a share of the investment necessary to build the infrastructure for these towers. One reason is that the telecom operators have not drawn a satisfactory profit from their mobile operations. The average revenue per user (ARPU) in Nigeria in 2012 was $9 per month. That is incredibly low compared with the United States, where the ARPU is $51.

The failure to adequately invest has resulted in poor service. And that in turn led, in May 2012, to the Nigerian Communications Commission (NCC) fining four mobile service providers a total of $7.38 million for failing to meet the minimum standard of quality of service.

Over the past several years Paga Tech and several e-commerce sites have stepped up to meet the challenge. Aided by considerable internationally sourced venture capital backing, they have started to invest in infrastructure and collaborate with the Nigerian government. This is what has made Paga and Nigeria's other tech startups significant. They are not just creating jobs and attracting investments; they are attacking the very barrier that has held their country back: poor infrastructure.

Paga Tech invests a significant amount in infrastructure development, committing 30 percent of its budget to the installation, upkeep, and repair of fiber optic cables as well as the purchase of generators that serve as backup during a power outage.

"You can't be going into this [mobile financial services] with an attitude that you will build the technology and the people will come," Tayo told me. "That's not going to work. We have to build the technology, go out and deliver it."

A handful of others agree, including a number of major US tech firms. Google launched Project Link, a wireless network, not in Nigeria, but in Uganda. Facebook, IBM, and Microsoft have also invested in African infrastructure.

The African Development Bank is spearheading an effort that will invest $360 billion through 2040 in African infrastructure.

Sim Shagaya, a Harvard Business School grad and former head of Google Africa, is another tech entrepreneur investing in improving Nigeria's infrastructure. Sim is the founder of Konga, an online merchandising site. It is a business that depends on logistics and the ability to move goods. Much as shipping and railroad magnate Cornelius Vanderbilt did in the United States in the late nineteenth century, he has used his own capital to upgrade cell phone service, install fiber optic lines, and repair roads. The opportunity, he believes, makes it worthwhile.

"We went from owning only a hundred fixed line phones (in the twentieth century) to owning hundreds and thousands of mobile phones," Sim told me. "I think we're going to see the same thing with e-commerce." The Internet, Sim pointed out, provides a channel for proprietors and customers to engage—an indispensable factor in moving markets. "All together we're going to build the engines and pipes that move commerce around this country."

. . .

RAIN FELL steadily on the morning that I headed out to meet several of the local agents Paga works with to deliver its financial services to people Tayo believes it is important to serve. These agents are the men and women, selected as trustworthy figures in their neighborhoods or villages, who recruit customers and ensure they are well served. They supplement Paga's mobile services, which are largely conducted via text message or online. These agents act as improvised bank tellers, facilitating money transfers as well as accepting bill payments and deposits. They help customers fill up their Paga accounts and act as a place for people to deposit and withdraw money.

Paga evaluates its agents based on several criteria. One is how effectively and honestly they can represent the company. Another is how well they can keep their books. Agents have to be reliable accountants. They have to record the amount of money received and cashed out at each transaction. Even though each Paga user is responsible for replenishing his or her Paga account, it is up to the agent to record and then report customer transactions.

Above all else, agents are evaluated on their ability to connect to the community and identify reliable customers. Knowing the customer and how he or she is using a particular service is an essential requirement for any financial institution. Agents have to procure relevant information from prospective customers. That reduces, though it does not entirely eliminate, the threat of money laundering, fraud, or terrorist financing.

Okeoma Obi, a shopkeeper and the first person I sought out, was delayed by the rain, which filled up potholes and drenched dirt roads. It created large puddles on roadsides and caused cars to stall. Lagos traffic froze, which delayed me as well and gave me a firsthand taste of life in a country in which the people have to contend day in and day out with poor infrastructure.

Okeoma had barely heard of Paga and mobile payments until a Paga employee called on him just a few weeks earlier.

Less than 15 percent of Nigeria's population uses mobile money.

This lack of awareness by so many people has forced Paga to rely on 1950s-style door-to-door salesmen and saleswomen to spread the word about the company and mobile money—and to identify and then recruit agents. The visit to Okeoma introduced him to the service as well as the prospect of receiving an Android-enabled smartphone and earning a commission on each transaction he processed. (Paga Tech has since done away with this service.) Paga Tech has a fixed, tiered fee per transaction. Those benefits, particularly the smartphone, which Okeoma would otherwise be unable to afford, convinced him to sign on as an agent. Okeoma is, at the time of this book's writing, one of nearly five thousand agents Paga has in twenty-nine of thirty-six states in Nigeria.

"When the person was talking to me about being a partner [with Paga Tech], even though the commission wasn't that big, I just wanted to be a part of this new move in the economy. I hear people talking about e-float—no more carrying around cash—I want to be a part of that change," Okeoma told me. "When people will come to understand Paga more, I believe somehow it will help my business to grow more."

The agent network is one of Paga's biggest expenses. Forty-five percent of the budget goes toward sales and marketing, which includes setting up and maintaining the agent network. These expenses, added to the 30 percent of the budget the company spends on infrastructure and investments, are the reason Paga struggles to turn a profit. Though it processed 918,000 transactions valued at $61 million in 2012, and 4.6 million transactions valued at $310 million in 2013, it barely broke even each year. Only when Paga reaches a critical mass of users can it start to see its profit and loss statement move well into the black. With nearly two million users, Paga is really just out of the starting gate when it comes to meeting Tayo's goal of twenty-five million users and thirty thousand agents. He believes that when he gets there he can kick back and regard Paga as a success.

Reaching this level of users and agents is a goal that Tayo believes will take more than $100 million to realize. The scale of the investment required has forced a number of Tayo's competitors to drop out. The Nigerian Central Bank has issued more than twenty licenses to operate mobile money, but only about a dozen of the holders are active in the market. The majority are banks that acquire a license. Many of those that have acquired a license have partnered with third-party vendors such as Paga Tech, willing to develop the business and bear the financial burden of customer acquisition. Akin Oyebode, a banking official with Stanbic Bank in Nigeria, has noted that "mobile money operators must be willing to lose significant revenues to drive growth."

A number of studies, including one from McKinsey and one from the accounting firm Ernst & Young, confirm this. "Our research suggests that even successful deployment requires three to five years to reach profitability," the McKinsey report reads. "Companies often have to commit more funds than expected to reach scale. Most successful mobile money launches have had the backing of millions of dollars." Vodafone's Safaricom, to take just one example, has spent $30 million on M-Pesa.

Convinced that the mobile payment space has enormous potential—particularly in the United States—a number of Silicon Valley investors have jumped in to help Tayo carry Paga Tech forward. The first person to back Paga was Tim Draper, a principal in the Silicon Valley venture capital firm Draper Fisher Jurvetson. Tayo met Draper through a Stanford business school classmate. After Tayo pitched his idea to the famous venture capitalist, Draper put several hundred thousand dollars of his own money into Paga as an angel investor in 2009.

In 2012 Adlevo Capital, a Nigerian-operated private equity firm with a $50 million seed fund for startups, led a $6.7 million investment round in Paga Tech. The Acumen Fund, Capricorn Investment, and the Omidyar Network, three US-based funds, joined the round. (Acumen and Omidyar are philanthropic funds.) Yemi Lalude, Adlevo's founder, initiated the deal. "Paga is building a new financial service from scratch," Yemi told me during a meeting in Lagos.

After spending six years at a Silicon Valley investment fund focused on China, Yemi, a tall and svelte engineer with a degree from Harvard Business School, turned his attention to his native Nigeria in 2007. Having witnessed the Middle Kingdom's rise shortly after the start of the new millennium, "long before" as he says, "China was sexy," he saw a number of signs that suggested that Nigeria had the potential to be a boom market.

"The leading indicator that something is going on in an emerging market is when the immigrants start moving back home," Yemi told me. Returning immigrants, he said, brought with them lessons learned, best practices, and a demand for excellence, which provide a framework for long-term growth. This not only builds startups but also helps repair conditions and overcome the obstacles that originally prompted emigration. The "brain gain" is what has propelled China and India over the past fifteen years. The Chinese and Indians returned and built their respective economies. Bülent Çelebi returned to Turkey to build AirTies. In Nigeria, the brain gain, combined with the country's huge population, is powering enormous growth.

Building, Yemi told me, is what Tayo is doing in Nigeria. "Financial services broadly is the one thing that is missing at all levels," he said. "The country lacks consumer credit; we [Nigerian investors] have no way of tracking the creditworthiness of individuals or for that matter of certain companies." Paga Tech, he said, is a conduit to a financial framework. Finance and financial tools are the areas he believes to be the biggest opportunities for emerging market entrepreneurs—and investors. Capitalism cannot function without credit.

"Paga Tech's solution overcomes the limitations of financial infrastructure in Nigeria by providing a convenient means for the unbanked to access (financial) services and conduct electronic transactions," he has also said.

Nigeria, like many places that suffer from poor infrastructure, struggles to fulfill its potential because it lacks credit, savings, and loans—it lacks a system in which money is not a mere unit of exchange but an asset to be leveraged.

Through its technology, Paga Tech is playing an important part in laying the groundwork for a financial framework. "They're helping to establish [financial] patterns in the market," Yemi told me. Paga is doing so by paving a path for financial inclusion for those left on the margins and collecting data and tracking patterns that can be used to better understand Nigeria's financial landscape and its actual finances. In a cash-based society, it is difficult to determine a market's transaction volume. It's hard to tell anything, really.

• • •

THE INTERNET has transformed our lives in many ways: how we communicate, how we read, how we consume news, how we listen to or buy music, how we watch television, how we shop, and how we learn. But it has not succeeded in changing how we pay for things and move money.

"A truly mobile wallet," said Jenna Wortham, the *New York Times* digital and startup reporter, is "one that would let you easily pay for restaurant meals, subway rides or beer at a bar with a quick wave of your cellphone—[and it] remains elusive." One reason she cites is banks and credit cards—functioning tools that have worked well, even if they haven't managed to create an entirely digital solution that would make payments as viral as content online.

Tayo Oviosu's Paga Tech, along with several other mobile payment platforms, is vying to be that digital solution. Current indications are that it has the potential to make significant gains. Paga has grown exponentially since its inception and has managed to continually attract investors. In addition to Tim Draper, Adlevo Capital, Acumen, Capricorn, and the Omidyar Network, Jim O'Neill, the former Goldman Sachs economist who coined the acronym BRIC (Brazil, Russia, India, China), invested an undisclosed amount in Paga Tech in April 2014.

Paga Tech has also managed to execute. That is in large part because of how Tayo Oviosu has applied his Stanford MBA, focusing on organizational structure and operations. Like Bülent Çelebi in Turkey, Tayo believes talent is crucial to Paga's success. Accordingly, he has attracted top talent— some from big companies in Nigeria, some from abroad— with competitive salaries. Perhaps more significantly, Tayo has engaged them in his efforts. Many of Paga Tech's employees told me that one of the things they appreciate about the startup is how Tayo listens to their concerns and ideas. Tayo holds weekly meetings with senior team members and holds frequent team retreats at which everyone understands where the company stands and where it is going. "They are my brand," Tayo told me when I asked him how he manages to get work done with team members taking advantage of his "open door" policy and interrupting him all day. "They are Paga's ambassadors. I give them the time and they give Paga their all. It's really a win for me if you think about it." After a while he added, "It's also about trust."

Trust is crucial to any startup anywhere. Gaining it in places like Nigeria, which are riddled with obstacles, is difficult. Obstacles impede faith and confidence. Talent is one way Tayo is building a trusted brand. Customer service is another. Paga Tech operates a twenty-four-hour help line, and Tayo himself is quick to respond to any concerns or complaints submitted via e-mail or the social media platform Twitter.

Paga's business development approach is a third factor in its success. Tayo has been selective about whom his company partners with. He has targeted a handful of big retailers, such as the South African–based MassMart, as well as a number of Walgreens-like pharmacy chains, fast food franchises, and Western Union. Paga Tech believes that its products—a payment platform, money transfer, and a savings account—can help attract customers to these retailers. In 2013 Tayo launched Paga Savings, a service that allows people to save money. The deposits are free, though there is a monthly maintenance fee. Unlike a traditional savings account housed at a bank, Paga Savings does not pay interest. It operates like a debit card. Retailers have welcomed Paga Savings, as it has increased foot traffic into their stores.

"The way I see it, for these organizations Paga is not only an up and coming brand with a relationship with lots of people in the market; practically speaking it is a product that could draw customers into their outlets," Jay Alabraba, Tayo's partner, told me.

Jay is a towering, imposing figure, well over six feet tall. I met him one day as he lumbered into Tayo's office. Malcolm Gladwell would call Jay the "salesman"—the charismatic soul that he describes in *The Tipping Point*, who can help "tip" an idea, trend, or social behavior into the mainstream. This is what Jay, perhaps because of his bear-like size or his ebullient belly laugh, is doing at Paga. He is the company's salesman, selling Paga's services to retailers. It makes him a complementary partner to Tayo. Jay plays Huckleberry Finn to Tayo's Tom Sawyer. Where Tayo tends to reflect and analyze, Jay acts—he's an offensive lineman who knows how to block and tackle. It is a trait that has helped Paga Tech gain traction and market share.

"The MassMarts and Shoprights are becoming the banking hall of the future. Finance is becoming connected to retail," Jay told me. People across Nigeria, he noted, are looking to conduct all their business in one spot. Especially given the country's poor infrastructure and wide distances between places, Nigerians, he said, want to shop, pay their bills, and withdraw or deposit money in the same location. Aggregation is the key. Industries and sectors had to combine efforts in order to scale up. That is what Jay is doing.

By far the biggest factor in Paga Tech's rising star has been the potential of the Nigerian market. Over the past decade, Nigeria's economy has grown between 5 and 7 percent annually. A large portion of that growth has come, interestingly enough, from services—not oil. Services account for 50 percent of Nigeria's GDP, and agriculture accounts for 23 percent. Oil is only 14 percent of the country's GDP.

"I tell people," says Tayo, "[that] the consumer opportunity of Africa is Nigeria." *The Economist* has noted: "Nigeria's promise has made it a test-bed for the Africa strategies of consumer-goods firms. This is not only because of its size. It is also because of the spread of Nigerian culture— its music and movies—around Africa." Nollywood, Nigeria's film industry, is second after India in terms of the number of movies produced. The United States is third (though it is first in revenues).

Despite ongoing infrastructure challenges, important manufacturers have expanded their presence in Nigeria. Procter & Gamble, one of the world's biggest producers of consumer goods, has just completed a second factory in Nigeria. SABMiller, a major beer maker, has built a brewery in the Niger Delta. Aliko Dangote, Africa's richest man and incidentally Nigerian, plans to build a $48.5 million food processing plant that would be the largest in Africa.

Startups have followed. Rocket Internet, a Berlin-based incubator that invests in "copycat" versions of American tech sites, rolled out the e-commerce site Jumia in 2013. It has inspired other Nigerians to venture into the startup world. I found a handful of them hovering over desks at the Co-Creation Hub, a startup workplace in Lagos.

As Seyi Taylor, a digital media entrepreneur and co-founder of Tech Cabal, a Nigerian startup news site (Nigeria's TechCrunch), pointed out to me, some startups are "figuring out how to create efficient processes—a lot of these startups are trying to create modernity." The challenge, he said, is for how long. Nigeria may have the largest GDP in Africa, but "there is so much growth that is still available within the country—and outside the country." Hence, the question is not who will create and innovate, but who can scale up what's already out there. Capital plays a big part in that, as much as infrastructure. "If we can figure out the money and figure out how to make it flow, then we've figured most of it out," he said.

Scale in mobile payments, as Tayo has figured out, involves the ability to access it. Wireless networks and broadband are one part of how and why mobile payments will succeed. Investing in that infrastructure—whether in Nigeria, New York, or Nebraska—is indispensable. Just as shipping ports, railroads, and the interstate highway system added value to the US economy, so too does the ability to connect to a digital network—continuously and without interruption. Mesh technology, as we saw in the first chapter—a technology that receives and distributes data through any wired device rather than a central access point such as a router—is something that both public and private sector officials should consider.

Equally important to the success of mobile payments is a critical mass of users. In Nigeria, as in Kenya and in other places where the majority are unbanked—without access to a place to store money—the agent network is critical to customer acquisition. In that business model agents receive a small percentage of revenues—a model similar to the one eBay, the online auction site, uses. Mobile money is unlike credit card companies, which charge proprietors for each transaction, and it will take off when a significant number of people find some sort of benefit in using it.

"I don't think we'll solve everything," Tayo told me on our last day together. We had attended the Card, ATM & Mobile Expo, a payments forum and conference, in Lagos. We toured a large exhibit hall where telecom companies, banks, phone manufacturers, and other mobile payment platforms had set up booths to market their products and services. "But I think we help people move." He paused.

After a few moments he added, "Yes, we help Nigeria move and synchronize." Unsure what he meant, I asked him to clarify what he meant by "synchronize."

In addition to poor infrastructure, Nigerians face a litany of other obstacles—a lack of talent, weak governance, corruption, and war. An insurgency set off by the Islamist extremist group Boko Haram in the north of the country—the group that kidnapped two hundred schoolgirls in 2014—has required businesses like Paga Tech to reassure investors and partners as well as customers that their investments and money, respectively, are safe. Convening people from otherwise disparate backgrounds on the Paga Tech platform—whether the banked or unbanked, the rural or urban—helps foster that assurance. The promise of transferring money, paying bills, and saving money "synchronizes" a large number of people behind a common voice and purpose. Poor infrastructure has forced Nigerians to fend for themselves. The ability to move money and have continuous and uninterrupted access to mobile networks and broadband has rallied a significant number of Nigerians—a majority—behind these vested interests. It has helped build a community, which otherwise has been difficult to do in Nigeria.

Community is precisely what Monis Rahman has struggled to create in another place beset by poor infrastructure and riven by war: Pakistan.

THREE

Steve Jobs Lives in Pakistan:
Tackling Insecurity and
Enabling Collaboration

Tell everyone the idea
Is to function together,
As good musicians would
In undefined future orchestras.

—BEN OKRI (*LINES IN POTENTIS*, 2002)

Lahore and Karachi

A haze hung over Lahore, Pakistan's second-largest city, on the March morning when Monis Rahman repeatedly tried to reach someone—anyone—at Naseeb Networks, the technology company he runs. It was half past nine o'clock. On any other day he would have already been at his desk. Operating two online websites, a matchmaking portal and a job search engine, in a country where Internet usage was rapidly increasing demanded that he start early. On this day, however, he acquiesced to his young family's pleas to have breakfast with them—just this one time. What could go wrong, they asked. Monis had built, painstakingly, an enterprise that could withstand unexpected difficulties, even a terrorist attack.

Monis's staff came face to face with what could go wrong when they tried to approach their office, located a block down from the city's main center, Liberty Square. Just before nine that morning, March 3, 2009, a pack of adolescents, armed with guns, grenades, and rockets, emerged from all corners of the square to attack a two-vehicle convoy. The convoy carried the Sri Lankan cricket team on its way to the nearby stadium, where it planned to play a match later in the day. For nearly half an hour, as the Sri Lankans took cover on the bus's floor, twelve terrorists fired their weapons furiously. Idyllic Liberty Square, adorned with orange, yellow, pink, and purple flowers, became a war zone, thundering with explosions and crackling with shots. Police shut down the entire area.

Monis, a normally calm and affable thirty-nine-year-old computer engineer, grew angry when he heard this news. No one on his staff of over a hundred was hurt. He knew that Naseeb's two sites would continue to operate. The company had backup servers located in the United States and contingency plans for the staff to operate remotely. What troubled him was the inevitable blowback from this incident. The Liberty Square attack would feed the negative reputation his country had gained over the past few years as a precarious place.

"This is not all that is happening in Pakistan," he would once again have to tell American investors that had backed his company. "Pakistan is not just about terrorism and violence." Terrorism and violence, he told me when we met at his two-story office on one autumn afternoon, are the "worst 5 percent" of what happens in Pakistan, but constitute 95 percent of what people read and hear about the country.

Five percent, unfortunately, has been sufficient to brand Pakistan as a failed state. That fact presents entrepreneurs like Monis—and others like him in other crime- and violence-prone places, including Brazil, Mexico, Nigeria, South Africa, and several US cities, namely Detroit, Michigan, and Camden, New Jersey—with a daunting challenge: how to conduct business, particularly on a serious scale, amid such notoriety.

Reputation determines one's acceptance or rejection. In the social media, all-news, all-the-time era, that has become even more applicable. On websites, blogs, Facebook, or Twitter, one misstep, one bad review, or one crisis can spread at record speed—and then be replayed on a loop incessantly. It can destroy any goodwill toward or effort by a person or place. People may not believe what they see or hear, but that they see and hear something negative is enough. Negative anything shatters confidence and sows doubt, which is what many feel when it comes to Pakistan.

"We [Pakistanis] have an enormous trust deficit with the rest of the world. . . . We've got this huge perception challenge globally," Monis told me. He wore a dark-colored *kurta*, a collarless shirt. The midday sun peeked through the vertical blinds into the glass-paneled conference room where we sat. The sun made his dark, deep-set eyes, which gave him a slight resemblance to the Egyptian actor and

Dr. Zhivago star Omar Sharif, squint periodically. A power generator hummed in the background, prompting him to pull his stocky body up straighter and project his voice. "Many investors and businesses don't want to be linked in any way to what's happening here," he said.

For the past decade Monis has been leveraging the Internet to show those investors and businesses, as well as others, particularly his own countrymen and women, a Pakistan beyond bombs and fear. The Internet has transformed, as Jared Cohen and Eric Schmidt note in *The New Digital Age*, "into an omnipresent and endlessly multifaceted outlet for human energy and expression." Monis is gambling that that energy and expression can build a network—a community and a space that bring people together—that can help recast Pakistan's reputation. His starting point are the two websites he has developed, Naseeb.com and Rozee.pk.

Naseeb is the Disney-fied version of Match.com. With great sensitivities about singles and romance, it is a Muslim-wide connection and collaboration platform that uses matchmaking site algorithms to allow people to become "friends" or even "court," but does not promote love. There's no hooking up here. The mixing of genders, let alone dating, in Pakistan remains taboo. So taboo that in 2012 Samaa TV, a major television channel, produced a reality show to probe into the relationship status of random couples on the street or in a park to expose "immoral behavior." The majority of Pakistani society expects unmarried men and women in Pakistan to refrain from physical contact. As a virtual platform, Naseeb circumvented that issue and became hugely popular among Pakistan's youth. It was so popular, Monis created a job search website where he could source technical talent to help him manage Naseeb.

Rozee is a combination of a job seekers' site like Monster.com, at which vacant positions are posted, and a virtual career fair, at which companies in Pakistan can promote their work. Pakistan has a robust and growing private sector. Several leading foreign multinationals, including Honda, Microsoft, Nestle, Philips, Procter & Gamble, Siemens, Toyota, and Unilever, conduct business in the country. The number of small- and medium-sized enterprises is on the rise. Over sixty thousand employers hire through Rozee. The site has processed 26.3 million applications and posts more than 110 new jobs each day.

Naseeb and Rozee give Pakistanis the opportunity to connect. Therein lies their value. Pakistan has two problems. One is that there are few public spaces where people—both men and women—can convene, collaborate, and create. The few gathering spaces that Pakistan does have are the mosque, the military barracks, and the cricket field—all of which segregate by gender.

The second problem is that Pakistan is split along four geographic, ethnic, and tribal lines: Punjab, Sindh, Baluch, and Pashtun. While not warring, these groups occupy different regions of mountainous and rugged countryside—where poor infrastructure isolates them further. Each holds individual and often opposing interests, which are controlled by powerful landowners and business leaders. These landowners and business leaders make it difficult for anyone to conduct his own business, much less for an entrepreneur to launch and scale up an idea. They act as de facto monopolists who squelch competition.

Naseeb and Rozee strive to be a virtual community space that Monis believes can widen, and, more ambitiously, serve as the basis to shift perspectives on and within Pakistan.

Much hope has been put on technology to improve our lives and solve problems—a phenomenon the digital activist and scholar Evgeny Morozov has called and criticized as "solutionism." In *To Save Everything, Click Here*, he notes:

> Today, virtually every story is bound to have an "Internet" angle—and it's the job of our Internet apostles to turn those little anecdotes into fairy tales about the march of Internet progress, just a tiny chapter in their cyber-Whig theory of history. "The Internet": an idea that effortlessly fills minds, pockets, coffers, and even the most glaring narrative gaps.

Many in the technology space, the *digerati*, have used the Internet and social media to fill in various narrative gaps and explain the supposed rise in social consciousness and activism around the world. The digerati proclaimed that the 2011 Arab Spring—wherein hundreds of thousands across several Arab nations rose up against their autocratic leaders—happened as a result of Facebook and Twitter. These same sites, they said, fueled protests against Wall Street that same year. When Islamic insurgents in Nigeria, Boko Haram, kidnapped two hundred schoolgirls in 2014, #BringBackOurGirls became a viral phenomenon.

Monis, though far more optimistic than most in Pakistan, is not so sanguine. He told me that while he believes the Internet can help "move things forward," in Pakistan and elsewhere, it alone will not transform Pakistan. "What I do know," he told me, "is that the Internet allows people to find and exchange information and get a better sense of what's actually going on." That, he rightly believes, is the Internet's value-add. It is but one tool that can help transform Pakistan, a country riddled with numerous disadvantages: poor infrastructure, a lack of competition, corruption, and weak governance. The rest depends on the country's people and its government—and their ability to collectively work together to create the conditions that will improve Pakistan.

• • •

PAKISTAN IS dysfunctional. With few exceptions, its institutions are weak. Only the army and the mighty spy agency, the Inter-Services Intelligence Directorate (ISI), operate with any degree of effectiveness. No Pakistani government has shown itself capable of running the country since its birth in 1947. Officially, Pakistan is a parliamentary democracy. In reality, it swings between kleptocracy and military rule, or combinations of the two, in which the media are tightly controlled.

As a result, its citizens are disengaged. Few pay taxes, including politicians. Pakistan has one of the lowest levels of tax collection outside of Africa. One of Pakistan's top political figures, current prime minister Nawaz Sharif, reported that he did not pay any personal income tax for three years ending in 2007. In the absence of tax revenue, the country, much like Nigeria, is bereft of basic services: clean water, reliable electricity, public transport, proper sewage, and policing. This has not only led to sustained poverty, illiteracy, and disease, but also has crippled emergency responses to natural disasters like the heavy monsoon rains of 2010, in which over two thousand died and millions were displaced, largely due to unpreparedness and a bungled relief effort. The weak state and derelict citizenry have also allowed the rise of militant groups such as the Taliban, the Haqqani Network, Laskhar-e Taiba, and al-Qaeda. It is no accident that Osama bin Laden felt confident enough to take refuge in Pakistan.

The rise in terrorism occurred after Monis Rahman returned to live in Pakistan. It was not something he had expected. He had always known that his country struggled to develop and had its share of troubles. But Pakistan itself was not a source of trouble; Pakistan was not an insecure or violent state. In fact, during Monis's childhood, Pakistan experienced periods of prosperity. In the 1960s and 1970s the country's textile industry grew and became globally competitive, making Pakistan a model for other struggling nations, including India. That is the Pakistan Monis believed he had returned to in 2000, after his father retired from the United Nations and moved back to Lahore.

Monis's father was an urban planner for the United Nations. That meant that little Monis lived in New York, Riyadh, and Vienna. Yet despite all of his international experiences, Monis did not develop an interest in diplomacy. He preferred making things. As a nine-year-old he took apart his mother's blender and ripped out its motor to build a remote car out of Lego and Meccano pieces. It was an ingenious invention that got him started on a creative path in technology and sealed his future as an inventor. From then on, Monis spent his time tooling around with gadgets. In high school, which he attended in Lahore at the international school, he worked on transistors, creating his own radio out of plaster for a science fair. By the time he graduated he had gravitated toward computers and the burgeoning field of computer technology.

Monis attended college at the University of Wisconsin at Madison. There he studied microprocessors, memory chips, and electronics, most of which, he noted, had been invented by scientists at Intel. "It became my dream to work at Intel alongside the legends I read about in textbooks," he told me. In 1996, after graduating from Stanford University with a graduate degree in computer engineering, he managed to land a job on Intel's microprocessor team. He specifically worked on the team that developed the revolutionary Itanium 64-bit microprocessor chip, the device that acts as a computer's nervous system, routing information and allowing multitasking.

Intel named Monis as an inventor on three patents for ideas he had developed. All involved the branch predictor—a digital circuit that channels information. It's the pipeline of a microchip. In Silicon Valley, however, these patents were not special. Everyone in Silicon Valley seemed to be working on one breakthrough or another. That was especially true in the late 1990s, when the Internet had become a phenomenon—what Michael Lewis described in *The New New Thing* as a "child's chemistry experiment," because young people were busy creating sites or software for the Web. It was the dot-com boom. Investors poured billions into all sorts of unproven projects. Not willing to be left out, Monis quit his dream job at Intel to start his own company in 1999. It was a chip designing and development firm, which he sold just a year later. But having caught what he described as the "entrepreneurial bug," he went on to launch his second startup, eDayCare.com, an online platform that streamed live feeds from daycare centers to parents, who could then monitor their children. eDayCare.com attracted $2.5 million in investments, including an investment from Ron Conway, a prominent angel investor in Silicon Valley. Conway invested in Google and PayPal in their early days. Despite receiving this money, Monis ran into financial trouble and was also forced to sell this company.

Both experiences taught Monis the value of management. Ideas alone don't enable startups to break out. As we saw in chapter 1 about Bülent Çelebi, they run on plans and with individuals who can properly execute on them. Monis's experiences gave him insight about the Internet. At the end of the 1990s people knew about the World Wide Web. What they didn't know was the potential it held— where the Internet would lead. Some said it wouldn't last. Monis, however, started to understand how the Internet grabbed people's attention, encouraged them to engage, how it could influence people's beliefs and behavior, and how it would eventually impact public attitudes and opinions and create new communities.

The dot-com bust in 2000 prompted Monis to follow his parents home to Pakistan. As stocks in the United States took a nosedive, companies lost their valuation. Investors lost money. Thousands of Silicon Valley startups were wiped out. Monis saw opportunity in Pakistan, where he believed that "all the curves were upward."

Also in 2000 General Pervez Musharraf, head of the Pakistani military, took control of the government in a military-backed coup and imposed a series of economic reforms. That presaged hope. These reforms boosted foreign direct investment and encouraged entrepreneurship. The country's economy grew at an average 7 percent annually thereafter. Close to seventy million Pakistanis, 40 percent of the population, moved into the middle class.

This middle class started experimenting with the Internet. At the start of the millennium, Pakistani interest in blogs and chat rooms rose considerably. The Internet proved to be a portal to endless associations and resources. Monis saw this as a ripe opportunity to be a so-called first mover— the first to market—in the country's still uncharted online market, as Pakistan seemed to be on an upswing, breaking from a troubled past and ascending. The same phenomenon had unfolded in neighboring India as well as other countries formally known as "developing": Brazil, China, and Turkey. After several scouting trips, convinced his country's reputation had improved, Monis moved to Pakistan in 2003, where he launched one of the country's first Internet companies.

Among the things his Silicon Valley experience taught Monis was the importance of revenue generation. It was not enough just to have an innovative product. When the dust of the dot-com bust settled, it was clear that there were some Internet business models that were very profitable in the worst of times. Job search engines were one. Matchmaking sites were another. Both relied on subscriptions rather than ads—a more reliable revenue stream. Though he eventually turned to a job search engine, entirely by accident, Monis zeroed in on the matchmaking site first. He was at the time a single, Muslim male—he wanted a site that would benefit him. In the early 2000s, social networking sites were just taking off. Enthusiasm for SixDegrees, Friendster, and MySpace—the first social networking experiments—showed an appetite for cyber connection.

Developing a platform for Pakistanis to connect to one another didn't require complicated coding or business development. It was simpler. To be sure, however, he sought out the advice of a few Silicon Valley veterans.

• • •

MONIS TAPPED Reid Hoffman, the founder of LinkedIn and a former PayPal executive, for advice. Reid had experimented with an online dating service that he called SocialNet. Though it failed, Monis felt Reid's experience contained important lessons.

Over a barbeque of Pakistani chicken *tikka*, Reid and Monis discussed how to make Naseeb.com flourish. Sitting on Monis's patio, the two entrepreneurs tossed around tech-speak about how the "connection" site would operate. They also discussed how Naseeb would engage users and win over repeat ones. Reid advised Monis to invest heavily in engineering and design. That led the conversation to capital. Reid asked if Monis had found his starting funds yet.

"I told him I didn't have the time," Monis said. Reid then took out his phone. Confused, Monis sat still. "Joe? It's Reid. Listen, I'm with Monis Rahman, who's starting a SocialNet (the startup Reid had launched but failed) in Pakistan. I'm going in on it. I think you should, too." Reid Hoffman had Joe Krause on the line—the founder of Excite.com, a Google-like search engine. Hoffman then dialed Mark Pincus, the future founder of Zynga, an online game developer. Neither had met Monis. Still, each put up a $25,000 equity stake in Naseeb. Monis sat there, stunned.

"Neither had seen any plans or PowerPoints on Naseeb," Monis recalled. That an "I'm going in" pledge by Reid Hoffman would suffice to bring in backers gave Monis pause. In Pakistan, only family and kinship could compel, out of loyalty, such support. This was trust, which simply did not exist in Pakistan on any social, economic, or political level. There was no opportunity or space to develop it. Pakistanis gathered at the mosque or else at one another's homes. There was no tradition of salons and few casual meeting venues at which people could brainstorm and establish relationships. The Internet transcended these limitations in a way that previous technologies had not. Unlike the landline phone, radio, and television, the Internet gathered unlimited numbers and allowed them to engage at the same time. It made it possible to learn, receive information, form bonds, and lay the foundations of trust.

The lack of trust and community in Pakistan is one reason, Monis realized, that his country navigates from crisis to crisis. "Its [Silicon Valley's] success was there in itself, not in the technology," he told me. Monis realized that if he—or anyone—intended to succeed in Pakistan, that ability to convene and have serendipitous interaction would have to be replicated. Just as Nigeria needs to build a financial framework, Pakistan needs to create community space. The virtual space he planned would be the place to start.

As a keen observer of all things digital, Monis was impressed by the website Eidmubarak.com. It was a holiday greeting site that millions of Muslims across the globe used. At the time, there were few sites that focused specifically on Muslims—a demographic of more than a billion people. The active and extensive engagement on Eidmubarak told Monis that a market for Muslim-focused content existed.

Monis acquired the site in 2003. That gave him an entrée to an extensive database of Muslims throughout the world. The site and the data Monis gathered from it enabled him to understand how Muslims interacted with one another and their preferences and sensitivities. There were many preferences and sensitivities, particularly around dating and sex, that eventually helped shape his idea for Naseeb.

Then Monis made a critical move. He arranged to keep his servers in the United States, away from Pakistan's unreliable power grid. Monis had to ensure uninterrupted service. A reputation for continued and reliable service was the only way he could earn the public's trust in him and Naseeb. It was a strategy similar to the one Tayo Oviosu pursued in Nigeria and that Dov Frohman, an Israeli engineer who worked for Intel and opened up a chip design center for the tech giant in Haifa in 1974, had adopted.

Living amid hostile neighbors, under barbed wire and the constant threat of suicide bombs, Israel is an improbable place for innovation to thrive. But when Frohman pushed Intel to expand into the country and then build the company's first semiconductor fabrication plant outside the United States in 1985, Israeli tech talent thrust itself into the limelight. Frohman and his team developed and designed smarter chips for Intel—and proved their grit and worth when they continued to develop and design those chips even when the former Iraqi dictator Saddam Hussein lobbed Scud missiles at Israel in 1991.

The United States had invaded Iraq in January of that year, launching what it called Operation Desert Storm—a military operation to emancipate Kuwait from Iraqi occupation. In retaliation, Hussein targeted the Jewish state. Frohman defied orders to shut down his operations. Instead, he carried out the contingency plans he had drawn up prior to the hostilities, which would allow his operations to continue. It was a simple plan: keep producing microchips. Israel couldn't avoid threats, but its people could band together to deliver cutting-edge products and services and, as Monis noted, "take the risk to help improve the situation and perception of the country." They came together as a community.

Israeli entrepreneurs created a narrative for their country that altered its reputation. Frohman kept producing microchips and went on to produce even more advanced ones, much to the surprise of his Intel colleagues back in Silicon Valley. As a result of his actions, no one could again look upon Israel only from the perspective of conflict with its Middle Eastern neighbors. In fact, he inspired other Israelis to launch technology ventures. Today, startups percolate throughout Israel, which still grapples with violence and war. The country has come to be known as *the startup nation*. Israeli entrepreneurs attract tremendous venture capital investment and investors. There are more than one hundred venture capital funds operating *in* Israel. After the United States, it has the most publicly traded companies on the NASDAQ.

It will take considerable time before something similar unfolds in Pakistan. The differences between Israel and Pakistan—historically, politically, economically, and globally—are huge, as are the respective efforts Dov Frohman and Monis Rahman have undertaken. Manufacturing chips is a far more tangible and winnable prospect than rallying people to a computer or mobile handset to connect with someone else—and then expecting public perceptions to change miraculously.

Monis had never thought of himself as leading a movement or cause. But having moved back to Pakistan as it slowly started to unravel again, he was in a position in which he had two choices. He could either leave and go back to Silicon Valley, or he could stay and fight on. If he fled he'd still have to grapple with the stereotype Pakistan had developed as a failed state. That he didn't want to do. The Internet may or may not change people's perceptions about Pakistan, including those of Pakistanis themselves. It could provide a space for collaboration. At that moment in time, however, he had nothing to lose. From a small room in his parents' house in Lahore and with $150,000 in hand, he proceeded with Naseeb, launching it on October 23, 2003.

. . .

"MOVING TO the city is the first step to getting filthy rich in rising Asia," writes the Lahore-based writer Mohsin Hamid in a fictional tale with the title *How to Get Filthy Rich in Rising Asia*, in a place eerily similar to Pakistan. It is a reflection of the actual rural to urban phenomenon that has taken place in Pakistan since the 1980s and the start of globalization. Millions of Pakistanis have left the countryside in search of better opportunities—jobs, schools, and health care—in the country's metropolises. Those opportunities have often occurred as a result of Pakistanis' own initiative—their own hustle. There are more Pakistani-owned small businesses and mom-and-pop shops today than at any point in the country's history. Small and medium enterprises constitute 90 percent of all enterprises in Pakistan. The service sector accounts for nearly 60 percent of Pakistan's GDP. By comparison agriculture, even with the country's bustling mango trade, makes up only 20 percent of the economy.

Yet because these businesses were "small" and "medium," job websites in Pakistan overlooked them. The thirty or so that existed poured resources into advertising positions for big conglomerates and multinationals. That's where the money lay. Small businesses, it was presumed, had small budgets that paid small salaries. Aggregating information about or for them seemed like a money-losing proposition. Especially by 2007, as violence in Pakistan started to increase, the number of job placements advertised dropped.

The sector looked to be headed for hard times. That, Monis concluded from his experience in Silicon Valley, was an opportunity to start a business. A number of Fortune 500 companies, including AT&T, Disney, Federal Express, General Electric, General Motors, and Microsoft, got off the ground when things were in decline. Two factors made it a good idea to launch a startup during a downturn: weak competitors are likely to drop out, and good people are looking for work.

If operating a startup in Pakistan is tricky, so is hiring qualified staff. Most experienced and well-educated Pakistanis opt to work for well-paying multinationals. Still, Monis knew that among the 180 million people in his country, only a handful would be qualified and interested in Naseeb. It required effort on his part to find them. Monis found classified ads in the newspaper too expensive a way to reach the talent he wanted to recruit. Nor did he think that the ideal candidates existed on the many job search engines populating Pakistan's market.

Geeks, as Monis personally knew, were a self-selecting group. To reach them, he decided to build a makeshift site for IT positions. After a few weeks, a number of other tech startups asked if they could post vacancies on the site. In six months this site went from makeshift to having hundreds of users. Job availability and mobility had played a critical role in Silicon Valley's growth. As Monis started to develop more of a mission to help his country, he saw how operating a job search website could contribute to improving Pakistan's reputation. It put on display opportunity and talent. It could help build a community.

Monis made Pakistani small and medium companies his niche. LinkedIn, the Silicon Valley–based business social networking service, had gained popularity among large corporations and executives in the United States and had started to gain traction abroad. While Monis knew that he would have to depend on foreign multinationals for revenue and reputation—and that in doing so he faced competition from LinkedIn—he felt that providing resources for the small- and medium-sized business segment would distinguish him and keep *Rozee*–livelihood, the site he launched in 2008, competitive.

Monis could, however, see that many small business owners did not perceive Rozee as a viable option when hiring. "A lot of them thought newspapers were the way to go," Monis said. Yet having witnessed the growth of job search engines in the United States, he concluded that that trend would spread, even to a place like Pakistan. Since he had returned home, Internet usage had gone up. The number of mobile phone users had skyrocketed. Job searches would inevitably migrate to the Web in Pakistan. Monis seized on the opportunity to launch such a platform with an emphasis on Pakistani-owned establishments.

To convince Pakistani businesses, Monis delved deep. Like Tayo Oviosu in Nigeria, he hired an army of salespeople, more than the number of engineers on staff, to help him reach out to Pakistan's small businesses. Monis needed to show them that Rozee was not merely a job board. Its mission was to advance and engage the country's private sector and promote Pakistan's marketplace. Monis made sure to provide essential data about hiring trends to Pakistani small- and medium-sized businesses. In addition, he partnered with university placement offices to create career pipelines for capable graduates. He also hosted job fairs.

The job fairs in particular proved important. Like Paga Tech in Nigeria, which uses agents to promote its mobile payment platform, these job fairs put a human face on Monis's virtual efforts. Pakistanis could see and talk to the very proprietors who advertised on Rozee. Digital did not have to equal impersonal. In fact, it could enhance human interactions and experiences, which is what Pakistan needs. Human interaction is the ingredient necessary for any innovation.

American-based e-commerce platforms, such as eyeglass retailer Warby Parker and the men's clothing line Bonobos, believe that to be true. Both started out as exclusively online sites but subsequently opened up "showroom" stores. David Gilboa, Warby Parker's cofounder and CEO, has said, "There's still something tangible that you can't replace, when you're walking into a store, engaging all five senses." People want connection to a product as well as with one another. Brands, ultimately, are about the people behind them—their vision and values. How people feel about those values and vision determines a brand's long-term success or failure.

Like Bülent Çelebi in Turkey and Tayo Oviosu in Nigeria, Monis wanted his product to enable Pakistanis to feel positive about their country and succeed. He treated Rozee as more than just a website. It was a community. Hosting job fairs took people away from their screens and put them in contact with other people—that was the entire point.

The ability to assemble and connect with others is the most fundamental basis of any society. It is no wonder that in authoritarian regimes, the state goes to lengths to intimidate and isolate a given population. Together, people effect change.

The ability to come together to share ideas and interact with others, Monis recognized, is what defined and helped create Silicon Valley. The lone entrepreneur, concocting ideas and building a game-changing business, is but a myth. Startups, just like change, happen when people connect and collaborate—whether in pairs or in a critical mass.

Silicon Valley happened when not one man but eight men, the "traitorous eight," walked away from secure jobs at the semiconductor company Shockley Semiconductor Laboratory in 1956, in order to form Fairchild Semiconductor a year later. It happened when Steve Jobs met Stephen Wozniak in high school and they shared a love of computers (and music). It happened when Sergey Brin sparred with Larry Page at Stanford University. Silicon Valley and the innovations it has spawned happened with people, conversation, and the experimentation of ideas that were imagined—together. It is a simple and natural process that everyone everywhere has been formulating complex theories about, particularly as it relates to places outside Silicon Valley.

Entrepreneurship and innovation have become the miracle cure to global challenges. They have moved beyond a simple product or service to become a salve that, when applied, can wondrously transform people, businesses, and even entire countries. As the world grapples with ongoing poverty, financial meltdowns, uprisings, insurgencies, and pandemics, there is a desperate need for a cure-all—a reset button that will fix everything. Entrepreneurship and innovation are, after all, what made a once sleepy, fifty-mile stretch of fruit orchards into Silicon Valley. They are now transforming places that were once dusty backwaters as well. China, India, Israel, Taiwan, and South Korea are all developing technological enterprises and, in the process, have become global economic powers.

Monis Rahman knew that for entrepreneurship—especially tech entrepreneurship—to succeed in Pakistan, the country needed to build community. The inability to convene is a significant factor in sustaining the negative stereotypes about Pakistan and fans the flames of fear. It is what prevents promising tech talent—Pakistan's Steve Jobs—from emerging.

• • •

IN 2007 MONIS received an e-mail from an investment group looking to acquire his Naseeb Networks, which had been generating several hundred thousand US dollars in revenue from Naseeb, the matchmaking portal. Pakistan, this investment group had found, appeared likely to be the next India or China—an emerging market that showed growth and where investors could make substantial returns. Pakistan had more than seventy million people, many of whom had moved into the middle to upper class. Pakistan had globally reputable universities, including the Lahore University of Management Sciences.

Monis refused the investment group's offer. Instead, he mapped out plans to build Naseeb further—into a broad online brand. He imagined becoming the South Asian version of the Berlin-based company Rocket Internet—a company that could clone Internet platforms that did well in the West but that had not yet gone beyond the English-speaking world.

He set out to raise investment capital for this idea in Silicon Valley. Pakistani banks wouldn't lend to him. They balked at extending credit to startups, even when contracts guaranteed return. That was also the experience of another Pakistani entrepreneur, Shakir Husain, the CEO and founder of the technology outsourcer Creative Chaos. When expanding his company in 2007, he requested a $100,000 loan.

"Put together collateral for $100,000, and we'll give you this loan," they said to him. Shakir replied that he had a $1 million contract from a client based in the United States. They still refused. "Had I been a textile company where I could produce a letter from my client, there would have been no problem. Being a software company, they didn't know how to collateralize that risk," he said to me when I visited him in Karachi. Shakir didn't have anything tangible for the bank to use as a guarantee for the loan. He eventually self-financed—the worst of all alternatives, because if the venture had failed, he would have been personally ruined. (Creative Chaos, in fact, has scaled up and has an office in San Francisco.) Once again, community mattered. In this case it was in the form of venture capital.

Venture capital is not just a financial transaction. It is, as its name suggests, venturing into an agreement to help an entrepreneur build a business. That includes mentoring entrepreneurs and opening up networks to help entrepreneurs build businesses. Venture capital certainly helped the "traitorous eight" build Fairchild Semiconductor. That is why Monis reached out to venture capital firms on Sand Hill Road in Silicon Valley. Not surprisingly, few wanted to hear about his company or idea. They all understood the Internet and had seen the potential for his offerings. But how those offerings could thrive in Pakistan piqued their curiosity. "The sell I had to make wasn't about Rozee or Naseeb," Monis told me. The sell Monis had to make was his homeland. He had to convince an otherwise skeptical group that it was more than a place of terrorism and bombs. He received two return calls. One was from Draper Fisher Jurvetson (DFJ), the other ePlanet.

"These were the best funds to help us because they had experience in emerging areas of the world," Monis said. The aggressive terms they presented suggested otherwise. Neither had invested in Pakistan, which one partner, Mohanjit Jolly, admitted was "risky." Jolly had just joined DFJ in order to establish the firm's presence in India, which was (and still is) a hot venture market. Priding themselves on being "trailblazers," Jolly told me that the firm was, in 2007, "eager to springboard to other parts of the region" ahead of everyone else. "As luck would have it, Naseeb Networks was one of the first deals I was asked to look at."

Bombarded with data and charts on the robustness of Pakistan's Internet, Jolly picked up on Monis's vision. He saw that Monis had created an interesting offering and had some level of traction. He was able to see it—and look past all the negativity about Pakistan because of his familiarity with the country. Jolly is of Indian descent. He knows about Pakistan's capabilities, as much as he is aware of its short-comings. Though India and Pakistan have been embattled neighbors, the two countries share much in the way of common history and culture. Pakistanis, Jolly knew, are just as capable as Indians. Jolly told me that over the longer term he recognized that Naseeb Networks would "bring in returns" because it was building a community. "This [Naseeb] is not just a play on tech. Monis is building partnerships that he can extend to other parts of the world; he's taking something and making it grow beyond Pakistan." After considering how much Monis actually wanted to raise, they agreed to invest. "In the scheme of things it wasn't a lot of capital."

There was an agreement to invest, but the deal took a long time to close. DFJ wanted one of the big five US accounting firms to audit Naseeb Networks. It was a process that anywhere else would have taken a month, but in Pakistan it took three and a half. No major accounting firm had experience valuing tech companies in places such as Pakistan, with outdated regulations. They could only assign numbers to hard assets, not software or intellectual property. The audit took place in the last months of 2007 when Pakistan was, as Monis describes, "turning upside down." The constitution was suspended. Bomb blasts had gone off in the country's major cities, Karachi and Peshawar. Just when it seemed that Pakistan had shaken off its past reputation, its troubles resurfaced. Former prime minister Benazir Bhutto, who had returned to Pakistan to campaign in the upcoming general election, was assassinated in 2007. Pakistan was all over CNN. It was no surprise that Monis received an e-mail saying that the partners were "reconsidering."

From Pakistan, Monis got on the phone and explained to a room full of experienced venture capitalists why they should move forward with their investment. "I went through the numbers and growth curves." In the last three months he'd seen historic high growth. Sensing that was not enough to sell them, he sat down to type an e-mail, the most important he had ever written.

Venture capital is about capitalism, not politics, he noted in his message. Like credit and loans, it acts as a facilitator. Sure, the market in which the venture capital is being vested is an important factor. "If you really calculate the risk [of a country], it's a rounding error compared to the inherent risk of a startup in the first place," Monis wrote. Venture capital has always been anchored in taking a risk on an individual and an idea. And risk, ironically, is exactly what Pakistan needs to encourage in order to jumpstart investments and the flow and retention of capital. Money in Pakistan, as in many struggling economies, does not stay in nor is it invested in the country. Remittances from migrants working in other countries, which totaled $15 billion in 2013, sustain millions of Pakistanis. Remittances are used to cover day-to-day expenses. It's cash flow into the Pakistani economy, but nothing more. It's not funding used as leverage to build infrastructure, invest in schools, or create new enterprises and, most important, jobs. Monis believed that for entrepreneurship to succeed in Pakistan, the country needed to attract and eventually develop a way to extend credit and turn money into an asset.

"I still remember getting that e-mail," Jolly told me. It led to a detailed discussion at DFJ that bordered on soul-searching. "The question we had to answer was, could we believe in Monis Rahman as an entrepreneur?" The answer to that was yes. Monis, as an entrepreneur, had an impeccable reputation. He was trusted—known to be a hard worker who delivered as promised. "It also came down to 'what is DFJ about?' We don't run away from situations most people would. Considering that we had effectively come this far and made this commitment, we didn't want to destroy our reputation and back out."

Since 2007 DFJ has worked with Monis to keep his operations moving. Like many businesses, Naseeb Networks felt the effects of global financial meltdown in the following year. Pakistani enterprises stopped hiring. People cut back. Jolly told me that Monis realized he couldn't pursue his dream of building multiple Web portals. Though it pained him, he pivoted to focus on one thing only, Rozee, the job site. "It was clear that Facebook and LinkedIn were spreading their wings throughout the world, including Pakistan and the Middle East," Jolly said. "Rather than go head-to-head against the giants, it made sense to leverage the local presence and knowledge to scale the Rozee.pk brand, which generated most of the revenue anyway."

· · ·

AFFIXED ON TOP of the Al Faisaliyah Center in Saudi Arabia is a golden ball. It appears to be poised to hurl itself, or else be hurled, along with the rocket-shaped building, past the expanse of sand and palm trees into the galaxy. The center is a celebrated landmark in Riyadh, Saudi Arabia's capital, and its third-tallest building. It is where Monis Rahman spent much of 2012 and 2013, shuttling in and out in order to acquire one of the companies that occupies space at Al Faisaliyah: a job search website called Mihnati.com.

Saudi Arabia is one of the world's largest recruiters. It and neighboring Gulf states hire hundreds of thousands of foreign workers. The majority of those recruits are from South Asian countries, especially Bangladesh, India, and Pakistan.

In June 2013 Monis acquired Mihnati. This is the first instance of a Pakistani tech startup acquiring a foreign company. Company acquisitions generally have taken place in the West, by established companies—Fortune 500 or Silicon Valley giants. This is one of the ways they have accumulated talent and assets, gained market share and competitive advantage, and entered new markets. At Intel, Monis saw how acquisitions helped strengthen the company's mission and capabilities, providing expanded distribution channels and access to know-how, and kept it ahead of the competition. Acquisitions are what Amazon, Facebook, and Google have done as well—sparking a separate question about these companies becoming monopolies and competition disappearing in their market spaces—a topic tackled in the next chapter.

Rozee had become the number one job search website in Pakistan, with the largest market share, and in June 2013 it reached twenty-two successive quarters of growth. The All World Network, an index started by Harvard business and management professor Michael Porter, ranked Rozee as the twelfth-fastest growing company in Pakistan in 2011, up from twenty-fifth the year before. Yet a number of investors I spoke to noted that Rozee doesn't have the numbers to match its market share. The company has less than a million dollars in revenues. Investors have doubts about its long-term success. They very well may be right. Still, Rozee, along with its founder Monis Rahman, is significant for the role it has played in Pakistan's budding tech scene and building an entrepreneurial ecosystem.

Brad Feld, an investor, entrepreneur, and founder of Techstars, a notable startup incubator in the United States, noted in *Startup Communities: Building an Entrepreneurial Ecosystem in Your City* that long-term commitment and active involvement of an existing entrepreneur are key to growing an entrepreneurial ecosystem. Monis Rahman exhibits both: he is an entrepreneur who sees Pakistan's expanding entrepreneurial scene, as Feld notes in *Startup Communities*, "as a game with increasing returns, in which the larger number of entrepreneurs involved, the more great things happen."

Rozee remains a player in the job search/human resources market, with potential to scale up. It continues to innovate new products such as InstaMatch—an online tool in which recruiters can use keywords to search through a database of CVs and find relevant talent. Regional expansion has increased its value.

"We saw an opportunity to add considerable value to Mihnati's customer base through our product portfolio, back office operations and business experience in online recruiting," Monis told me. Acquiring the company "shortcut" expedited Rozee's entry into Saudi Arabia and provided the added benefit of having a local team and local partners.

Not just an exhaustive expanse of pale desert, Saudi Arabia now has shiny, futuristic buildings and well-manicured, green gardens. It is a place where one expects saucer-shaped cars to fly in and out of the many towers that occupy the skyline. Wall Street bankers and lawyers fit right into its callous commercial glory. Dig deeper, however, and Saudi Arabia's true nature is exposed. It is a place still dependent on oil, where women have few rights, and the people have little say in governance. The Saudis have built structures but still largely lack spaces for creativity and community. Buildings alone do not make community, nor can they alone spark creativity. Community happens when people can and do come together. That is something Detroit is discovering—after failing at it for so long.

Since the decline of car manufacturing in the "motor" city and its fall into bankruptcy, Detroit has struggled to stem the tide of people relocating elsewhere. Its population has declined from 1.8 million in the 1950s to fewer than 700,000 today. Yet an influx of young people eager to take advantage of the city's low rents is turning things around.

And the city, the state of Michigan, the federal government, a number of universities, and a handful of wealthy Detroit-born patrons are helping.

TechTown is one example. Backed by state and federal funds as well as a handful of foundations, it is an accelerator/incubator offering a variety of resources over a twelve-block radius. These resources include workshops, workspace, and connections to investors. Similarly, Detroit Creative Corridor Center is, as its website states, "a partnership between Business Leaders for Michigan and the College for Creative Studies." It has philanthropic and government backing to support creative works.

Dan Gilbert, a Detroit native, moved his company Quicken Loans, an online mortgage lender, to downtown Detroit to help revitalize the city. Quicken Loans employs about 11,500 people in the city. His investing group, Rock Ventures, has bought up $1 billion worth of property, which his real estate company, Bedrock Real Estate Services, is renovating. Gilbert has dubbed his efforts "Opportunity Detroit," which as the *New York Times* noted is "both a rescue mission and a business venture that, if successful, will yield him a fortune."

Monis Rahman is hoping his efforts in Pakistan will yield both him and Pakistan a fortune. He is one of a handful of tech entrepreneurs in Pakistan who collectively are working to put the issue of technology and entrepreneurship front and center in Pakistani minds, particularly those in government and at the top echelons of business.

To push technology and entrepreneurship, Monis has spearheaded a number of initiatives and organized a number of conferences. One held in 2010, entitled "Unleashing Change," brought together Pakistani entrepreneurs as well as the country's business and government leaders.

The gains Monis is making are substantial and have caught the attention of senior Pakistani officials. As much as Monis believes a critical mass will help alter Pakistan's reputation, Monis himself requires a critical mass around him to push that forward faster.

American involvement in Pakistan centers on terrorism and drone strikes. But there is a more long-term upside in assisting individuals like Monis Rahman: not through mere USAID programs that display social enterprises, but through serious high growth and scalable companies that stand a chance to move the proverbial needle forward.

The Internet presents a chance to reframe Pakistan's reputation from "frontier of apocalypse," as Monis called it, to "international marketplace." It offers an otherwise fragmented, poor, and isolated population a forum in which the anchor is ideas, not ideology, and the participants are innovators, not insurgents. It presents the potential for many to experiment and seek support to build an idea. Ideas beget ideas. That is what is behind the phenomenon of so many social media platforms—from Facebook to Twitter to Instagram to Pinterest and Tumblr. It is what is behind the success of Meetup, a startup focused on convening communities of people around an issue, a topic, or an idea. These startups are not breakthroughs in and of themselves. But they are in what they have enabled their users to do— and where they have pushed the Internet.

Naseeb and Rozee strive to be a virtual community space that Monis believes can widen, if not shift, perspectives on Pakistan. They can rally an ethnically and politically divided Pakistan into an informal network in which ideas, experiences, and knowledge are exchanged—with one another and perhaps even the world. "Pakistan can compete with the best of the best," Monis told me. "Maybe not today, but one day."

Competition is key to entrepreneurship—something our next entrepreneur, Enrique Gomez Junco, recognized in Mexico.

FOUR

Goliath-n-David:
Complementarity Over Competition

The most common way people give up their power
is by thinking they don't have any.

—ALICE WALKER

Mexico City, Monterrey, and Acapulco

Every April *Forbes*, a New York–based financial publication, releases an annual list of the richest people in the world: "the billionaires." In 2007 that list placed Microsoft founder Bill Gates, who at the time had wealth valued at $59.2 billion, in the number one slot. Eduardo Garcia, a Mexican journalist and founder of the online daily *Sentido Comun* (*Common Sense*), suspected that was wrong. Garcia had actively eyed Mexico's stock exchange, tracking companies owned by Carlos Slim.

Carlos Slim is Mexico's richest man. In 2007 Garcia determined that Slim was, in fact, the richest man in the world. The price of the stock of America Movil, Slim's mobile network company, surged 27 percent in July of that year. Garcia knew that the portly man of Lebanese descent, who still lived in a modest middle-class house in Mexico City, Mexico's capital, and drove his own car, had edged out Bill Gates for the biggest billionaire title on *Forbes*'s famous list.

In 2007 Carlos Slim owned more than two hundred companies across a variety of industries: banking, retail, airline, bottling, cigarettes, and hotels. However, what underwrote Slim's wealth were TelMex, Mexico's main telecom company, and America Movil, the mobile phone network. Slim had acquired TelMex in 1990 when the Mexican government privatized a number of industries to raise much-needed revenue. The privatization did not deregulate these industries, including telecommunications. TelMex, which controls more than 70 percent of Mexican landlines, went from being a state monopoly to being a private one. America Movil's monopolistic dominance—it controls 70 percent of Mexico's mobile subscribers—parallels that of TelMex.

Monopolies—both state and private—have dominated Mexico's economy for decades, as they have in many emerging market countries. A handful of family conglomerates have dominated places like Turkey, Nigeria, and Pakistan. In Mexico, as Ruchir Sharma, an investor at Morgan Stanley and author of *Breakout Nations*, has noted, monopolists are powerful not only in business but in politics as well. The Institutional Revolutionary Party (PRI) in Mexico held power for seventy-one years.

The monopoly has stood as a symbol of Mexican sovereignty. Indeed, Mexican monopolies came about as a direct response to Mexico's troubled history. For centuries, foreigners invaded Mexico and appropriated the country's resources. The Spanish exploited Mexico's gold resources and sent them to the monarchs in Madrid. Catholic priests seized property to enrich the papacy. American expansionists claimed territory for their "new world"—the United States. Each historical episode triggered uprisings and even revolution—and an even more powerful central state. In the twentieth century Mexico focused on salvaging as much of its natural resources as possible for itself, protecting its private sector, and bringing stability. It developed what Mexico-based business consultant Lawrence Weiner described in *The Atlantic* as an "us versus them," deep-seated paranoia: to keep outsiders out and keep a firm hold on Mexican property.

Yet in controlling entire industries—cement, electricity, food and beverage, oil, and telecommunications—Mexico has strangled competition and efficiency. While the country's main objective has been to stand in the way of outsiders wanting to take advantage of Mexico's resources, what it has done is to stand in the way of those eager to build anything beyond a mom-and-pop shop. The monopolies' tactics have created an economic system that exacerbates inequality and in which people pay high prices for low-quality products and services. Ruchir Sharma has said that "private cartels produce about 40 percent of the goods Mexicans consume and charge prices that are 30 percent higher than international averages." A can of cola in Mexico costs more comparatively (commensurate with local purchasing power) than a can sold in the United States.

"The economic institutions that made Carlos Slim who he is," note Daron Acemoğlu and James Robinson in *Why Nations Fail*, "are very different from those in the United States. If you're a Mexican entrepreneur, entry barriers will play a crucial role at every stage in your career. These barriers include expensive licenses you have to obtain, red tape you have to cut through, politicians and incumbents who will stand in your way, and the difficulty of getting funding from a financial sector often in cahoots with the incumbents you're trying to compete against. These barriers can be either insurmountable, keeping you out of lucrative areas, or your greatest friend, keeping your competitors at bay."

Enrique Gomez Junco, the forty-something founder of an energy saving company (ESCO) called Optima Energia, which is focused on optimizing electric power, fuel, and water consumption, knew that starting a business, much less succeeding, in Mexico was difficult. Too many monopolies stood in the way. Yet he recognized that globalization had changed many things, including erasing economic borders. Perhaps, he thought, it could also erase corporate ones. Big businesses and monopolies were commonplace and, in fact, encouraged in places like Mexico throughout much of the twentieth century, when competition wasn't among individual businesses but among countries—namely advanced Western ones. Enrique knew that in the "globalized" world, competition had become something different. Maybe that meant that monopolies would have to become something different, too.

Monopolies—wherever they exist—have favored the rich, to the great disadvantage of the remainder of the public. This is the main reason that the United States enacted legislation at the start of the twentieth century to break up the holdings of an elite few, collectively known as the Robber Barons, the powerful American industrialists who spearheaded big businesses at the end of the nineteenth century, such as John Jacob Astor, Andrew Carnegie, and John D. Rockefeller. This antitrust legislation has helped, until recently, to protect the American marketplace and the American consumer.

The growth of technology firms such as Amazon, Apple, eBay, Facebook, and Google has put that protection in question. In fact, they have resurrected the question of whether there is any competition at all. Under the guise of "go big or go home," these firms dominate the various market verticals they occupy throughout much of the globe. This is particularly true of Amazon, Facebook, and Google.

Enrique saw that while he couldn't go up against Mexico's monopolies, he could complement them and thereby succeed. In the globalized twenty-first-century economy, monopolists could no longer dominate any one industry in one country alone. Today, the competition is not between countries but between companies—giants like Alibaba, Amazon, Facebook, and Google. This is a fact that Mexican monopolies themselves have come to acknowledge.

Enrique honed in on energy efficiency, a space that no one in Mexico had occupied. In turn, Mexico's top monopolist has teamed up to collaborate with Enrique. Enrique has become one of the country's top entrepreneurs and has helped fan the flames of entrepreneurship in Mexico. And that has forced Mexico's monopolies to loosen their grip on wealth. Mexico—its government and its monopolies—is waking up to the reality that monopolies do not in fact protect the country, but are holding it back.

Breaking up monopolies or changing how they operate will improve quality and reduce prices. More important, it will allow Mexico to engage with the outside and economically interconnected world. Over the past decade Mexico's leaders have taken steps to integrate Mexico into the global supply and production chain. This has led Mexico to become the thirteenth-largest economy in the world and the second-largest economy in Latin America, after Brazil. As entrepreneurs like Enrique—in a diverse array of industries—have gained traction and outside investments, Mexico's leaders have started to recognize their value and have turned their attention to them.

• • •

DEITIES ONCE believed to have decided the fate of humanity stare down from the walls of Mexico City's world-renowned archaeological and anthropological museum. Stern and impassive Olmec heads share space with exquisitely carved jade figurines dug up from Mayan temples. An ornate, twenty-five-ton Aztec calendar looks both backward and forward—an apt symbol for modern Mexico. Mexico takes pride in its roots but is eager to conquer the future.

Enrique Gomez Junco, the founder of Optima Energia, had passed through these ancient halls many times before. On the May morning in 2013 when he traveled from Monterrey, a city in northern Mexico where he lives and works, and stepped back into the building, he did not know what to expect.

The president of the United States, according to the invitation from the US embassy, had requested his presence for a discussion on entrepreneurship. Walking into one of the museum's grand halls, which had been temporarily decorated with American and Mexican flags, that seemed hard to fathom. The Museo Nacional de Antropología honors the past. Presidents, especially the one who runs the world's greatest power, normally focus on Mexico's long-standing and well-known problems of debt, drugs, economic instability, illegal immigration, gang violence, and poverty. President Barack Obama's interest in entrepreneurship in Mexico surprised Enrique. Until recently entrepreneurship has rarely been discussed with any enthusiasm or emphasis in Mexico. The country's leaders have traditionally favored the big businesses and monopolies controlled by people such as Carlos Slim.

Fourteen other entrepreneurs, a mix of men and women from a variety of industries, joined Enrique at the museum. They gathered in a hall where several rectangular tables had been covered in dark navy blue cloth and joined together to form a square. A name placard made of heavy white parchment had been placed at each place setting. Aside from a single White House photographer, there were no cameras to capture this event.

As the clock inched past 11:00 a.m., the US officials—the ambassador to Mexico, Anthony Wayne, and White House senior adviser Valerie Jarrett—who had greeted Enrique and others asked everyone to be seated. President Obama had not yet arrived. He had much to squeeze into his twenty-four-hour trip to Mexico before traveling on to

Costa Rica: meetings with Mexico's political and business leaders and an address to the Mexican people.

Enrique, who bears a striking resemblance to light-eyed and light-haired *Silver Linings Playbook*, *American Hustle*, and *American Sniper* star Bradley Cooper, had been assigned a seat at the far corner of the table—a spot, I suspected after spending time with him in Monterrey just a month earlier, he would have gravitated toward anyway. Broad-shouldered, he has a football player's physique that tends to dominate any space. Mindful and considerate—someone who rarely forgets to say "thank-you" and "please" and bows his head at the slightest compliment, as men did in an era when movies were shot in black and white—Enrique prefers to deflect attention from himself.

From this distance, Enrique listened as Ambassador Wayne and Ms. Jarrett spoke about the importance of entrepreneurship for job creation and economic growth. This was among the top issues President Obama discussed with Mexico's president, Enrique Peña Nieto, they said. The American president wanted to explore partnerships between American and Mexican startups. He especially wanted to find ways to support individuals starting new ventures in Mexico.

New ventures have the ability to create jobs. They also have the ability to foster change—to transform the economic and political landscape. Take Henry Ford. The industrialist changed more than just the auto industry with his Model T car. He launched mass-market production, revolutionizing every industry and thereby the US economy. Steve Jobs changed more than just the telephone with the iPhone. He helped lay the groundwork for the rise of other startups such as Instagram, WhatsApp, and Uber, which have spawned what has come to be known as the "sharing" economy—an economy that bypasses formal businesses and encourages peer-to-peer exchanges. In the cases of Ford and Jobs, the means of production and wealth shifted. The dynamics of business, and of government, changed. What was once held in a certain set of hands moved into another set. That is what has happened in Mexico as well as in other parts of the world.

Starting in the 1980s, Mexican leaders relaxed top-down control in certain industries and shifted that control into private hands. They simply realized that government wasn't the best entity to operate businesses. Members of government lacked the knowledge and experience to do so. Yet even as Mexico's leaders loosened the reins on the country's economy, they still held a tight leash on competition. Competition in Mexico remained limited. Assuring that Mexican banks, cement factories, and telephone lines remained in the country's hands mattered more than whether those hands could add value—to the customer, the economy, or both.

Not surprisingly, they didn't. Though savvy businessmen replaced bureaucrats in a number of industries, Mexico's market remained straitjacketed. Those at the top determined the output and cost of goods—to the great disadvantage of the Mexican consumer and Mexico's economy.

What's more, their products and services tend to lack variety and quality. Monopolies feed on the ability to exploit the customer, not strive to fulfill his or her satisfaction.

They are reluctant to sacrifice high margins and to reinvest earnings in talent, research and development, and innovation—and they loathe what they consider "upstarts" with startup visions that upset this existing state of affairs.

The upstarts attending this historic event at the museum understood, perhaps all too well, the power that monopolies in Mexico wield. Though each had dared to launch a startup, no one went directly up against Mexico's big businessmen. Instead, they built what a business school textbook would call "B2B" ventures: business to business enterprises, which complement or support existing businesses rather than delivering a product or service directly to consumers.

Complementing rather than competing has not only given these entrepreneurs a role in their country, but it has also started to make entrepreneurship possible. Over the past decade, Mexico's monopolies have been willing not only to tolerate men and women launching their own products and services, but also to do business with them, especially when those products and services add value to their own efforts. Entrepreneurship has contributed to the slow expansion of Mexico's marketplace—and even the potential for eventual competition.

Complementarity is how Enrique's company, Optima Energia, has gained traction in Mexico. The company has delivered energy-saving solutions to various businesses such as hotels and municipalities. It has done this through "performance contracting." In this model the company only earns when the client saves. Optima Energia's revenue is taken as a percentage of the savings the project generates. The company develops and designs energy efficiency solutions, such as air conditioners that have heat recovery that can be re-used and street lights that operate on LED bulbs.

A number of Mexico's monopolies have embraced Optima Energia. More significantly, a number of its prominent businessmen, including Carlos Slim, have even provided the company with financial backing. Together they have started to transform Mexico's electricity landscape—and to drive a wedge into Mexico's electricity monopoly—a point that Enrique made to President Obama when the American leader finally arrived for their meeting.

• • •

OVER THE PAST decade, and after more than a century of playing America's junior, and often ignored, partner, Mexico has taken on new importance in both Washington and Wall Street. In 2013 Mexico and the United States traded $507 billion worth of goods, making Mexico the third-largest US trading partner, following $707 billion with Canada and $579 billion with China.

Mexico increasingly is becoming a manufacturing hub for US businesses. With a population of 120 million, Mexico is the world's top consumer of Coca-Cola per capita and has more Walmarts per person than the United States. Chrysler, Ford, and General Motors all have factories in the country. NASA and the US Department of Defense commission security equipment and space satellites made across the southern border. With rising labor costs in China and elsewhere in Asia as well as the continued fluctuating price of oil, computer, mobile phone, and flat-screen television makers are moving their production operations from Asia to Mexico, where labor remains cheap and the transport distance is considerably shorter.

"If the United States and Mexico are working together, we can sell a whole lot of things on the other side of the Pacific Ocean where the fast-growing economies are taking off right now," President Obama said in an address to the Mexican people hours before meeting with Enrique and the entrepreneurs gathered at the museum.

"Let's not just sell more things to each other, let's build more things together. . . . Let's answer the hope of a young woman—a student at the National Polytechnic Institute—who spoke for many in your generation, so eager to make your mark. She said, 'Give us jobs as creators.'"

Enrique arrived in Mexico City early enough to hear the president's speech. "It was the first time I heard an American president talking about Mexico in this way," he said. It filled him with anticipation. Though he had met his own country's president, as well as a handful of other world leaders, Enrique felt that his meeting with Barack Obama would yield something different.

While not life changing, the meeting with the president was distinctive. For starters, despite the magnificent surroundings, there was no receiving line. About a half hour into the discussion at the museum, President Obama appeared without any warning or fuss. Dressed in a dark suit and silver gray tie and flanked by several Secret Service agents, he walked in and right up to a few of the entrepreneurs, then continued to make his way around the table, past the various artifacts and imposing statue of a Tenochtitlan warrior, which he paused to admire for a moment.

Enrique stood at his corner of the table, stunned by the lack of ceremony.

Second, there were no lectures. After shaking everyone's hand, President Obama took a seat near his advisers, delivered a few remarks, then picked up a pen and prepared to take notes. He told the fifteen entrepreneurs that he had come to learn from them. He asked each to tell him about his or her business.

One person talked about designing cars in Mexico. Another spoke about the radio frequency technology (RFID) he produces to help businesses keep track of any number of assets: equipment, products, services, or customers. A biologist turned entrepreneur told the president about his effort to bring sustainable biotech solutions to Mexican agriculture.

When his turn came, Enrique talked about his work in energy efficiency. Despite being an oil producer and having nearly nationwide electricity capacity—meaning nearly everyone in Mexico has access to electricity—Mexico produces energy at remarkably high prices, and even has to import it from the United States. Mexicans pay more for fuel and electricity than do people living in the United States, just as they pay more for phone service and most consumer goods.

In Mexico, the Comisión Federal de Electricidad (CFE), widely known as "la comisión," has dominated the consumer electricity market. It is the second most powerful state-owned company in Mexico after Pemex, Petróleos Mexicanos, the national oil company. Pemex is the world's second largest nonpublicly listed company and Latin America's second-largest enterprise. Brazil's national oil company, Petrobras, is the first.

The CFE has a solid hold on electricity transmission and distribution throughout the country and is given minimal oversight. Though SENER, Mexico's ministry of energy, sets the country's energy policy, and the Energy Regulatory Commission (CRE) is responsible for licensing and outlining energy guidelines, neither has jurisdiction over the CFE and its subsidiary, the distributor Luz y Fuerza del Centro (Central Light and Power). The CFE is a self-regulated body. These factors give it free rein, allowing the CFE to charge high prices while providing minimal services. While the company, at the behest of Mexico's leaders, hands out subsidies to residential consumers, it charges businesses, which are responsible for 59 percent of the country's electricity consumption, between 25 and 60 percent more than the international average. This has hurt business and thus economic growth in Mexico.

Despite the massive amounts of revenue it generates, the CFE has hesitated to reinvest profits in upgrades and innovations. It built one nuclear power plant in the eastern part of the country, but largely relies on oil and natural gas for electricity. Seventy-five percent of Mexico's electricity is produced using oil reserves. Hence the CFE has been slow to seek energy alternatives. A 2008 law mandating that it develop a strategy for sustainability has forced the body to focus on clean technology as the country's energy needs grow, at a pace of 3 percent annually. Within a decade the CFE will lack the capacity to keep up with Mexico's energy demands.

"We believe that energy efficiency should be prioritized," Enrique said. "We need efficient companies to compete worldwide."

Enrique told the American president that he had found that Mexico's cities and towns spent an exorbitant amount on electricity, rather than security, schools, and infrastructure development. The bulk of a municipality's budget, Enrique told President Obama, went first to paying salaries and second to paying electric bills. To change the latter, Enrique put together a performance contracting solution that reduces any given municipality's energy consumption by 60 percent—without the need of an initial investment from the municipality. His company finances public streetlights. Specifically, Optima Energia extends loans to municipalities that allow them to purchase and install LED bulbs— long-lasting lights that cost more than standard florescent ones but use less electricity.

"My main objective was to point out to him that financing can really change the possibilities of Mexico to develop sustainable projects," Enrique told me. By possibilities he meant job creation and additional cash flow into other social programs. "Financing will be the driver for municipalities to be able to develop energy efficiency programs and stop wasting energy," he added.

As Mexico's manufacturing capacity grows, so too does its demand for energy. Factories need power to operate machines. Over the next several years the country, along with many others throughout the world—including the United States—will have to increase energy production several fold. A number of large companies, such as Nissan and

Cemex, Mexico's cement monopoly, pushed for a law in 1992 to allow private companies to generate their own electricity. Thousands of small- and medium-sized businesses had been waiting for the government to push through reforms that would open up Mexico's energy sector to private sector collaboration and competition. That finally happened in December 2013.

President Obama listened to Enrique intently, resting his hand on his chin and occasionally looking through his notes as Enrique spoke. He periodically muttered to his advisers.

Optima Energia was an ideal choice for a partnership with the Overseas Private Investment Corporation (OPIC), a US federal agency, and the Export-Import Bank of the United States (EXIM), an independent body. These organizations work specifically to improve business conditions and opportunities for US entrepreneurs and companies abroad. Optima Energia offered a persuasive solution for a number of Mexico's challenges: financing, security, sustainability, and, in a roundabout way, monopolies.

Obama's advisers wanted the president to leave Mexico with a number of achievements that would build the US-Mexican relationship. Brokering partnerships between US organizations and funders and entrepreneurs like Enrique offered that opportunity. Moreover, President Obama separately saw a chance to make headway on climate change. In 2008 and 2012, the president had campaigned on and strongly urged reducing the US greenhouse footprint as a larger policy matter. Obama had identified energy as a domestic priority. Partnering with Mexico on an energy-efficiency project would contribute toward that goal.

As President Obama departed and shook hands with Enrique and the other entrepreneurs, Enrique felt a renewed determination about how to make Optima Energia's struggle in its new market segment work. One of the funders for its lighting project, the Inter-American Investment Corporation (IIC), a development bank, had reneged on its promise to provide $6 million in credit. The possibility to work with new partners—partners in the United States—gave him new inspiration. Amid all the big businesses, finding a partner in Mexico, much less a funder, had been difficult. Entrepreneurship in the country wasn't something people wanted to do; it was something that they had to do to survive. It had become a solo one-man or one-woman effort. Like Monis Rahman in Pakistan, Enrique knew from his own experience that success usually came through a larger network of people—a team and community.

• • •

ENRIQUE GREW up in Monterrey, a city about an hour's drive from Texas. His father, a journalist also named Enrique Gomez Junco, had settled there in the early 1970s. Enrique senior had been a part of the family business in Mexico City, the newspaper *El Norte*. Numerous management changes as well as a family tug-of-war forced Enrique senior to break out on his own. Rather than try to navigate Mexico City's complicated bureaucracy and the even more cutthroat, patronage-prone private sector, he headed north to Monterrey, where he helped build *El Diario*, which is today the daily newspaper *Milenio*. Enrique senior's example was a model for Enrique's career.

Monterrey had been one of Mexico's active business centers since the mid-twentieth century. It was close to the United States, and many companies—Mexican and foreign—chose to set up shop there, especially after the establishment of the *maquiladora*, factories in a free trade zone in northern Mexico, in 1965. American companies flocked to set up factories in the region and take advantage of cheap labor and the cheap peso. This has given Monterrey the feel of a small town in the Midwest. Unlike Mexico City, there are no grand boulevards or squares with elaborate fountains or ceramic sculptures in Monterrey. Instead, single-story dwellings with satellite dishes affixed to rooftops and windowsills dot the landscape. It is not a pedestrian-friendly city, either. People get around by driving and go to strip malls and fast-food joints.

Since the start of the new millennium, Monterrey has been reincarnated as one of the country's cutting-edge technology hubs. Before drug cartels tainted the city's image over the past few years, Monterrey competed with Guadalajara, a city in the north heavily involved in manufacturing, to be Mexico's Silicon Valley. The Monterrey Institute of Technology, Technológico de Monterrey, helped build this reputation. A group of local businessmen started the school after struggling to hire the right talent—managers and people to fill more senior and operational positions—for their enterprises. Set up as a technical training school in 1943 to prepare people for positions at Mexican conglomerates, Monterrey Tech has become Mexico's premiere center for entrepreneurship and business education. What Stanford is to Silicon Valley, MIT to Boston, and Technion (the Israel

Institute of Technology) to Israel, Monterrey Tech tries to be to Mexico.

Monterrey Tech is comprised of a high school and college; the latter offers both undergraduate and graduate courses in twenty-five cities across the country. It was the first school in Latin America to connect to the Internet, in 1989; has become a leader in filing patent applications; and has expanded its campus abroad, most recently to China. It has graduated a series of top businessmen, including Lorenzo Zambrano, the late CEO of Cemex, Mexico's cement monopoly. Today the school is firmly focused on encouraging entrepreneurship.

Enrique attended both Monterrey Tech's high school and college. In 1986, right after receiving his bachelor's degree, he enrolled in an entrepreneurship program the school had just rolled out as a pilot. It changed him.

For his entire life, Enrique had believed necessity drove entrepreneurship. That is what he saw in Mexico. People set up storefronts and traded goods in order to earn an income. For them, entrepreneurship was a reaction against unemployment and poverty. It didn't include growth, investments, innovations, or scale. It merely focused on hand-to-mouth survival.

In Monterrey Tech's pilot program, he discovered a different kind of entrepreneurship, driven by invention and ideas—the kind of entrepreneurship embraced by the *Yanquis* (Yankees) in the north, which produced groundbreaking innovations and globally competitive products and services, created hundreds of thousands of jobs, and generated millions in revenue. Entrepreneurship seemed to be the source of American dynamism.

Enrique never had considered starting a business. Like many graduates in Mexico, he looked forward to a professional job in an office. *That* was the Mexican dream. The year spent studying entrepreneurship at Monterrey Tech prompted him to think about what it would be like for him to start a business—and the importance of young Mexicans such as he doing so. Entrepreneurs, Enrique learned, created jobs. That is what Mexico needed. The more he thought about it, the more he wanted to become an entrepreneur. His timing, however, was questionable.

In the late 1980s Mexico's economy, still largely closed, still struggled. Reforms enacted earlier in the decade had failed. In 1982 the country declared bankruptcy. Millions of people fell into poverty. Public coffers ran dry.

Opportunity, however, as Enrique had learned during his year at the pilot entrepreneurship program at Monterrey Tech, came during economic downturns and hardship—as Monis Rahman had learned in Pakistan. Disney, Federal Express, General Electric, IBM, and Microsoft all started during times of uncertainty. General Electric's foundation, for example, coincided with the financial panic of 1873. Though it had eventually listed on the Dow Jones Industrial Average—one of the original twelve companies to do so—it was not at all clear whether General Electric, in its early days, would survive. Electricity was a new concept, its uses and limits untested and unexplored.

In the late 1980s Enrique started to hear about the new sector of alternative energy. A decade earlier, in 1974, *Time* magazine had run a story about climate change. In 1975 the Washington-based National Academy of Sciences had released a major study on global warming and the greenhouse gas effect. Talk in scientific circles centered around the earth's rising temperature and the destruction of the atmosphere. Innovators marveled at new breakthroughs that harnessed natural resources such as the sun, wind, and possibly even other biological material for energy.

Harnessing alternative sources of energy seemed to be just the innovative idea that could gain traction—growth, investments, and scale—especially in a place like Mexico, where energy cost so much. Enrique explored the topic from this perspective, as a business opportunity, rather than as a chance to tackle global warming or climate change. Environmental concerns did not factor into his thinking.

Armed with an elevator pitch, Enrique went to friends and family with a promise to create the first world-class Mexican solar energy company. With their financial support, he would manufacture solar panels—equipment that captures and harnesses radiation from the sun into energy— and sell those panels to Mexican businesses. Because of the Mexican state's monopoly over the energy sector, Mexican businesses, he had found, spent a lot on energy costs. Solar panels could help reduce those costs, create more jobs, and generate significant revenue.

The reality was not that simple. Building solar panels required specialized parts and resources. That required a lot of upfront costs—cash for necessary purchases. This is where Enrique needed the support of friends and family. Mexican banks, heavily regulated—in fact, among the most regulated in the world—did not lend to individuals or make small business loans. Angel investing, along with venture or seed financing, did not exist as a concept in Mexico in the late 1980s. Though a number of Mexico's elite had set up family offices and foundations, they did not consider investing in businesses local people were trying to get off the ground.

Enrique's friends and family did consider investing in him. Convinced by his energy, they lent him several hundred thousand pesos to start CelSol. The company burned through funds quickly. That would not have been a problem if Enrique had managed to make sales and earn revenue. But the high costs of producing electricity through solar panels discouraged potential customers. Energy produced with solar panels at the time cost $156.90 per megawatt-hour to generate. That was more expensive than coal-generated electricity, priced at $99.60, and natural gas, priced between $65 and $132 per megawatt-hour.

That was not the only problem. Electrical output from solar panels went down at night and when there was cloud cover during the day. To fix this problem, the panels had to be complemented with a generator or battery that could store energy. In the late 1980s those batteries cost tens of thousands of dollars. That made it difficult for CelSol to convince ordinary Mexicans, the majority of whom already lived near or at the poverty line, and Mexican businesses, the majority of which struggled to stay open, to put in the investment. Unlike many US solar panel manufacturers that have tried but failed to make the business work, Enrique made CelSol succeed, only he did not do so solely selling solar panels. Hotels were the key to his success.

· · ·

ON A FAMILY trip to the beach one summer not too long after launching CelSol, Enrique hit on the idea of focusing on hotels. While developing his business, Enrique had repeatedly heard Mexican businesspeople discuss reducing energy expenses. A number asked Enrique if he could help them do that.

Enrique recalled the complaints about the high price of operating machinery and queries about alternative solutions to air conditioning. As he sat on the sand, watching his wife and three children, two girls and a boy, frolicking in the Pacific Ocean, it occurred to him that the hotels that lined the boardwalk behind him probably faced the same problems—especially with air conditioning. Enrique went back to the hotel he and his family were staying in and began to ask questions.

Along with manufacturing and oil, tourism is one of Mexico's largest industries. Enrique learned that hotels in Mexico did indeed spend a lot on air conditioning, lighting, refrigeration, and water. Building solutions that would help hotels save on those items could be the focus of his company. No sooner had he returned from his family holiday than Enrique set out to realize his plan.

He reached out to his board of directors. Boards are an afterthought at most startups. Entrepreneurs are busy building a business. Yet if assembled correctly, the board is a network that provides essential guidance and support to the CEO and the company. From what Enrique had learned at Monterrey Tech, he knew that a board can fill in the gaps that he, as the entrepreneur and founder, could not. That is what Optima Energia's board did when Enrique laid out his new vision. They advised him to rename his company Optima Energia—optimum energy—and then sought out engineers and designers who could help him find energy-saving solutions.

It worked for a while. Enrique signed agreements with dozens of hotels, including the Ritz Carlton, Hilton, and Omni in Acapulco, Cancun, Los Cabos, Puerta Vallarta, and Tulum. This time he offered them comprehensive solutions to reduce their energy costs.

Energy bills at hotels began to go down—as much as 50 percent. Optima Energia began to pull in profits. Over a decade, Enrique saved his clients 1.6 million cubic feet of water, 64 million kilowatts of electricity, 8.8 million liters of natural gas, and 11.8 million liters of diesel, all adding up to more than $15.7 million in savings. He generated revenues of nearly $10 million. Investors came calling at his door. With their support, Enrique continued to roll out new products for his clients, including a twenty-four-hour computer monitoring system.

During my visit to Optima Energia's orange-and-gray decorated offices, Enrique guided me through the room where he kept this monitoring system. The room could have doubled as the control room of a television studio—or, as I imagined, the National Security Administration's headquarters. Multiple flat screens hung on a glass wall and from the ceiling. Each displayed pie charts, bar graphs, and various numbers. The system monitored the air conditioning, water levels, and electricity at various hotels.

Data are essential to Optima Energia's work. With the advancement of cloud computing, companies like Optima

Energia, which collect data on energy efficiency, are increasing in value. "We created this system to facilitate our job fulfilling our performance promises," Enrique told me. The system helped Optima Energia track how each hotel used water and electricity and create an energy-saving solution based on those patterns.

But in 2008 and 2009 things unraveled. Not only did Wall Street's meltdown in 2008 negatively affect Mexico, but a global flu pandemic—severe acute respiratory syndrome (SARS)—spread throughout Mexico in 2009, hurting tourism. Winter-weary northerners from the United States and Canada canceled vacation plans. Hotels emptied out and sat idle. The gains Optima Energia had made disappeared.

One of Enrique's investors, Inbursa, a bank that Carlos Slim, Mexico's richest man, owned, encouraged Enrique to broaden his reach. His board of directors agreed. Energy efficiency is a nearly $200 billion industry worldwide, with the potential to grow to $350 billion over the next ten years. Increasing concern about greenhouse gases, which has multiplied since the industrialization and rise of emerging markets, and climate change is a driving factor. Emerging markets have contributed 90 percent of the total increase in greenhouse gases over the past decade.

The increase in greenhouse gas emissions is impacting food production, health, infrastructure, and water supplies. According to the United Nations, global temperatures have risen nearly 1.5 degrees Fahrenheit (.85 Celsius) since 1850. This "global warming" is damaging crops, increasing disease, and setting off severe weather—"super storms." Hurricane Katrina, which devastated New Orleans in 2005, caused $108 billion in damage. Hurricane Sandy, which devastated Connecticut, New Jersey, and New York in 2012, caused $50 billion in damage.

In response, Western leaders, particularly in the United States and Germany, are working to reduce their dependence on fossil fuels such as oil and gas. They are pushing for stricter efficiency standards for cars, factories, power plants, and workplaces, standards that reduce emissions. As more and more people crowd into urban centers, mayors are pushing for "greener cities." The increase in regulation has encouraged those eager to turn rice husks and animal waste into biomass fuel, erect windmills along coastlines, and experiment with solar- and thermal-powered devices.

To be sure, energy efficiency and its corresponding sector, clean tech, is no easy jackpot. Both sectors have struggled to generate a return on investment. Indeed, a number of clean tech startups have outright failed. Solyndra, the US solar panel maker, is the most notable, defaulting on a $535 million government-issued loan in 2011.

Still, many entrepreneurs and venture capitalists, particularly in Silicon Valley, remain focused on alternative energy. Vinod Khosla, a cofounder of the technology giant Sun Microsystems, has raised several "clean tech" funds for his venture capital firm Khosla Ventures. John Doerr, a partner at Kleiner, Perkins, Caufield & Byers—a venture capital firm that has invested in Amazon and Google—has said that "going green may be the 'biggest economic opportunity of the twenty-first century.'" His venture firm has invested $200 million in alternative energy startups.

Elon Musk, a South African entrepreneur who co-founded PayPal, has galvanized excitement around clean tech through his electric car venture, Tesla, and SolarCity, a supplier of rooftop solar panels. Tesla and SolarCity have mobilized investors to pour more resources into startups that are working on innovations in biofuel, electric, solar, and wind. In 2013, $13 billion went into solar projects in the United States.

Inbursa investors encouraged Enrique to think creatively about energy efficiency—to go beyond merely the innovations and systems to cut costs. They also encouraged him to think beyond individual clients and businesses—to think big. Municipalities, Inbursa's investors told Enrique, paid for certain public utilities such as street lamps. Carlos Slim had made a number of investments to revitalize downtrodden municipalities in Mexico. Inbursa's investors advised Enrique to work with Mexico's thirty-one municipalities to figure out a way for each to save money on streetlights.

• • •

ENERGY IS AN emotional issue for Mexicans. Take oil. The oil giant Pemex has been a symbol of Mexican sovereignty and stability. Elementary school textbooks portray the 1938 nationalization of the oil industry as one of the country's most important historical events, so important that it is commemorated every March 18 as a national holiday. There is even a hymn that credits oil with "saving our fatherland."

Electricity is held in the same regard, though perhaps not with as much fervor. It is a national treasure. A decade into the new millennium, however, Enrique knew that the country could no longer cling to such sentiment. Globalization had linked markets and people throughout the world. The North American Free Trade Agreement (NAFTA), the 1994 treaty among Canada, Mexico, and the United States that eliminated trade tariffs and barriers, had reoriented Mexico's economy to look externally. NAFTA integrated Mexican markets with global ones, with both negative and positive effects.

At a time when Mexico's economy had already moved away from agriculture and toward industrialization, NAFTA added to the already dire situation Mexican farmers faced from fierce competition from subsidized farm products flooding the Mexican market. Unable to compete with low costs for beans, corn, grains, milk, and sugar, nearly 1.3 Mexican farm laborers lost work. At the same time, however, Mexico benefited from US manufacturers' eagerness to expand operations into Mexico, where labor costs are cheaper. Mexico added tens of millions of new jobs.

NAFTA increased foreign direct investment in Mexico, amounting to $150 billion in the first fifteen years after its implementation. That helped Mexico's private sector expand. Mexican multinationals opened up factories that produced everything from clothing to cars to consumer goods. Mexican exports increased fourfold. This prosperity would eventually depend on a number of variables, including increased and effective energy production—something Enrique knew state-controlled entities could not provide alone—and competition, or the breaking up of Mexico's monopolies.

Though Mexico became Latin America's largest exporter, and its economy grew dramatically, the export multiplier effect, which, as Shannon O'Neil, a scholar on Mexican politics and author of *Two Nations Indivisible: Mexico, the United States, and the Road Ahead,* notes, "measures how exports expand the overall economy, is much lower in Mexico than in countries such as Brazil, and is about half what it is in the United States." The effect is lower, she argues, because the country lacks a competitive marketplace. The wealth that Mexico generated from increased exports lined the pockets of an elite few. It was not distributed throughout the population.

"There is a lack of trust in Mexican society of market oriented policies and I don't think we understand quite well what it means to be a well-functioning market system where business people benefit but also consumers gain from that kind of trade," Eduardo Perez Motta told me. From 2004 until 2009 Motta served as the chairman of the Mexican Federal Competition Commission (CFC). Mexico's leaders established the CFC in 1993 specifically to eliminate monopolies and "other restrictions to market efficiency." Motta, however, struggled to achieve this goal during his tenure.

"When you look at the reasons that Mexico is not growing as fast as it should, it is not a lack of endowment or resources—such as human capital and physical capital. The main problem is a problem of productivity. It is a problem of not using [in] the most efficient way our resources," Motta told me.

Mexico's government, and to a certain extent, Mexico's monopolies have been blind to the benefits accruing from productivity. Instead, they have been focused on their own narrow interests and the benefits they receive through corruption, an obstacle tackled in the next chapter. Yet as globalization set in and countries engaged and collaborated with each other, Mexico's leaders started to reconsider methods that produced businesses that were big and personally lucrative but not globally competitive or innovative. Mexico had no Apple, Facebook, or Google. And, as a result, the country was losing out on billions in profits.

Over the past decade Mexico's leaders have tapped startups to help add value and improve efficiency throughout the market and ensure that Mexico can compete on the world stage. Still, various elements in both the government and monopolistic enterprises have resisted a complete change in the status quo. As entrepreneurs like Enrique have witnessed, the monopolies may want certain improvements, but they still want to remain monopolies. Enrique's experience in Acapulco is a case in point.

• • •

When Frank Sinatra and his Rat Pack traveled outside of Las Vegas or Hollywood, they headed for Acapulco. The city on Mexico's west coast was a mecca for the rich and famous throughout the 1950s and 1960s, appearing on magazine covers and movie screens as "the" in place. Elizabeth Taylor, John Wayne, Brigitte Bardot, and Lana Turner were among the regular jet set in Acapulco. Then senator and later president John F. Kennedy took his bride, Jacqueline

Bouvier, to the Mexican beach resort for their honeymoon in September 1953. (Another Democratic president, Bill Clinton, would also take his bride, Hillary Rodham, to Acapulco for a honeymoon.)

By the mid-1970s, however, serious overdevelopment had hijacked the city's haloed status as a paradise on earth. Cheap motels shoehorned themselves in between high-priced resorts. These attracted shady characters and eventually drug dealers, who found Acapulco an ideal location from which to move drugs abroad. Today, drug cartels that roam Acapulco's streets have made it one of Mexico's most dangerous and dark places—literally. Most of the city's streetlights do not work. "Out of 45,000 lamps, they had 18,000 out of work," according to Enrique. The city of Acapulco could not provide any statistics.

Both Mexico's federal government and Acapulco's local municipal officials have worked hard to reverse the city's misfortunes. The Mexican Tourism Office has launched new air service to the city, along with investments in the rail system going in and out of Acapulco.

More recently, Carlos Slim has invested in Acapulco's revitalization. He has backed infrastructure projects, including local transportation services. He has also encouraged bank loans to the poor and pledged to raise money to build new hotels.

Enrique's team selected Acapulco as one of the first places to test his new street lighting endeavor. They got in touch with Acapulco's municipal leaders and brokered an agreement that would allow Optima Energia to finance a street lighting project worth several million dollars. The company had already signed a contract with several other municipalities in Mexico. These contracts stipulated that Optima Energia would provide the financing to municipalities to lease LED lights and, where necessary, install new poles for a period of ten years, after which the municipality would take on the responsibility for the streetlights.

Financing streetlights would require considerable capital. Inbursa put up some of it, but in order for Optima Energia to reach scale it would have to extend efforts in other municipalities. Enrique needed more financing himself. He approached the IIC, which is a member of the Inter-American Development Bank (IADB), focused on promoting private sector development in Latin America and the Caribbean. Toward that end, the IIC extends loans, grants, technical assistance, and research to small- and medium-sized enterprises.

Enrique had worked with the International Finance Corporation (IFC), the investment arm of the World Bank, in 2010. The IFC had granted Optima Energia a $10 million loan to support its work to reduce energy use and carbon emissions at hotels.

When Enrique approached the IIC, the multinational bank welcomed him. Optima Energia was known for its various awards, media mentions, and memberships, including its selection for Endeavor Mexico, the local arm of the New York–based nonprofit that supports high-impact entrepreneurs worldwide. The board of the IIC was excited when Optima Energia expanded its scope to include public projects. The board wanted to work on a project with Optima Energia—especially one that had a clearly defined purpose and multiple benefits. Streetlights advanced safety. Safety instilled confidence and trust, two key elements of any vibrant economy.

"Normally, a project scores high in one [of the evaluated areas of financial impact and development impact] but not the other," Goldie Shturman, the investment officer in charge of Optima Energia's account, told me. "Optima Energia had one of the highest rankings in both financial and developmental impact." As a result, the project breezed through several of the IIC's committees that screen proposals. Without hesitation, the IIC agreed to provide Optima Energia technical assistance to carry out a feasibility study. It also approved a $6 million line of credit for Optima Energia's public lighting projects. This credit encompassed not only Acapulco but also projects in other Mexican municipalities.

Yet IIC never extended the credit. It pulled out after consulting with CFE officials in Mexico City, who said they did not want the project to move forward. Efficient LED streetlights would save municipalities money, whether in Acapulco or elsewhere, and that would undercut the CFE's revenue. The IIC backpedaled, covering its tracks with a confusing statement about how it belatedly realized that local banks in Mexico could provide Optima Energia with credit. The trouble was, no commercial bank would extend credit to Optima Energia, especially not after the IIC abandoned the project. "It was hard for us to explain why the I[A]DB left the operation," Enrique said. This negatively affected the company's ability to raise the necessary finances to proceed.

· · ·

DURING ENRIQUE'S meeting with President Obama, the president noted that he wanted to create a commission dedicated to US-Mexican cooperation on energy projects, especially ones focused on sustainability and efficiency—and ones that had a hard time finding financial and technological support. This commission would assess the resources needed to back such projects. Since then it has taken steps to do just that. Optima Energia certainly qualified for such investments.

In September 2013 OPIC stepped into the breach. It extended Enrique and Optima Energia approval to start a due diligence process for a $50 million loan guarantee for five street lighting projects in Mexico. "This project will have a positive development impact," OPIC noted, "by unleashing high quality, energy efficient public lighting equipment to municipalities in Mexico. Improving the quality and reliability of public lighting will result in safer communities, which will also benefit the local economy by increasing night-time commercial activities."

Since then, Optima Energia has been moving forward, rolling out its street lighting project in six other municipalities. It has received the support of local banks and other international funds, including a Chicago-based venture capital firm, True North. That is a noteworthy accomplishment. Mike Ahearn, the cofounder of First Solar, an Arizona-based solar power company that is listed on the NASDAQ, founded True North. He has said that he did so in the belief that startups in "disruptive" sectors such as alternative energy need expert guidance. According to Enrique, that is exactly what the venture capital firm has provided. "They have made me work hard; to see things I didn't think were possible; they have helped me to think big," Enrique told me.

Enrique has risen to be one of Mexico's "big" thinkers, poised for success. His company, Optima Energia, has withstood Mexico's political and economic vacillations and has managed to survive the challenges thrown into his path by the country's electric monopoly. Much like Bülent Çelebi in Turkey, Tayo Oviosu in Nigeria, and Monis Rahman in Pakistan, Enrique Gomez Junco has done so by nurturing talent and culture and focusing on management.

Interestingly, the board of directors Enrique has put together for Optima Energia has also played a pivotal role. Aware of how difficult and time consuming it is to get things done in Mexico, Enrique pulled together a diverse array of businessmen with unique expertise and connections that have opened many doors and smoothed over many deals for the company. They have become Optima Energia's champions. "Enrique used to be his own boss," Roberto Jaime, a retired Mexican businessman and Optima Energia board member, told me. "He gave that up in order to move the business forward." Jaime noted that this is hard for an entrepreneur. An entrepreneur's natural state is to act on instinct, not take direction. Yet as Jaime pointed out, in order for the business to scale up, he or she can no longer revel in risk and ideas. The entrepreneur needs to plan and strategize. Enrique has managed this, even if, as Roberto Jaime noted, it wasn't always easy for him. Today, Optima Energia is a multi-million-dollar company with healthy prospects for growth—even beyond Mexico. The company is considering expansion into Central America.

• • •

MEXICO HAS been moving forward to improve how energy is supplied and utilized in the country. On the night of December 11, 2013, the energy reform bill that Mexican President Enrique Peña Nieto had made a cornerstone of his presidential campaign and presidency finally reached the floor of the Mexican legislature and was passed. Peña Nieto, the head of the Institutional Revolutionary Party (PRI), had worked with the opposition party, the National Action Party (PAN), to ensure that it would. Though the two parties have been locked in a bitter political rivalry since the late 1980s, they united on the matter of breaking up the monopolies, not only in energy but in telecom and television as well. Both have recognized that Mexico's prosperity hinges on its having a competitive market. Hence, they have agreed to set aside their rivalry and collaborate so that their country may compete.

Passage of these reforms, which have been compared to the "trust busting" that Teddy Roosevelt championed during his US presidency in the early 1900s, has the potential to unlock billions needed in investments and increase Mexico's annual growth by as much as 2 percent.

"Competition unleashes investment and innovation, fostering economic and social dynamism," said President Peña Nieto.

Investors have taken notice. At a time when venture investments in Brazil, Europe, China, and Israel have declined since 2008, the number of funds investing in Mexican startups has increased. From 2012 to 2013 investment in Mexico doubled. In 2013, the Latin American Venture Capital Association (LAVCA) released a "scorecard," a bellwether of the region's startups and investments, which showed vast improvements in Mexico's entrepreneurial activity. LAVCA notes that venture capital investments in Mexican startups have increased steadily since 2010. In 2010 Mexican startups raised $211 million for nineteen deals. In 2011, they raised $459 million for twenty-two projects. In 2012, $684 million went into twenty-one Mexican enterprises.

Reforming Mexico's financial structures was key, Rogelio dos Santos, a serial entrepreneur and partner at the Mexico-based Alta Ventures, told me when I visited him in his office in Monterrey. Mexico needed to "get the money flowing," he said. Monopolies in the energy, telecommunications, and food industries, and until 2000, one-party rule by the PRI, obviated investments. With little to no competition, wealth accumulated in a few hands rather than circulating to the broader population. "We needed to do what happened for the [venture capital] industry in 1978 in the U.S. We needed to put the savings of Mexicans to work for the private sector," Santos said.

These investments followed a variety of government reforms and initiatives throughout the 1990s and into the early 2000s. None was more critical than revising rules in 2004 to allow pension funds to invest in different assets—bonds, securities, equities, and eventually venture capital funds— which started to pop up soon after this change. In 2006 the government launched its own fund of funds, Fondo de Fondos. Largely intended to be a private equity vehicle, Fondo de Fondos has backed a number of investors who have raised seed and growth stage venture funds.

"We are in a fragile stage," according to Fernando Lelo, the cofounder of an accelerator and seed fund called Venture

Institute, located in Mexico City. "We need results in the next few years to consolidate this [venture capital] asset class." That, he told me, is a "game of numbers." But not just any numbers.

"Normal numbers work against us [in Mexico]. We [investors] have to play differently; we have to play with more single hits rather than huge home runs," he said.

Single hits rather than home runs have transformed Mexico into Latin America's dark horse. Unlike Brazil, which started out as the go-to Latin American country for all things startup and investment, Mexico has been methodical at the government and investor levels, taking incremental steps to reform. More important, it has worked to build an ecosystem that investors can trust—and profit from. The World Bank's *Doing Business* report puts Mexico at number 48 on its scale of ease of doing business. Brazil, in contrast, has a ranking of 130.

Of the seven countries whose efforts to develop an entrepreneurial core are at the center of this book, Mexico holds the most promise. China may churn out the greatest number of startups—including the most multibillion-dollar "unicorns," but Mexico has a promising entrepreneurial ecosystem. Mexicans at various levels in both the government and private sectors have worked to improve incentives and policies that enable and encourage entrepreneurship. They have raised funds, created collaborative spaces, rolled out entrepreneurial education, built mentor networks, and reformed laws.

Not long after I returned from Mexico, *New York Times* columnist Thomas Friedman visited the country and came away with a similar conclusion about Mexico. "In India," he wrote, "people ask you about China, and, in China, people ask you about India: Which country will become the more dominant economic power in the 21st century? I now have the answer: Mexico."

These predictions are not guaranteed. Over the past decade, violent drug cartels and gangs have seized many towns as well as travel routes. This has made moving around and moving things in the country dangerous. The Mexican government largely has failed to counter their force.

Mexico also has a poor track record on seeing that reform results in change. The country's history shows that past efforts to redirect Mexico out of its poverty trap have failed. The lure of monopolistic bribes and methods has proved too powerful, and changing the status quo too difficult, a topic explored in the last chapter. Yet they have not been more powerful than the will of individuals like Enrique Gomez Junco.

Enrique started a business fully aware of the challenges his country presented, in an industry he knew little about. What he did know was that he didn't just want to sit around and wait for things to change. His father had not waited. Nor had any of the American entrepreneurs he learned about at Monterrey Tech. "Progress does not march forward like an army on parade; it crawls on its belly like a guerilla," Michael Lewis wrote in *The New, New Thing*, the story of Jim Clark and the rise of Netscape, Silicon Valley's earliest tech startup. Enrique got on his belly to crawl and find the thing that no one else had. That is hard. Especially in today's competitive marketplace, there is a rush to build a better

Facebook, Google, and Uber. Indeed, it is not uncommon to hear twenty-somethings in Silicon Valley and New York's Silicon Alley say that they have built the "Uber of. . . ." Identifying the gap and finding the pain point—and then turning that gap and point into a viable business—take patience, research, and time. Mexico's monopolies most certainly have posed a problem for Mexico's entrepreneurs, but not any more so than the fear that prevents many individuals from going beyond their comfort zones, that paralyzes their ability to think "big," and that perpetuates the status quo.

That is something Shaffi Mather, an entrepreneur from India, taught me when I visited him in Mumbai.

FIVE

"A Little Bit of Extra . . . ": Ending Corruption

Always do right. This will gratify some people and
astonish the rest.

—MARK TWAIN

Mumbai and New Delhi

In the dimly lit entry hall of Mumbai's state-owned telecommunications company, the smell of mold oozes from floors
and walls. Middle-aged bureaucrats, *babus*, dressed in col-
lared shirts, hide their potbellies behind desks covered with
rubber stamps and piles of paper, some slightly yellowing.
On one morning in early 2005 when Shaffi Mather arrived
at the office, he felt he had passed through a time warp. He
resisted an urge to turn and walk out.

Improving this—India's public service mess—was the
dream that had brought Shaffi to the shabby offices of Mah-
anagar Telephone Nigam Limited (MTNL). A gangly lawyer
with wire-rimmed glasses, a receding hairline, and a slight

overbite, Shaffi carried with him a plan for an ambulance service. It would be, he believed, a startup that could save lives while helping to modernize health care and perhaps India, too.

Focused on his mission, Shaffi squeezed past a crowd in the entry hall. All he needed, he reminded himself, was something the bureaucrats in the ministry gave out every day: a phone number. Shaffi approached what seemed to be a reception desk. With difficulty he managed to attract the attention of the man sitting behind it.

"I'm starting an ambulance company and want to register for an easy-to-remember phone number that sick or injured people could call in emergencies," he said.

Every day in some corner of sprawling Mumbai, there is an accident or emergency—a man falls off a roof, a child is hit by a car, a woman doubles over in pain, or an elderly person has a heart attack. In the West, one can easily call an ambulance for help. Until very recently that was not possible in Mumbai, or in any of India's cities. In fact, it was not possible to call for an ambulance in any of the country's twenty-nine states, which have the primary responsibility for caring for India's 1.2 billion citizens.

Shaffi Mather, along with four friends, intended to fill the gap the government could not. None were activists or had a background in health care or public service. They were lawyers, investors, and marketing executives—well-to-do thirty-somethings. Like most people of their generation, they had embraced a social consciousness. That consciousness, along with a number of personal encounters that magnified the importance of emergency response care, led them to take an interest in their county's lack of ambulances. An ambulance service, they believed, could not only improve India's health care; it could mobilize change in India's public services—transform them to be more accountable, trustworthy, and service-oriented. As he continued to talk and the man, the *babu*, before him gazed at him coldly, Shaffi sensed that getting that simple phone number to make his dream a reality would be more difficult than he had anticipated.

He was right.

"Where shall I go?" Shaffi asked the bureaucrat after explaining his mission. A fan sputtered overhead. "What should I do?

"Wait your turn," came the brusque reply.

Waiting his turn involved not just a few minutes or a couple of hours, but several months. Unable to secure a toll-free number on his many visits to the telecom office in Mumbai, he traveled to India's capital, New Delhi—first to the Delhi branch of MTNL and eventually to the Ministry of Telecommunications. These trips yielded nothing. After finally securing an appointment with the minister himself, he received news that the number he sought was ready. It was a four-digit number, 1299. He had wanted a three-digit number, like 911, used in the United States, but those were only given for government operations and services. Shaffi had no choice but to choose a four-digit combination between the numbers 1251 and 1299—those were the combinations given to a private service. While he found this and the constant runaround tiresome, he also felt that it was nothing more than a small inconvenience. That he could tolerate—he had his entire life. India's government offices waded in bureaucracy, multiple levels of regulations and permissions or what long ago had been dubbed "the License Raj."

He found what came next, however, to be intolerable.

"Good news," a bureaucrat at the telecom ministry said to Shaffi one day when he came in to see if the toll-free number he had requested, 1299, had been approved. "Your number is ready." Shaffi sighed in relief. His head was filled with thoughts about the next steps he and his partners needed to take to get their ambulance service going.

"That is great news indeed," he replied. "What must I do now?"

"Now," the bureaucrat helping Shaffi said. "You will tell me how you would like to support this number."

There was no fee to register for a toll-free number—a fact that was clearly stated in the ministry's paperwork, and which Shaffi had confirmed on his numerous visits to the office. Still, the bureaucrat expected Shaffi to pay 200,000 rupees (approximately $4,000) in order to access it. This would be his "compensation."

It was the amount, more than the "request," that took Shaffi aback. Having grown up in India, Shaffi was no stranger to bureaucrats or anyone in the country asking for *chai paani*—change for tea—or what a friend of mine calls "a little bit of extra." "A little bit of extra" is how everyone in India navigated—and to a certain extent still navigates—everything in the country. Government workers, repairmen, landlords, store proprietors, street vendors, and, from my own personal experience, even taxi drivers think nothing of squeezing out a few more rupees from a customer—or a lot from a gullible one. On one taxi ride I took, the driver not only gouged me for the fare but demanded payment for the use of air conditioning, which he said was a separate charge.

Everyone in India is ready to push the limit—India unbounded. The bureaucrat's request for the equivalent of $4,000, however, stopped Shaffi in his tracks. He and the friends he planned to launch the ambulance company with had agreed that they would "build the ambulance project the right way or not build it at all." Bribes were a red line.

"I cannot pay that sum," Shaffi said. He explained to the bureaucrat that the ambulance he planned to launch required lots of up-front capital. It required a large fleet of vehicles, gas, medical equipment, radios, and other technical gear essential to coordinate patient pickups and hospital drop-offs. He had staff to train and had limited funds to do that with. At that time, the ambulance company had not planned to generate a profit.

Shaffi wanted to launch the ambulance service as a charity. His aspiration was to assist people like the bureaucrat himself. Unlike lucrative industries such as construction, mining, real estate, technology, and pharmaceuticals, there was no money or promise of money in ambulances. Emergency response sapped money. Shaffi had founded the company out of a desire to "give back."

"Even if one life is saved, isn't it worth it?" Shaffi asked, convinced that would resolve the situation. The bureaucrat, Shaffi thought, surely had enough reason to understand that. Moreover, Shaffi believed, his greed surely had a limit. Yet perhaps sensing that Shaffi came from a privileged background or perhaps in resentment of Shaffi's white-collar professional job, the bureaucrat remained unmoved. He told Shaffi if he didn't pay the 200,000 rupees, he would not receive the toll-free number he had requested.

"I could not accept this," Shaffi told me when I visited him one steamy August afternoon in his company's offices in the northern reaches of Mumbai, about a half hour drive from downtown. We sat in a cramped but busy space in a building that stood amid a row of squatter settlements made up of tin siding and blue tarpaulin.

Puzzled and frustrated, after the bureaucrat's request for the bribe Shaffi got up. "I will be back," he said to the bureaucrat and walked out. Outside the sun blazed and the air was thick with humidity, giving the sky a grayish-blue hue. Central New Delhi and its grand roundabouts teemed with cars, yellow and black rickshaws, and people dressed in a rainbow of electric colors. Shaffi had planned to head back to Mumbai and the sleek office tower where he worked on mobile communications for one of India's top conglomerates, Reliance Industries. Instead, he walked for a while, trying to work off the adrenaline that rushed through him. He had firmly decided that he would not pay the bribe. The question running through Shaffi's mind, however, was *what depths had India's corruption stooped to?* 200,000 rupees signified more than "a little bit of extra." It spoke of a bigger problem.

It was.

This form of corruption—tit for tat—has always existed in India, as it has and does everywhere that excessive bureaucracy compensates for weak institutions. It serves as a convenient opportunity and the easiest path to move ahead—for both payer and recipient. Bribes and kickbacks fill in where public services do not. They make it easier for someone eager to get a license or avoid excessive paper-work, much to the delight of the person tasked to help. "In some parts of the country," economist and Nobel Laure-ate Amartya Sen has noted in reference to India, "nothing moves in the intended direction unless the palm of the de-liverer is greased."

Throughout the twentieth century, when India was choked on poverty, bribes between bureaucrats and busi-nessmen were small. A rare few in the country had significant wealth. Hence, bureaucrats and politicians only requested *chai paani,* a little bit of extra. No wonder then when, in 1989, a scandal involving a Swedish arms company, Bofors, paying India's ruling party kickbacks believed to be worth $10 million, dominated headlines for weeks. The scandal certainly stunned many. But what truly shocked Indians was that one company could possess $10 million for kickbacks. This was much more than "just a little bit of extra."

India's economy was liberalized in 1991. When it started to take off in the mid-1990s, so too did the op-portunities to manipulate it. Corruption grew from chai paani to influence peddling and manipulation on a grand scale. By 2005 India had catapulted, according to GDP, to the number ten slot of the global economic ranking. It had become one of Wall Street bank Goldman Sachs's BRIC darlings—a country with a growing and prospering economy. With these developments, bribes in India, and corruption of all kinds—embezzlement, extortion, graft, and nepotism—skyrocketed. Transparency International, a global corruption watchdog NGO, has ranked India at the bottom of an annual index that measures perceptions of global graft for the past decade—slipping further down each passing year as India's GDP has risen. In 2007 the country ranked 70 out of 163 countries. In 2009 it ranked 84 out of 180. In 2011, it ranked 95 out of 182. In 2013, it ranked 94 out of 177.

"In the past two decades, there's been a shift toward grand corruption: the recent scandals [in India] are just qualitatively and quantitatively bigger than anything we've seen. And a big reason for that is India's rapid growth," Milan Vaishnav, an expert on South Asia at the Carnegie Endowment for International Peace, has noted. Instead of moving the country ahead, India's economic gains have become a boon for those in government, both at the lowest and highest levels, who are willing to take advantage of it. It has especially become problematic in elections—a problem with parallels to the out-of-control financing of political campaigns in the United States. In India, as in the United States, people gain access to and influence over politicians through large "donations." Public officials in India, according to *Corruption in India: The DNA and RNA*, pocketed as much as $18.42 billion, or 1.26 percent of the country's GDP of $1.82 trillion, through corruption in 2010–2011 alone.

The 200,000-rupee request for a simple toll-free number for a small ambulance startup helped clarify for Shaffi that corruption is what held India's public services back. Corruption stands as one of the country's biggest obstacles to progress. That, Shaffi felt, posed a threat greater than the absence of emergency response care.

"Bribes and corruption have both a demand and supply side," Shaffi told me. "The supply side being mostly greedy corporates, unethical businesses, and the hapless common man. On the demand side being mostly politicians, bureaucrats, and those who have discretionary power invested in them."

Public services in India would never improve so long as this supply and demand persisted. In fact, Shaffi realized they were the reason India's public services had not modernized. As he thought about it, he came to see that corruption paralyzed huge parts of India's economy. As *The Economist* magazine noted in March 2014, it produces "bad decisions," and concern over corruption "produces indecision." Corruption equals gridlock. Worse, on the scale it had reached in India, corruption contributed to gross inequality. The rich could buy influence as the poor sat in silence.

The social consciousness that Shaffi and his friends embraced had to extend beyond picking up and caring for the injured and sick. It had to take on India's "a little bit of extra" and break up the chain of those supplying and demanding bribes. He had to do what the titans of India's IT sector had done decades earlier: build an organization with defined and uncompromising values.

Narayana Murthy, an unassuming and bespectacled engineer, was one of a handful of Indians who had done just that to India's private sector two decades earlier. Borrowing $250 from his wife in 1981, he launched Infosys, a business processing and technology outsourcing firm that catered to foreign clients based on trust. Murthy ensured that his company championed corporate governance, honored contracts, heard customer concerns, and punished graft and personal use of company assets. Today, Infosys is a billion-dollar company that has created hundreds of thousands of jobs and spawned an industry that has turned India into a major technology center.

Infusing trust in India's public sector, Shaffi felt, would require a similar gesture. What transpired when Shaffi returned to the telecom ministry the following day was just that.

"I'm glad to see you're back," the bureaucrat who had requested the 200,000 rupee bribe said when he saw Shaffi. "I hope that you have come with some support."

"I have not," Shaffi replied.

"I see," the bureaucrat said after a short pause. He bobbed his head in a figure eight, a common gesture in India that, combining both yes and no, conveyed something along the lines of acknowledgment. "That's just as well. It seems that the number you requested, 1299, is no longer available. The option you now have is 1298 or 1297."

Shaffi chose 1298. "I guess he thought that 1298 was not a good number," Shaffi told me. "We would reveal to him that this was not the case." Shaffi and his friends plastered the number 1298 all over their fleet of bright yellow-and-green ambulances. Then they went out to tell everyone what had happened at the telecom ministry—and incidentally talked about emergency response care. "That number became not just for people to call," he said. It became the name of their startup, Dial 1298, and the crusade to move India away from "a little bit of extra" and toward accountability.

"Dial 1298 showed our intolerance to such actions and ways," he told me.

• • •

SHAFFI MATHER had come face to face with India's lack of a functioning 911 system one night in 2002. He had returned to his family back in Kerala, one of India's southernmost states. It is a place that holds the highest rank on India's human development index and life expectancy, and where a large number of elected officials belong to the Communist Party. Interestingly, Kerala has the lowest incidence of corruption in India.

On that night, Shaffi's mother had prepared dinner for him and all his family: wife and daughter, father, brother, and sister. It was nearly midnight, and everyone had retired for the night. No sooner had the doors shut, however, than shouts brought everyone back together. Shaffi's mother had fallen, and Shaffi's father called out for help. Shaffi ran to his parents' bedroom and found his then fifty-two-year-old mother writhing on the floor, clutching her chest and gasping for air.

"I panicked," Shaffi told me. "She was choking on something. And the thing is, I didn't know what to do. None of us knew what to do." He had heard of the Heimlich maneuver but didn't know how to perform it. He tried dialing India's 911, but no one answered. Likewise with Kerala's ambulance service. No one picked up the phone when someone called. Ambulances in India only functioned as hearses, to transport dead bodies. Few hospitals in the country, even those abundantly endowed, operated ambulances. In India, people in an accident or with a life-threatening injury had to depend on goodwill or else privately run responders, which were not always available to the general public.

"I didn't know how else to help her. I just picked her up, put her in the rear seat of the car and drove like crazy," he said.

Shaffi took his mother to the hospital, where doctors helped her and her choking cleared. She was, however, in bad shape. She had stopped breathing. The doctors kept her in the intensive care unit for several days.

A few weeks later, another emergency compelled Shaffi to focus on India's lack of ambulance services. Ravi Krishna, a close childhood friend, called him in distress.

Ravi's fifty-something-year-old mother had collapsed in a hotel lobby in New York City. Stepping off an elevator, she fell into septic shock. He told Shaffi that if paramedics hadn't arrived on the scene when they did, she might have died. When Shaffi asked how long after her collapse the paramedics arrived, he was amazed to learn that it took New York emergency technicians only ten minutes after someone called 911.

What happened in response to Ravi's mother's collapse as compared to what happened in response to his own mother's choking put into perspective for Shaffi the vast differences between India and the West.

India had made a lot of progress economically—enough to capture the attention and interest of the United States and Europe. In 2002 the country's GDP stood at $492.4 billion. It had become a lead destination for business process outsourcing and technology support. Infosys and another technology firm, Wipro, had become globally renowned. Tata Consulting became a much sought after business partner. Other Indian companies started to appear on the Fortune 500 list and the NASDAQ. The leaders of several of these companies appeared on *Forbes*'s list of billionaires. The country had created jobs and wealth. It mesmerized many— technologists, bankers, and investors. India was hailed as the next China. Its renaissance was part of the evidence that persuaded Thomas Friedman, a columnist from the *New York Times,* that the world had radically changed—that it was actually "flat," a place where location no longer mattered in terms of economics and commerce. Everyone in every part of the world could build businesses and trade and, thereby, progress. Friedman believed India occupied considerable space on that landscape.

Yet despite all of India's gains, the country's citizens could not rely on public services. Roads remained strewn with potholes. Trains and buses broke down regularly. Teachers failed to show up to class. And as Shaffi knew, no one could successfully call for an ambulance in an emergency. He found that unacceptable—and unnecessary.

India had not only become a global power, it had a persuasive historical narrative that many rallied around: self-determination. It was a narrative that had been gathering momentum in the early twentieth century and was penned in the early 1940s when a bespectacled barrister named Mohandas Gandhi stood up to British colonial rule, arguing that Indians need not be ruled. They possessed the capacity and disposition to rule themselves. Gandhi helped shake off centuries of imperialism to establish the world's largest democracy in 1947. Such a nation, Shaffi maintained, possessed the ability to reform and update its public sector; it had the ability to provide paved roads, clean water, reliable electricity, police protection, education, and ambulances.

Shaffi and Ravi decided to take the matter of emergency care in India to the authorities. Indians had long entrusted their social welfare to government. Yet health care stood out as a fraught and largely neglected topic in New Delhi. For much of the 1960s and 1970s it only translated into family planning and population control. In 1983 Indian lawmakers finally adopted legislation for a national health policy.

Two decades later, they still grappled with the matter—attempting to improve policies and increase expenditures. The Indian government allocates to health care the same percentage of resources—between 1 to 4 percent of the country's GDP—as do the poorest governments of the world, including Afghanistan, Haiti, and Sierra Leone. To make up for this insufficient amount of money and seize an obvious market opportunity, the private sector in India stepped up to pour resources into health care. As these companies did so, they made money. India's private sector has turned health care into one of the country's most lucrative revenue generators. Private health care in India, which includes medical tourism, is valued between $65 billion and $80 billion—a figure projected to double in size by 2020. Indeed, health care is in great demand.

Unfortunately only 15 percent of India's population has access to private health-care coverage. That has left one billion people to compete for grossly underfunded public services. Emergency response care, Shaffi and Ravi believed, offered a compelling way for the government to engage in the health-care industry. Emergency response care depended heavily on logistics. With oversight over roads, police, and communications, the government could execute on logistics better than a private firm.

In early 2003 the two friends gathered relevant information about the importance of emergency response care. They took time off from their jobs in Mumbai, Shaffi from Reliance Industries and Ravi from another one of India's top conglomerates, where he headed up the corporate affairs division. Together, they traveled to New Delhi. "We had data from reputable institutions that made a clear case that the number of people saved when there is an ambulance service available is considerable," Shaffi told me. Ambulances, they argued, could reduce the number of fatalities from accidents and heart attacks considerably. And that would add value to a growing and accelerating India by keeping citizens healthy and in the workforce. They lobbied officials at the health ministry as well as parliamentarians. They pleaded that funds should be allocated for each of India's states to operate ambulances and a response service.

As India progressed economically, more people crowded into cities and the number of accidents increased. More than 80 percent of Indians injured in road accidents don't get critical care in the hours after those accidents, leading to close to 160,000 deaths annually.

As Indians became wealthier and moved into the middle class, their diets became richer. Communicable diseases such as cholera, malaria, smallpox, and typhoid, which plagued India for much of the twentieth century, account for only a small percentage of deaths in India today. With a prevalence, and now abundance, of fried and butter-laden foods—*samosas, daal, chapattis*—and little exercise, heart disease is the leading cause of death in the country. Heart attacks kill 25 percent of Indians between the ages of twenty-five and sixty-nine. India, with more than 1.2 billion people, is estimated to account for 60 percent of heart disease patients worldwide.

None of the arguments Shaffi and Ravi made, however, moved the parliamentarians to take up the cause of emergency care. "We failed miserably," Shaffi said. "We failed in impressing upon the policy leadership to undertake this matter." This did not, however, dissuade them from forging ahead. If the government would not take up the cause of emergency response care, Shaffi and Ravi would—though they had no real idea how difficult that would prove to be. "We thought that we could start a working model that could be replicated around the country," Shaffi told me.

• • •

SIZE—IN LANDMASS and population—delays and slows down everything in India. Ineffective government adds complications. Yet somehow, daily life in the country inches on. Ad hoc systems, comprised of strong networks of family and community, are a major reason. India, as anthropologist Edward Hall described in *Beyond Culture*, is a "high-context" society, one in which members fall back on their strong bonds, depending on one another rather than on outsiders, much less the government.

Jugaad, Hindu for an innovative fix, is another reason. Left to their own devices, Indians have found resourceful solutions to basic challenges such as lack of electricity and poor sanitation.

After striking out with the government in New Delhi, Shaffi and Ravi began to think about how they could move Indians to think about how they could channel their networks and *jugaad* to improve emergency response care. Given the right incentive, the friends concluded, their fellow citizens could be motivated to rally behind an effort to improve health care for all. That was especially important as the country's demographics changed. No longer were families living as cohesive units in small rural communities. More and more Indians lived apart from their parents and grandparents, cousins, aunts, and uncles—in cities and in city apartments. Indeed, India's future lay in cities—places with naturally weaker social networks and more individual lifestyles.

Mumbai alone had become what writer Suketu Mehta calls "the Maximum City"—a city dense with people, buildings, cars, and activity and struggling to accommodate it all. With a population in its metro area of over nineteen million inhabitants crammed into Mumbai's 169 square miles, in parts of the city the population density exceeded a million per square mile. Shaffi and Ravi concluded that Mumbai, like many cities around the world that had become overwhelmed by, and indeed victims of, urbanization, needed to adapt to the "brave new world," in which it had become a major player. The city needed many things: stronger infrastructure, reliable electricity, improved schools, clean water.

They identified emergency response care—ambulances—
as their personal crusade.

Because it was personal, Shaffi and Ravi stopped thinking about emergency response care as something that
someone else—the Indian government or a charity or hospital—should do. While an ambulance itself required well-
trained health practitioners, running an ambulance service
involved operations and systems—things that Shaffi and
Ravi knew plenty about. They were business professionals
with management experience. Taking that collective know-
how—and driving forward with their passion—they decided
to roll out a modest ambulance service for Mumbai.

To get started, both hit the library. They read up on everything related to ambulances. They visited hospitals and
talked to friends as well as friends of friends who were doctors. In 2004, when Shaffi Mather had the opportunity to
spend four and a half months at the London School of Economics (LSE), where he had been accepted into a visiting
scholars program, he reached out to the London Ambulance
Service.

Always academically oriented, Shaffi was eager to attend
classes anywhere he could. He had earned degrees in law
and business administration, and in 2008 would earn a master of public administration at Harvard. And prior to that,
while at LSE in 2004, he had conducted original research
on a project that would have a positive social impact in India. The lack of emergency response care in his country
was an ideal topic. Channeling Fred Smith, the founder of
FedEx, who wrote about his idea for a shipping and logistics

company as an undergrad at Yale, Shaffi spent his year in London learning how an ambulance system worked, to meet his goal of creating one for Mumbai.

In London, Shaffi spent days riding shotgun in a number of the bright yellow vehicles dispatched throughout the British capital. The London Ambulance Service had two types of ambulances, an advanced life support vehicle equipped with a defibrillator for cardiac patients and a basic life support vehicle. He shadowed National Health Service staff at the organization's headquarters and its high-tech call center, which manages seventy ambulance stations throughout greater London. Shaffi took detailed notes on how the London Ambulance Service mastered such a massive operation and then shared his findings with Ravi. They then reached out to a few more friends and persuaded them to join their endeavor.

Together, the group of five pooled an initial $100,000, which enabled them to make an initial purchase of two vehicles and test their concept. As the pilot succeeded, the London Ambulance Service offered to donate its three-year-old vehicles, but Indian customs regulations did not allow used ambulances to be imported into India. The friends then raised an additional $400,000 from friends, family, and other angel investors to purchase eight more vehicles, buy medical equipment, hire staff, and set up a twenty-four-hour call center. This was not a straightforward process, either. Indian customs wrongly classified the defibrillators as regular equipment, which came with a 30 percent customs charge. "If we paid them a bribe, they would have reversed the charges and classified the defibrillators as life-saving equipment, as they should have been," Shaffi told me. Instead, Shaffi and his partners appealed to the high court to have the defibrillators classified appropriately. They won.

Dial 1298 could not operate without hospitals. In Mumbai, as in other cities throughout India, hospitals overflow with people. On a visit to one, Prince Aly Khan Hospital—a private facility in Bycalla, a neighborhood in Mumbai— I counted nearly seventy people waiting, at ten o'clock in the morning in its open-air emergency care unit. Receiving patients from an ambulance would require the hospital to dedicate space, already at a premium, and to invest in the necessary equipment to coordinate with the ambulance. Hospitals in Mumbai are known not to do much without "a little bit of extra."

Indians had already been in the habit of paying "a little bit of extra" for otherwise banned prenatal tests to determine the sex of a child and paying off medical personnel to falsify medical reports in the case of an honor crime death or rape. The competition for health care has only increased the number of bribes to doctors in order to be treated or to hospitals to find space.

Interestingly, however, because Dial 1298 had access to a pool of patients with life-threatening conditions, hospitals offered bribes to first Shaffi and Ravi and then some of Dial 1298's drivers and medics to divert patients to their facilities. Life-threatening conditions, particularly cardiac cases, bring in thousands in billing revenue for hospitals. Shaffi and Ravi refused.

In May 2005, after navigating India's bureaucracy, including the country's customs offices, and resisting hospital bribes, Shaffi, Ravi, and their friends managed to put together the framework for a real emergency response care operation. The only missing piece was a toll-free number.

• • •

THE REQUEST FOR a bribe at the telecom ministry not only sobered Shaffi, it gave him new purpose. "There are two types of corruption in this world," Shaffi said to me one evening. "The first is the Bernie Madoff kind, where the person is motivated by pure greed. The other is the kind driven by entitlement—this sense that 'I deserve extra money because of who I am and who you are not.' This is what I believe must end in India." It was the "a-ha" moment that pushed him to change course.

He had temporarily set aside his original name for the ambulance service, Ziqitsa, a fusion of the Sanskrit word *chikitsa*, meaning medical treatment, and *zigyasa*, meaning quest for knowledge, for Dial 1298. "Our brand philosophy is based on the great thought of Gandhi that 'saving a life is one of the most rewarding experiences a person can undergo in his/her lifetime.'" Instead, he heeded the advice of a mentor who had advised him months earlier that he and Ravi should not operate their ambulance service as a nonprofit.

An ambulance is a difficult business to profit from. Shaffi certainly had no intention or desire to do so. He wanted an ambulance to operate regardless of a person's ability to pay for its use.

One of India's leading business figures, Sam Pitroda—an engineer and former adviser to the Indian prime minister on public information and infrastructure and innovations—challenged Shaffi to reconsider his thinking. Pitroda is known to be India's leading innovator and proverbially the godfather of the country's telecom revolution. Shaffi had turned to him for advice on 1298, specifically what its revenue model should be.

"You have to get it out of your minds that this work can only be done by a nonprofit," Pitroda told Shaffi. "Profit is not bad, profiteering is."

Shaffi had a grand vision: he was going to transform Indian emergency health care and, therein, possibly all of India's public services. Pitroda asked Shaffi if he thought that as a nonprofit operating on a minimum and frugal budget, he could achieve those results. Nonprofits, Pitroda reminded Shaffi, chased after grants and spent their time reporting to donors. They also did not pay their staff well, which was one of the key reasons many in the nonprofit sector and in government were inclined to ask for *chai paani* when the opportunity presented itself. Talent, Pitroda pointed out, migrated to places that offered adequate compensation. Especially because it involved people's lives, he encouraged Shaffi to offer whatever he could to attract the best people to his enterprise.

"For a sustainable, vibrant, efficient organization to reach its highest potential it needs to be a for-profit enterprise," he said. That, Pitroda explained, didn't mean merely profit. It had to create value. Value is what the best-run companies and institutions focus on.

Shaffi and his Dial 1298 partners adopted a sliding scale model—a model used by many in the health-care sector as well as in education worldwide. In the United States, many state universities operate on a sliding scale model—requiring full tuition for those from outside the state's boundaries and extending a discount to residents. It was a model that an unknown ophthalmologist named Govindappa Venkataswamy had employed back in 1976.

Venkataswamy had seen too many afflicted with unnecessary blindness because of cataracts. To address that challenge, which India's health-care system couldn't, he opened up an eye hospital. At the Aravind Eye Hospital, as he named it, he performed cataract surgery on rich and poor alike, using a tiered pricing structure and a menu of options. Wealthier patients paid more than poor ones. In fact, the wealthy, eager to stay in the workforce and remain productive, patronized Aravind in such large numbers that Venkataswamy expanded.

Today, Aravind Hospitals operate on hundreds of thousands of patients yearly. As of 2013 they had cared for 3.1 million people. Sixty percent of procedures are free, and the company makes a gross profit margin of greater than 35 percent. Aravind takes no donations or charity and makes enough profit to fund a new hospital every three years.

Following Sam Pitroda's advice, Dial 1298 bills those destined for a private hospital the full amount. Anyone requesting to be taken to a public facility is charged on a sliding scale, or a subsidized fee. In certain instances, such as emergencies, the service is free.

When they started, Shaffi and Ravi had not worked out a system for how subsidies would be granted or collected. Moreover, they had not considered the fact that an emergency itself would make billing and payment collection all the more difficult. A university or even an eye care hospital can discuss and deliberate prices. Cost is not the central consideration in an emergency.

Initially, Shaffi and Ravi had empowered the driver and the emergency medical technician on hand to handle fees and their collection. A year into Dial 1298's operations, Shaffi and Ravi realized that this served as a loophole. Without oversight, opportunistic staff members pocketed a portion of the full fares they collected from legitimate trips to private hospitals, while recording discounts for imaginary trips to public ones.

"When we looked at the pattern of movement, we noticed that there was a high proportion of visits to public hospitals—and that we weren't getting much revenue from many transports," Shaffi said. That struck Shaffi as strange. The phone dispatchers taking incoming calls all talked about the high volume of requests for private hospitals.

Moreover, he knew that the poor hesitated to use an ambulance service. Because Shaffi wanted Dial 1298 to be egalitarian and reach everyone, regardless of background, he spent time marketing to the poor. In doing so, he learned that few of them could be convinced that a shiny and well-equipped ambulance was available for them to use—for a discount. India's poor had no experience with centralized and coordinated health care, much less emergency response care. In a crisis, India's poor called a family member or a neighbor. Expecting them to reach out to a complete stranger required a change in behavior—and a leap of faith.

"We realized that the freedom granted (to the driver and EMT) was being misused," Shaffi told me. More than that, however, he and his Dial 1298 partners realized that they had failed to convey their purpose to their own employees. Dial 1298's story about fighting India's *babus* and the prevalence of "a little bit of extra" could not just be a public one. The company had to internalize it.

Shaffi and his team laid out new rules. First, drivers and technicians had to call in their destination to Dial 1298's headquarters. Second, the company firmed up its internal oversight, hiring staff to supervise the books. Moreover, just as Bülent Çelebi had done with his company AirTies in Turkey, Shaffi and his team spent time creating and developing a culture—a values system—that each Dial 1298 employee could rally around and could champion at all times, especially during a crisis.

• • •

DARKNESS HAD enveloped Mumbai as two inflatable speedboats pulled into the city's harbor on the night of November 26, 2008. They landed at the Gateway of India, a monument that commemorates the landing of the British king George V on that site in 1911. Behind it stood the regal, five-star Taj Mahal Palace and Tower. Nearby, high-end boutiques and restaurants lined the streets, including the fashionable art deco Leopold Café. Ten men jumped from the boats and rushed for these and a handful of other sites, including the Oberoi Trident Hotel, another posh stomping ground for the rich and famous. At each location, these men fired shots and lobbed grenades, unleashing havoc. As they did, a number of victims caught in their crossfire managed to pull out their mobile phones and call 1298. The ambulance service dispatched every available vehicle to the handful of sites.

On that night, 1298's vehicles attended to 125 people—a fraction of the 600 victims injured. A number of other ambulance services arrived on the scene and attended to several dozens more. Yet none could meet the immediate need. For that, the Indian government came under fire—most significantly within the country—for its poor response to the crisis.

As India's fortunes have risen over the past decade and a half, so, too, have the demands and expectations of its citizens. "Everywhere it has emerged a modern middle class causes political ferment," wrote political scientist Francis Fukuyama in June 2013, referring to the Arab Spring uprisings in Tunisia and Egypt in 2011, then later the street protests that gripped Turkey and Brazil in 2013. "Middle class people want not only security for their families, but choices and opportunity for themselves."

Those choices and opportunities, they recognize, come from "fighting the power," which with increased disposable income and, more important, awareness, they are able to do. Increasingly urban and connected to cable television and mobile phones, ordinary Indians are, as corporations long ago recognized, a viable market, and to the chagrin of politicians, a discerning constituency. Age-old traditions and caste divisions in India no longer have the sway they once did; *chai paani* no longer has mass acceptance. Indians want functioning public services and reliable governance. In fact, they believe functioning services and reliable governance are their right.

The demand for functioning public services has included improved health-care services. Health-care startups, in general, particularly ones focused on low-cost or affordable care and preventive care, have proliferated in India—as they have around the world. According to the Omidyar Network, the philanthropic investment fund started by eBay founder Pierre Omidyar, "affordable health care" drives about $20 billion in revenues in India alone. Overall, Indian health care is a $65 billion to $80 billion industry, with projections that it will grow up to $155 billion by 2017. While that is minuscule compared to US health care—a market estimated to be $2.8 trillion—the opportunity for growth in India's health-care industry is huge.

Around New Delhi's Qutub Institute, an area near the Indian Institute of Technology, something called "MedTech Row" has emerged. There, one can find ventures that range from assisting patients in finding trustworthy service providers to engineers building hardware devices that improve diagnosis, treatment, and even surgery. Much like Silicon Valley's venture capital firms, located on Sand Hill Road, a number of Indian-led investment funds sit on MedTech Row. The Bill and Melinda Gates Foundation, the Dell Foundation, and the Omidyar Network, philanthropic organizations focused on improved health care, have offices there.

Along with their demand for improved health care, India's middle class has taken up arms against corruption. That is not a surprise. Transparency directly corresponds to the delivery of public services. In fact, transparency is essential to it.

In 2009, when Ramalinga Raju, chairman of the technology company Satyam, confessed to tampering with the company's accounting ledgers and financial records in a way similar to, though not on the same scale as, the Enron scandal of 2001, India's public called for his removal. When investigators revealed that government officials had squirreled away hundreds of thousands of rupees from rigged construction bids for the Commonwealth Games in 2010, there was a significant public outcry. A short time after, audits revealed that the telecom ministry had undersold licenses to operate on a 2G mobile network at a $40 billion loss to the treasury. The Indian public took their anger to the country's political leaders. India's leaders have responded.

Arvind Kejriwal, a former bureaucrat in the Indian tax office, has led one of India's most effective campaigns against India's corruption. In 2011 he orchestrated a hunger strike with a seventy-four-year-old activist, Anna Hazare, to push for the passage of the Lokpal Bill, a bill to create an ombudsmen office. They have succeeded in doing so.

Representatives of India's key political parties, the ruling Congress Party and the leading opposition party, the Hindu nationalist Bharatiya Janata Party (BJP), have promised to end India's "little bit of extra." Narendra Modi, the BJP leader, campaigned on a jobs first and "neo-middle class" platform that promised to increase transparency and end corruption—corruption that he says the Congress Party has long taken part in and been responsible for in India. He now serves as the country's prime minister.

· · ·

GOOD TO GREAT is a bible of sorts for business executives and twenty-somethings launching startups. Its author, Jim Collins, a prominent business consultant, examines the question of how a good company becomes a great one. Collins lists a number of observations about the importance of talent, culture, community, originality, focus, and leadership, including the following:

> Yes, leadership is about vision. But leadership is equally about creating a climate where the truth is heard and the brutal facts confronted. There's a huge difference between the opportunity to "have your say" and the opportunity to be heard. The good-to-great leaders understood this distinction, creating a culture wherein people had a tremendous opportunity to be heard and, ultimately, for the truth to be heard.

A desire to bring emergency response care inspired Shaffi Mather to launch Dial 1298. India's culture of *chai paani* or a "little bit of extra" prompted Dial 1298 to be great. Shaffi recognized that for his social enterprise to succeed, it needed to confront the brutal fact that corruption perverts governance and undermines progress. Infosys and Wipro had become billion-dollar plus tech enterprises because they refused to engage in corruption. Dial 1298 set out to take on that corruption. Combating corruption, Shaffi had decided, is what would "tip" India from "good to great."

Shaffi has been an outspoken advocate on this matter, appearing at TED, the popular Technology, Entertainment, and Design conference, which has become chic. He has attended the Clinton Global Initiative and been a guest at the White House Summit on Entrepreneurship. In 2009 he launched Bribe Busters, a nonprofit focused on battling corruption. These efforts, along with a growing collective consciousness about emergency response care and corruption, has helped scale up Dial 1298's business.

A number of India's states have stepped forward to work with Dial 1298 and roll out an ambulance service for their constituents. In addition to Maharashtra (Mumbai), 1298 operates in seventeen states in India and provides full coverage in Kerala, Odisha, and Punjab. In Bihar, 1298 operates on behalf of the state, as an official public service. This, along with a number of investments, has helped Dial 1298 expand from a five-person endeavor with two ambulances to a 5,558-staff operation with 860 vehicles. In 2007 Dial 1298 raised a first round of $1.5 million from the New York–based Acumen Fund, which backs international social enterprises. (The Acumen Fund also backed Tayo Oviosu's Paga Tech in Nigeria.) Since then Dial 1298 has raised a number of debt investments from both inside and outside of India. HDFC (one of India's biggest banks), the India Value Fund (a private equity firm), and the IDFC (an Indian financial institution like the International Finance Corporation) have put a combined $4.25 million into Dial 1298.

Increased interest in emergency response care has allowed Dial 1298 to broaden its scope. In addition to running ambulances for and within various Indian states, the company operates ambulances for hospitals and private businesses. It also works with various businesses to provide basic emergency response care training, such as cardiopulmonary resuscitation (CPR). In 2014 Dial 1298 expanded its model to Dubai and has plans to do so in other Asian cities, including Singapore, Dhaka, Bangladesh, and Rangoon, Myanmar.

As Shaffi works on Dial 1298's expansion plans, he has also launched another startup focused on emergency response care, MUrgency, which is a Facebook-like global emergency response network. First responders will be able to join the service and connect with other first responders worldwide, to share best practices as well as assist in individual emergencies and provide on-demand emergency care. He is working on that in Silicon Valley.

Other entrepreneurs are attacking corruption as well. Swati and Ramesh Ramanathan, a husband and wife team, launched the website Ipaidabribe.com in August 2010. The site collects anonymous reports of bribes requested and paid. As a result, it has become an instant hit with millions—and not just in India. Ipaidabribe has been replicated in Kenya, Pakistan, and Russia. As of this writing, it has logged in India several hundred thousand reports of bribes paid, to the tune of hundreds of millions of rupees.

Technology in general has made it more difficult for *babus*—bureaucrats—to ask for *chai paani*. More government services—issuing a license, registering for property—can be done online and away from the extended hand of a struggling government worker.

Still, it is foolish to believe that corruption will disappear entirely—from India or anywhere else. Money, whether it is *chai paani* or millions of dollars, buys power and influence the world over, most often in legal forms. Moguls buy up newspapers and news outlets. Political action committees

(PACs) in the United States channel money from corporations and wealthy individuals to support a particular candidate and/or push for a policy or cause.

What will counter corruption, as Shaffi Mather has pinpointed, is accountability and strong governance. Prosperity has thrived in those places where people, as economist Chris Blattman has noted, have "the means to be mobile and exercise voice, and hold leaders accountable." It comes from strong institutions and the rule of law. No one knows that better than Russian entrepreneur Yana Yakovleva.

SIX

Order in the Court:
Political Participation and the Rule of Law

The duke cannot deny the course of law.
For the commodity that strangers have
With us in Venice, if it be denied,
Will much impeach the justice of his state,
Since that the trade and profit of the city
Consisteth of all nations.

—WILLIAM SHAKESPEARE,
MERCHANT OF VENICE (ACT 3, SCENE 3)

Moscow

Yana Yakovleva's long, curly, auburn hair had not fully dried when three men and one woman approached her on a crowded street in central Moscow one evening in early June 2006. The city's skyline, usually gunmetal gray, shone bright blue on that day. The sun danced off a gold-covered church cupola nearby. Yana, at the time the thirty-five-year old co-founder of Sofex, a chemical trading and manufacturing business, had just stepped outside of the gym. Outfitted in a white skirt and heels, she was headed to dinner with a boyfriend. The four strangers—plainclothes police officers—forced her to miss that date.

"It is so pleasant to detain such a respected woman," one of the men said as his three other colleagues surrounded Yana. Several passersby stopped to stare. Yana remained calm.

"Give me your keys," another officer ordered and directed her to walk toward her car. All five piled in and drove to 38 Petrovka Street, Moscow's main and infamous detention center. Without an appearance before a judge, they threw her into a holding cell. They didn't provide Yana with any information about why she had been arrested, when she would appear in court, or how long she would be incarcerated. Consulting with a lawyer was out of the question. They only offered to allow Yana to contact her family.

"Papa, they have me in jail," Yana said before she was forced to hang up the phone.

Months earlier, officials from Russia's drug enforcement agency—the Federal Drug Control Service—had begun showing up repeatedly at Yana's office on Moscow's gritty, industrial east side. First they took an interest in her financial records. Then came questions about her business dealings and Sofex's chemical suppliers. The intent of each visit was clear. It was to test Yana's nerves. With corruption accepted as the norm in Russia, she suspected the ultimate goal was the typical *vzyatka*—a bribe or kickback.

It was.

The "Drug Control" officials wanted Yana to pay kickbacks on acetic anhidrid, a chemical used to process heroin—or else supply it to them. Yana flatly refused.

The police visits to Sofex went on for weeks. They questioned staff and combed through the accounting books. On one occasion a whole busload of police officers—weapon-wielding men and women alike—pulled into the company courtyard. They ordered the staff out and went about the all-too-familiar ritual of seizing documents and computers.

Members of the *siloviki*, officials from the higher ranks of Russia's top security and law enforcement bodies, started following Yana and her cofounder, Alexei Protsky. All these tactics of harassment and intimidation did not surprise Yana. Her arrest, however, did.

Yana had not thought that in the new "democratic" Russia she was really a target for arrest. The country had, after all, made some strides to abandon its iron-fisted past and Westernize—to open up its economy and respect international norms. Besides, she had broken no laws. On that June evening in 2006, Yana learned that in Russia laws did not matter.

Over the past decade—and arguably throughout the history of the Soviet Union—Russian authorities, particularly those at the seat of power, the Kremlin, have exercised power with impunity, using their offices along with the police and the country's courts to exert their control.

Some have called this *bespredel*, a term originally used to describe organized crime gangs that ravaged Russia in the years after the fall of the Soviet hammer and sickle. It translates into "without limits." Today, it is not surprising to hear this term used in reference to Russia's leadership and its ruthless authoritarianism. Whatever the label, Russia's leadership has succeeded in usurping authority and throttling the rule of law.

The rule of law is the most essential factor in and foundation of entrepreneurship. Entrepreneurs, as we have seen in previous chapters, can work around the absence of talent, infrastructure, collaboration, competition, and transparency. Yet without a strong rule of law, entrepreneurs and their startups risk, at best, paralysis and stagnation. At worst, they are subject to corruption, extortion, and intimidation—a mafia state, which is the case in Russia today.

The Kremlin has targeted entrepreneurs and businesspeople—individuals with vision and drive and, in some instances, money and influence—and accused them of white-collar crimes or "economic crimes."

Russian courtrooms overflow with these individuals with money and influence—who can pose a direct threat to Russia's leaders. More than 100,000 entrepreneurs and businesspeople have been incarcerated or been brought before a court in Russia since the early 2000s. Sergei Magnitsky, a lawyer who alleged that the Russian police had engaged in fraud and money laundering, and Mikhail Khodorkovsky, the former head of Yukos oil, are the most famous. Magnitsky died in prison in 2009. After being imprisoned for a decade, Khodorkovsky was freed by Russian president Vladimir Putin on the eve of the 2014 Sochi Winter Olympics.

As Boris Titov, Russia's ombudsman for business rights, notes, it is hard to find "another social group persecuted on such a large scale." And that, as Yana pointed out to me when we met in Moscow one damp and drizzly November morning, is crushing the country's entrepreneurs.

A common refrain of those in Silicon Valley is that "government should get out of its way." It is a mistake, however, to equate government with regulation. In reality, Silicon Valley could not exist without the government. The US government and each of its fifty states ensure the proper functioning of the laws, courts, and police forces of the country's justice system. That justice system provides the basis—the trust—for anyone to open up a storefront; enter into and, more important, enforce a contract; and protect his or her idea or ideas through patents. The US justice system has broken up monopolies and worked to safeguard competition in American markets. Indeed, while US regulations and certain economic policies have caused concern, if not consternation, the US justice system has allowed businesses—small and large—to get off the ground, to take risks, and even to fail without fear.

Yana Yakovleva's story highlights the importance of that system and the importance of entrepreneurs engaging in it.

• • •

HAVING HAD several video chat conversations over Skype with her, I immediately recognized Yana's petite frame as she walked past the doorman sporting a bowler derby at the historic Hotel National just across from Red Square. Unlike most women in Moscow, she wore no makeup and did not coif, let alone tame, her hair. A blue cable sweater added to her simple, down-to-earth looks. Yana is no-nonsense.

She started toward me, clearly identifying me as well. Most of our Skype chats had been lengthy conversations about Sofex and the Kafkaesque ordeal that had turned her into an activist—a Russian Norma Rae. In addition to running Sofex, which was now struggling, Yana founded Business Solidarity in 2007, an organization that champions the rights of entrepreneurs.

Business Solidarity is what made Yana stand out. While Sofex gave her experience and insight into entrepreneurship, Business Solidarity helped her understand it. "I understood at that time [in setting up Business Solidarity] that entrepreneurship is freedom," she told me. That it is the manifestation of self-determination. Entrepreneurship exists where people are free and inspired—it exists where there is the rule of law.

Though a strong oil- and gas-rich country, Russia has long lacked the rule of law. And that has been a key reason that the country, even though it is the eighth-largest economy in the world, has not fulfilled its potential as a startup haven. Yana stressed that point after I mentioned that I had just returned from "Open Innovations," a government-sponsored conference focused on technology, with a particular emphasis on Russian startups and Russian technological competitiveness.

"Open? Innovations? Really?" she said. "This is not possible. It is not possible for us [Russians] to have innovation." While Yana believed that Russians possess the talent to conceive cutting-edge breakthroughs, she is not convinced that in the country's current political environment they can do so. "This country won't let you become Steve Jobs."

Russia possesses the energy, native talent, capital, mentors, and networks necessary for innovation-rich entrepreneurship—far more than most emerging market countries;

far more than any of its fellow BRIC countries: Brazil, India, and China. Its engineers and technical minds have long been world class, winning Nobel prizes in chemistry, economics, medicine, and physics. For much of the Cold War, these minds rivaled those in the United States in defense, science, space exploration, and technology. Today, Russians are producing world-class companies such as Google's rival search engine Yandex, the cloud-computing company Parallels, and cyber security giant Kaspersky Lab. Yota Devices, a Kremlin-backed technology firm, produced the world's first dual-faced smartphone in 2013. Nginx, a Moscow-based software company, powers many of the world's top websites, including Airbnb, Facebook, LinkedIn, and the *New York Times*. Seventeen-year-old Moscow-based Andrey Ternovsky created the popular and at times controversial online webcam chat site Chatroulette in, he claims, "two days and two nights." Russian minds are behind the Silicon Valley–based software giant Evernote.

The Russian government has built Skolkovo, a multibillion-dollar, high-tech center modeled after Silicon Valley, in a suburb outside Moscow. The one-thousand-acre campus is dotted with sleek modern buildings, research labs, and schools—including one affiliated with the Massachusetts Institute of Technology. This shows an earnest desire to innovate, which government officials, including former president Dmitry Medvedev (in office 2008–2012), confirmed in discussions at "Open Innovations." Russia would not "sit on the sidelines," Medvedev noted, as "certain countries" (alluding to the United States) moved ahead in technological growth.

"They all say the right things," Yana told me. "But the government considers business people in Russia criminals. Look at the laws. The main law governing the life of the Russian businessman is, unfortunately, the criminal code."

There is no question that Russia's leaders want their citizens to innovate and compete on the same level as the engineers and techies in Silicon Valley. Yet they want them to do so within a framework of authoritarianism and control. Dating back to the Soviet Union, the law in Russia has long served a single purpose: as a tool to control the masses. The Russian justice system, as Moscow-based journalist Joshua Yaffa has noted, "is permeated by a sense of inevitability." That is, regardless of right or wrong, the state decides all matters—nearly always in its own favor.

The criminal code is the main body of law governing Russian life. It is exhaustive, especially when compared with the civil code pertaining to individual relationships and interactions such as marriage, divorce, and employment.

Less exhaustive are the country's commercial and business laws. These have only been drafted and on the books since the establishment of the Russian Federation in 1991. They are, as a result, vastly underdeveloped and lack judicial and administrative guidance. There is little precedent for the court system to work with. Not surprisingly, Russian civil and commercial laws are applied inconsistently, if they are applied at all. In the absence of commercial and business laws, thousands of Russian entrepreneurs have been jailed on charges of violating any number of articles of the country's criminal code.

Bigger businesses have exploited Russia's weak justice system. Using their money and influence, they lodge complaints and make accusations about competitors—however small a competitor might be—with the police and courts, rather than resorting to a lawsuit or civil action. Until recently, these complaints and accusations led to the arrest and incarceration of fledgling entrepreneurs and the suffocation of their businesses.

It is therefore not surprising that this weak justice system and absence of the rule of law have been obstacles to entrepreneurs. According to the Global Entrepreneurship Monitor, which assesses entrepreneurial activity worldwide, in 2013 only 5.8 percent of Russians were either nascent entrepreneurs or business owners. Compared to other emerging market countries, that is extremely low. Total entrepreneurial activity in Brazil is 17. 3 percent, in China 14 percent, in India 9.9 percent, in Mexico 14.8 percent, and in Nigeria 39.9 percent. In the United States it is 13 percent.

The majority of Russians opt for jobs, first in government and second with multinational corporations. According to the *Economist*, "small and medium-sized firms account for only a quarter of Russian employment compared with half, on average, among countries belonging to the OECD [Organisation for Economic Co-operation and Development]." Most of those who have started businesses over the past ten years have registered their companies offshore, where the Russian state cannot touch their assets—something Yana, whose company Sofex is registered in Russia, covets. Investors have spurned Russia. In 2013 over $60 billion in capital and assets flowed out of the country.

Though entrepreneurs break rules and "disrupt" norms, they need incentive—as do their investors. An environment in which ideas are insecure and unprotected is not one where there will be much willingness to innovate or invest.

"It is why it's not possible for us to produce the iPad," Yana said.

. . .

YANA'S AMBITIONS were modest when, as a shy twenty-two-year old in 1993, she cofounded the chemical trading and manufacturing company Sofex. She wasn't trying to create something as paradigm-busting as the iPad, but simply to make a living. It was two years after the collapse of the Soviet Union. Having the freedom to sell and trade basic commodities—especially in the open—was novel enough. So novel, few knew how to do it. Even fewer wanted to. Decades of communism had denied Russians the mind-set and the necessary desire, experience, and psychological drive to be entrepreneurs. They felt more comfortable taking orders than exercising initiative.

There were some, however, who thrived on recklessness. Most were hustlers who had long defied Russian authorities and operated an underground economy. Some were from the elite—party members and those connected to the state. They exploited loopholes in laws even before the Soviet Union collapsed. These people stood ready to seize and profit when it finally did. They had managed to amass significant capital that eventually allowed them to take over banks, oil and gas reserves, and other industries. Some became the country's biggest billionaires—the oligarchs.

Others, with fewer political connections but bold dreams, settled for becoming middling entrepreneurs who identified opportunity and created industries.

Alexei Protsky was one such individual—a hustler with few connections but tons of ambition. After earning a PhD in chemistry, the boxy scientist approached Yana, whom he knew from their eastern Moscow neighborhood, about delivering chemical products to recently privatized factories. He had been working in a research lab and knew the factories that produced chemicals and those that received them. His idea: to be the go-between for these factories and the chemical producers.

The new Russia jettisoned the previous command economy through "shock therapy" of overnight economic liberalization. No longer did the government operate factories, plan the production of goods, or set prices. Everything was left to the "invisible hand," including supply and distribution chains. "We saw that factories needed raw material and different products but nobody could supply it," Yana told me.

It was entrepreneurship 101: pinpoint the gap, something that sounds easy to do but rarely is. Most eyes instinctively turn toward the center—to the place of action. It is harder to look off to the side, where no one else stands and, worse, where no one believes there is possibility, and start to build. Yet that is what Yana and Alexei did. While most others in Russia focused on big money industries, they pursued logistics, since they believed this was a field in which they could excel.

Entrepreneurship 102, building an enterprise, happened serendipitously. Neither Yana nor Alexei had any of the financial or management skills necessary to operate a business. Instead, both benefited from the tremendous leeway given to startups in the early days of the new Russia, when there were few laws governing business and little government interference. Though the old Soviet bureaucracy still burdened everyone with red tape and endless procedure, shock therapy left the new leaders of the Russian Federation no time to map out legislation regulating business or adjust institutions to provide proper support and oversight. History moved faster than constitution. Many deliberately wanted to keep government at a distance. The transition to economic liberalism, these individuals argued, would only work if lawyers and bureaucrats stayed out of the way.

Time showed, however, that the challenge of building a new Russia wasn't getting Russian entrepreneurship and the free market started. Building a new Russia—one that would be prosperous and stable—required getting people willing to take the risk to operate within an established framework and under the same ground rules. Without legal and, more important, judicial structures, Russia's nascent private sector fell prey to every opportunity and to every opportunist. What philosopher Thomas Hobbes described in *The Leviathan* had come to life. The country lacked trust. That prompted "protection rackets"—gangsters—to pop up alongside oil oligarchs and banking barons. Russia became a quasi mafia state, with crime rising between 20 to 25 percent each year between 1989 and 1992.

Amid the new Russian Federation's Wild West framework, Yana and Alexei managed to slip under the radar. The protection rackets that arose during the early days of new

Russia had no interest in the chemical trade—it wasn't lucrative enough (lower level police officers would later go after this segment). After raising several thousand rubles from friends and family as startup capital, Yana dove into the role of entrepreneur, though she did not consider herself to be one at the time.

"We didn't know what going into business meant or how to handle things," Yana said. There were no mentors to turn to or examples to learn from. She operated on instinct—reaching out to factories and then chemical manufacturers to arrange the pickup and delivery of supplies. This quickly became a regular process in which the manufacturers contacted Yana. Sofex hit its first startup milestone when it acquired clients. "They [manufacturing houses] would call us and ask 'Do you have this chemical?' and I just said, 'Yes, I have it.'" Then she scrambled to find it.

"If we bought for a dollar, we sold for two," she said. That sustained them for a while. But by the mid-1990s, competitors started to spring up. What Yana and Alexei knew about competition came from their experience as avid, albeit amateur, boxers. A single punch rarely wins the match—agility and multiple combinations do. They needed to do more than merely trade chemicals.

"At that time there were lots of factories producing new production lines," Yana told me. She learned that these lines depended on silicone—the compound used in everything from insulation to breast implants. Given Alexei's background as a chemist, he and Yana started to manufacture their own silicone products. Manufacturing silicone products in Russia, rather than supplying them from Europe, heartened Russian factories. Not only did this provide Russian factories with a steady and quick supply of silicone, it also provided them with a cost-effective product. And that helped Sofex grow.

It also helped Yana and Alexei weather the deep Russian political and economic crisis that by 1998 resulted in the country's decline. The country was in severe debt. Several hundred billion rubles were missing from state accounts. Former state enterprises went bankrupt. The Kremlin defaulted on its international and domestic liabilities. The Moscow stock market crashed. The ruble lost all value. Banks shut down. Those who had deposits lost everything. Nearly 11.3 million Russians were unemployed. Those who had jobs had their salaries suspended.

While Yana and Alexei managed to keep Sofex going, as small business owners they suffered. Orders shrank as factories went out of business. Sofex's profits plummeted. The duo managed to bring in a steady stream of income from clients based in Western Europe, particularly in Germany and the Netherlands. Sofex had even started a partnership with US-based DuPont. That kept them going. Still, by 1999 Yana and Alexei, not to mention the entire country, were ready for serious change.

That readiness resulted in the emergence of a new leader, Vladimir Vladimirovich Putin.

Boris Yeltsin, Russia's first president, had tapped Putin, a former KGB agent, to be the country's prime minister in 1999. He had first met Putin in 1997 when Putin joined the president's staff. Putin did not stand out, which is exactly what appealed to Yeltsin, whose popularity had deteriorated by the late 1990s. Moscow's moneyed men held Yeltsin and his drunken mismanagement responsible for Russia's decline (but at the same time, they knew Yeltsin was responsible for their meteoric rise). Yeltsin hoped that Putin, an unassuming bureaucrat, could focus on rescuing the country from crisis.

In his first years Putin was a welcome relief, especially from the perspective of the small business owner. The oligarchs had gotten out of control. They had grown so big and powerful that they pushed up housing and property prices in Russia and made small business a difficult endeavor. The average entrepreneur scraped by, never able to scale beyond a certain level. Few had access to loans or investments. While Putin had shady dealings with the oligarchs for what appears to have been personal economic gain, he also shone light on the challenges of the common man in Russia. Putin presented himself as an advocate for the struggling farmer and worker.

After a few years, however, Putin started to display a heavy hand. He started to push back at Russia's oligarchs, warning them to mind their own business and stay out of politics—that was his domain. Russia's rich could go on conducting their business however they wanted, so long as they didn't challenge the Kremlin. When they did, Putin retaliated. He had already begun to rebuild the country's state sector, taking over banks, oil companies, and television stations. One oligarch, however, refused to bow to Vladimir Putin.

"All these troubles began with Khodorkovsky," Yana told me.

She was referring to Mikhail Khodorkovsky, one of Russia's original oligarchs, who amassed vast wealth, first in banking and then through oil and his company Yukos. In February 2003 the crew-cut coiffed Yukos boss, dressed in a dark shirt and dark suit, turned what should have been a routine photo-op for government and business leaders into a showdown. All had gathered for the annual meeting of the Union of Industrialists and Entrepreneurs, a lobbying group. With cameras pointed over a circular table in a brightly lit room, furnished in the hallmark Kremlin trimmings of white and gold, he launched into a half-hour harangue about the Russian government and its tyrannical grip—its corruption and what he said was its "indifference to the law." This landed him in jail several months later on charges of fraud and tax evasion, and later embezzlement and money laundering. He remained behind bars even before the start of a yearlong trial that, by all accounts, was conducted fairly—even if its outcome was preordained.

Still, that it was conducted at all raised eyebrows. Other oligarchs most certainly broke the law at times. They avoided customs duties and taxes, greased palms, accepted kickbacks, fixed prices, and put family members on the payroll. Yet because they submitted to the Kremlin's commands, these oligarchs stayed out of trouble. The police did not touch them. Khodorkovsky, on the other hand, having challenged Putin publicly, found himself with a verdict of guilty. As the judge addressed the courtroom on a rainy May morning in 2005, Yana Yakovleva listened to the radio, taking a momentary break from the pile of papers on her oversized and messy desk. "I can't believe that such a guy like Khodorkovsky can be in prison," she recalled thinking. Then two members of the *siloviki* paid her a surprise visit a few months later.

"What do we have here?" one said, holding up an order she had received from a Dutch factory worth several hundred thousand rubles. Turning to his partner he commented, "It looks like a mini-Yukos, wouldn't you say?"

Yana had not had such dealings with the police before. There were inspectors who came through to review Sofex's accounts, but none ever made threats or illegal propositions such as those made by the two officers who walked into her office that morning.

"They wanted us to give up our clients," she recounted. "And then they wanted me to help them with a drug operation. They talked about sharing profits; that they would give me envelopes of money. I could not accept this." This led to Yana's arrest a few months later, on that warm June day in 2006. After a few hours in a holding cell at 38 Petrovka she was transferred to a female penitentiary. There she shared a cell with forty-six other women for seven months.

• • •

"THE SYSTEM IN Russia is so broken," Victor Yakovlev warned his daughter. "It is not possible even to pay a bribe," he said and advised his daughter to fight—to confront the government so that it no longer had the incentive or power to intimidate innocent citizens. That, he argued, was the only move that could possibly set things straight.

Getting a lawyer to take on such a strategy was a problem, however. After giving her the runaround, Yana's first lawyer tried to strike a plea bargain. The next two simply didn't respond to her requests to meet. Finally, after the fourth try she had found someone who, as she says, "understood that there is no justice in Russia." This lawyer supported Yana's decision to fight the charges.

Remarkably, others joined in. Yana's approach struck so many in the Russian justice system as bizarre that word spread. As it did, it sparked media interest. Before Yana knew it, people organized on Moscow's streets and squares on her behalf. Newspapers wrote about her. Television broadcast her plight.

Prominent human rights figures came to Yana's defense. They included Moscow Helsinki Watch Group's Lyudmilla Alexeyeva and Alexander Lebedev, one of Russia's billionaire oligarchs—owner of the British-based newspaper *The Independent* and part owner of *Novaya Gazeta*, a Russian opposition newspaper. *Novaya Gazeta* had famously employed slain Russian journalist Anna Politkovskaya, who wrote about the Kremlin's abuses in Russia's war in Chechnya starting in 1999. Yana may have only had Alexei to lean on when getting Sofex off the ground. But with this campaign, she had what she felt was her own personal army. It filled her with both trepidation and a sense of purpose. She had seen herself as an ordinary girl from an ordinary family who had never gotten into any serious trouble. Even when the Berlin Wall crumbled and her Gen X peers rushed into Moscow's parks and squares to demand more *perestroika* and *glasnost*, she hung back. Politics didn't interest her. "But it turned out, it was interested in me," she said. However reluctantly, Yana became an activist.

"I think to myself, 'Yana you are Russian; you are an entrepreneur; you have the power to change this situation,'" she said.

So she did.

On February 16, 2007, seven months after she had been incarcerated, Russian officials dropped the charges against her and released Yana from prison. No businessperson had walked away from a Russian court with a declaration of innocence before. Yana became the first entrepreneur to be exonerated. She vowed not to be the last.

Just as in her early days as an entrepreneur, Yana embraced the new, unfamiliar circumstances she found herself in. She spoke about her plight at rallies and in the media. Yet unlike the dissidents who opposed the Soviet state and its ideology, Yana remained rooted in practicalities. Rather than taking on the Kremlin and Putin himself, she questioned the Russian government's policies toward business. Putin, she knew, wanted a globally dominant Russia. Entrepreneurship, she argued, played a key role in contributing to that goal. It should be something the government championed, not hindered.

That is what Business Solidarity has focused on. Within a year of her exoneration she set up Business Solidarity— a crusade, as she described it, for entrepreneurial rights. "When my story is finished and we won, I thought I have to share my way with the people who don't know what to do; I have to talk with other people needing this kind of advice." The organization has provided legal guidance and support to other entrepreneurs and businesspeople falsely accused of white-collar crimes. It has also made a point of galvanizing media attention. Yana has made it a point to publicize unlawful situations. She has also made it a point to push for entrepreneurial change.

"I see a new generation of entrepreneurs who came back to Russia," she told me. They are twenty-somethings returning with degrees from Cambridge and Stanford and dreams of starting the next Facebook or Google. Many have flocked to spaces that encourage entrepreneurship. Digital October, a locale like the US-based General Assembly that hosts tech and startup focused conferences and workshops, is one. Farminers, an incubator started by Russian tech entrepreneur Igor Matsanyuk—one of the original team members of Mail.ru—is another.

"They are creating businesses on the Internet. And they think that because they create on the Internet there is no asset the government can take away from you." They don't grasp the extent of the government's mistrust and fear of entrepreneurs. "I tell them, 'This Facebook guy [Zuckerberg] does not just create business for profit. He makes change. You must be after change too, not profit.'"

Change has become an overused term in entrepreneurship. It is a point that repeatedly comes up in any discussion about startups, to the point that its meaning has blurred, morphing from idea to label. The majority of entrepreneurs seize on change more as a tagline rather than resolve.

Mark Zuckerberg has certainly been accused of that—as have other Silicon Valley startup founders. Evgeny Morozov, a scholar of digital activism, has been the most vocal critic. His book, *To Save Everything Click Here*, takes Zuckerberg to task for "pseudo-humanitarianism": using Facebook to "root out human misunderstanding" and improve "just about everything under the sun: politics, citizens, publishing, cooking."

In an op-ed piece for the *New York Times*, Morozov extends his digital critique to all of Silicon Valley:

> Silicon Valley was once content to dominate the tech world. But recently, its leading companies have ventured deep into areas well outside its traditional bailiwick, most notably international development—promising to transform a field once dominated by national governments and international institutions into a permanent playground of hackathons and app-fueled disruption.

Others have agreed. Malcolm Gladwell, a staff writer for the *New Yorker* magazine, noted in a critique of the role of Facebook and Twitter in the Iranian "green" revolution in 2009. "Innovators tend to be solipsists. They often want to cram every stray fact and experience into their new model." That has included "change."

These critiques are important—as are the majority of critiques. Criticism is a form of checks and balances. It keeps things in perspective and, to the extent that it is constructive, holds individuals and their efforts to account. Amid the startup world's over-effusive proclamations about "changing" and "saving" the world, that is necessary. Not all startup are having such an impact, nor can they. Entrepreneurs, Yana pointed out, need to consider how their startup is being used and could be used—by and among individuals, businesses, and governments.

Entrepreneurs, Yana insisted, are more than just businesspeople. They are different from small and medium business owners, who like her, started a business in order to make a living. Entrepreneurs create tools that can catalyze both advancement and progress and, at the same time, repression and control. As a result, they need to look beyond a profit-and-loss statement. They must engage with the community in which they operate and, most important, in governance. Business and politics are, for better or worse, inextricably linked.

Engagement is the basis of democracy and representative government. Without it, the powerful—regardless of country—push forward their interests at the peril of the masses. Russia is an obvious example. Mexico and India are other places where the rich and connected manipulate government to their own advantage.

But, so too, is the United States. Powerful corporate interests and lobbyists work to influence US lawmakers and legislation. They do so to protect their own interests, often to the detriment of others, particularly startups. Rather than begging the government "to get out of the way," they seek out government and use it to maintain the status quo, and we will see in the next chapter that the government is happy to oblige.

The Stop Online Piracy Act is a case in point. Drawn up by US lawmakers—at the urging of Hollywood production houses—angry at "rogue" websites that post content such as movies, music, books, and articles without permission, it was a bill that would have stopped copyright infringement and thereby have saved the millions of dollars that are lost to piracy. The act would have allowed the government to go after and block websites and search engines that post or link protected content without permission. While China, as a notorious and continuing violator of intellectual property rights, was its intended target, the law would also have affected legitimate startups such as Facebook. Following an enormous and organized backlash against the bill, the House Judiciary Committee announced that it would postpone consideration of the legislation "until there was wider agreement on a solution."

Russia, with its corrupt police state that equates startups with criminality, begs for similar results. Activists and entrepreneurs, among others, possess the means to affect "change" in Russia or "fight," as Yana put it, "the cockroaches."

In December 2012 the cockroaches crawled back into Yana's world.

· · ·

SIX YEARS AFTER stepping out of the gym and landing in a holding cell at 38 Petrovka, Yana Yakovleva once again found herself under pressure from government authorities. Once again, she took them on.

A few weeks after I left Moscow, in December 2012, an inspector from Russia's tax office called on Yana at her Sofex office. He asked to review her accounts and profit and loss statements. After reviewing them he claimed that her company owed $100,000 in "extra taxes." She would have no choice but to pay them—"or else."

Unlike the episode in 2006, when she stonewalled the Federal Drug Control Service, Yana told the inspector that she would comply with his "request." Since launching Business Solidarity in 2007, Yana knew that there was a growing intolerance for such requests, that the Russian government wanted to quash the growth of "a little bit of extra." Hence, Yana agreed to the inspector's request in order to expose him. She has lobbied for legal reforms, including the establishment of an ombudsman and the bolstering of anticorruption police.

In addition to Yana, a number of other Russians have raised their voices against corruption and the country's weak rule of law. Alexei Navalny, a lawyer and politician, is the most prominent. He became known through several platforms and a spirited run for mayor of Moscow. Navalny started LiveJournal, a blog that questioned and at times exposed police brutality and the Kremlin's heavy hand and uncovered criminal dealings at major Russian oil companies, banks, and government ministries. He is also the founder of RosPil, a site that listed public documents for public scrutiny. He agitated for government accountability and the reduction of its monolithic and top-down hold on power. His activities resulted in a court in Moscow charging Navalny with stealing and money laundering; he was arrested in 2012 and convicted in 2013. (For reasons that are unclear, Navalny was released a day after his conviction.)

The tax inspector's bribe request presented a "moment of truth" of sorts—a test to see whether Yana's and Alex Navalny's efforts had had any effect. As soon as the inspector left her office, Yana contacted the anticorruption police. "It surprised me that they listened," she said. The police instructed Yana to arrange a meeting at a restaurant, where she would wear a wire and hand the inspector a suitcase of marked money. The operation resulted in his arrest.

It also resulted in small steps to strengthen Russia's rule of law. In 2008 then President Dmitry Medvedev, a huge proponent of innovation and startups, formed an anti-corruption council that pushed forward a campaign to eradicate bribes, nepotism, and graft from the country. Among the council's key tasks were legal reforms and legislation to advance and protect business. One of the laws the body succeeded in pushing through stipulated that anyone arrested has the right to a lawyer upon detention. In addition, no longer can Russia's police carry out and demand checks of a company's financial records and business activities.

The police corps, long called the *militsiya*, the militia, underwent an overhaul. Medvedev rechristened Russia's police *politsiya*. To tackle corruption, he trimmed Russia's police force by 20 percent and raised the salaries of the remaining officers by 30 percent—leaving them, hopefully, with less incentive to shake down civilians.

In June 2012 Vladimir Putin appointed a presidential commissioner for entrepreneurs—an ombudsman to improve Russia's business environment. A few months later, in August, Russia joined the World Trade Organization and expanded its commercial code. It adopted new regulations on bankruptcy, investments, and loans, which have relieved entrepreneurs from the risk of being unnecessarily dragged into criminal detention.

These developments have yielded positive results—which have kept Yana pushing forward and other Russian startups incentivized. They have shown her that, as an article in the

Wall Street Journal noted, "[w]hile much of civil society has been squeezed by the Kremlin in recent years, some elements are having a measure of success." The article pointed to Business Solidarity as an example.

Russia has advanced on the World Bank's annual *Doing Business* ranking. It jumped nineteen places, from 111 in 2013 to 92 in 2014. *Fortune* magazine noted that toward the end of 2013, "many respected money managers were excited about Russia—if not bullish." The country, while far from democratic, showed—for a while—a willingness to comply with international norms and strengthen its institutions.

Still, Russia continues to suppress representative government and the rule of law in favor of heavy-handed authoritarianism. That authoritarianism only deepened in 2014 with Russia's illegal annexation of Crimea from Ukraine, its subsequent role in arming separatist rebels eager to carve out Ukrainian territory and integrate it with Russia, and its role in the downing of Malaysian Air flight 17. These events have isolated the country and hurt its economy. Though Russia has a comfortable amount of money in its reserves, it is, by all accounts, headed for an economic crisis. Many Russian companies are in trouble. The few European venture capitalists that had expressed interest in Russian tech talent have turned their attention elsewhere. In the first three months of 2014, investors diverted more than $60 billion in capital out of Russia. Russia's stock market declined 20 percent. The Russian ruble shrank in value. The International Monetary Fund, the international development agency, cut its growth forecast for Russia for 2014 from 1.3 to .2 percent. Many people in the country are leaving.

Nonetheless, Yana, along with a number of other entrepreneurs, has chosen to stay in Russia. "This is my home," she told me when I asked why she didn't leave—she had and has ample opportunity to do so. "I will stay and fight."

Amid a dark political and economic setting, Russia's handful of entrepreneurs is betting that Putin won't be able to hold onto power forever. They recognize that Russia's current wealth is built not on the production of goods and services but on oil and gas. And as oil and gas prices continue to plummet, they may be right. They are racing against the clock to ensure that there is something else that continues to move Russia forward. As a geographically vast country with enormous energy resources, Russia will exist—at least for the near term—as an important global player. Time will tell whether it can produce innovators, and whether those innovators can produce an equitable system that engenders trust and helps strengthen the rule of law.

Entrepreneurs, by the very nature of what they do—disrupt and innovate—provide a necessary check and balance on government that no one else can—not businesspeople, not NGOs, not civil society organizations. They help remake the social order and help move progress forward, giving rise to new ideas, new industries, and new possibilities and forcing change. That is what has made them both heroes and villains that many in power feel the need to keep in check. That is something that Lei Jun is trying to change in China.

At the Edges:
Disrupting the Status Quo

Progress is a nice word. But change is its motivator. And change has its enemies.

—ROBERT KENNEDY

Beijing and Shanghai

Only a few coughs and nervous laughs could be heard after China's Premier Li Keqiang, the second in command, asked a group of academics, corporate executives, and entrepreneurs to "speak out—directly, without using euphemisms." They had gathered at Zhongnanhai, China's White House, in January 2014 to get a preview of the country's Government Work Report. This report, delivered every March, is China's equivalent to the US State of the Union address.

"Speak out!" the premier, dressed informally in a dark zip-up jacket and white shirt, repeated after a few minutes. In particular, he asked those gathered—in a large and garishly lit conference room with a series of concentric horseshoe-shaped conference tables, replete with tacky red-covered seats—to share their insights on the country's economy. Still the bemused crowd sat silent, this time turning their heads to look at one another.

One academic broke the silence. He spoke about the risks of an economic downturn. Another followed about the need for regulation to improve confidence in the market. Their answers revealed little about what they thought about China's economy, however. Rather, these initial comments—meek generalities—reflected what is still one of the biggest challenges to entrepreneurs in China: political obstinacy.

Even as hundreds of millions of Chinese citizens have moved out of poverty and into the middle class, a socio-economic grouping known for its political awareness and engagement, China's Communist Party continues to hold a strong grip over every aspect of society. And it is making every effort to keep things that way. China's leaders may have prioritized growth and prosperity, including the economic advancement of its citizens. They have not, however, shown any leeway on loosening the reins and changing the political status quo.

Maintaining the status quo is not unlike preventing competition. Just as monopolies and big businesses don't want to see any rivals cut into respective market shares, those in the establishment—in both the public and private sectors—don't want to see a challenge to their authority or position. While they might advocate innovation, progress, and social mobility, change in the social order—in their very own position and authority—is anathema.

China is far from alone in this regard. As startups "disrupt"—that is, transform existing industries and ways of doing business—industries and governments worldwide, from the top to local levels, are revealing their paradoxical relationship to entrepreneurship and innovation. On the one hand governments—whether in China or, ironically, the United States—encourage and enable the citizens they rule over to take initiative, launch ventures, and prosper. At the same time, however, they—at varying levels—have been unable to keep up with the pace of change. Current laws, policies, and institutional structures drawn up in the twentieth century do not accurately reflect the reality of the digital age. Taylor Owen, a professor of digital media and global affairs, notes in *Disruptive Power: The Crisis of the State in the Digital Age* that the state used to have a monopoly on the ability to shape the behavior of large numbers of people. This is no longer the case. "The state is losing its status as the preeminent mechanism for collective action," he writes. As a result, many governments have shown signs of discomfort as citizens become empowered and begin remaking the economic and political orders altogether.

The startups that have introduced the "sharing economy" in the United States and that have scaled up rapidly are a case in point. Companies like the car ride sharing app Uber and the accommodation site Airbnb, which encourage peer-to-peer collaboration and provide an alternative to taxis and hotels, have rattled their respective industries, from South Korea to India and from Germany to the United States.

The same is true of ventures that have introduced new business models and approaches in what is often dubbed the "new economy." Amazon has upset the book publishing industry through its online e-commerce platform. Electric car manufacturer Tesla upset the auto industry by selling its cars directly to consumers instead of through dealers and showrooms. The now defunct Aereo sent broadcasters into a tizzy by streaming cable content to viewers without their involvement (or consent). Distraught bankers fear that bitcoins, the cyber currency, will upend the financial industry. Even the food truck has caused the restaurant industry to shake its fists in protest.

Not surprisingly, those in established industries have started to rise up against these "new kids on the block" vigorously. Their weapon of choice is regulators, who are known to cry, well, regulation. From every level of government, regulators across the globe have made a case against a number of startups in the shared and new economies. They have argued that companies such as Uber and Airbnb circumvent laws designed to ensure quality and protect the public good; that they violate copyright, labor, safety, tax, or zoning laws—and perhaps all of them.

Among the priorities of a regulator or government official is to protect the consumer. It is not to keep things static, suppress change, or hamper innovation. Rather, to quote from US President Lyndon Johnson's "Great Society" speech, it is "to build a society where progress is the servant of our needs."

Progress, as we have seen in previous chapters, thrives in places where there is talent, proper infrastructure, and the ability to collaborate and compete; where there is opportunity, transparency, and a strong rule of law. Yet there are other elements that underpin progress and are of particular importance to entrepreneurship and innovation, elements that are counterintuitive, if not outright abhorrent to those in authority: the devolution of power, the embrace of disruption, and the redistribution of wealth.

As technology advances, it shifts the economic landscape by improving individual capability and capacity. The automobile, the airplane, the railroad, the steam engine, the telegraph, and the telephone were breakthroughs that connected people and helped free them from manual labor and drudge work. Technology also helped reshape the economic landscape, giving people the time and space to think and imagine. Innovation unleashes individual potential. And as individual potential grows, so too do awareness and engagement, sparking the desire for more rights and independence. That is something that frightens China's leaders. Having more rights and independence diffuses and thereby redefines power. It shifts it away from the hands of those in charge into the hands of those who participate and engage in the political process. In that scenario power morphs from a tool of authority into one of accountability. Social and economic advancement becomes a democratizer.

China's leaders are eager to move their country's economy into the future. So eager, in fact, they have scuttled many core principles of communism that otherwise would prohibit private enterprise. Yet while they have opened up China's economy, welcomed capitalism, and encouraged entrepreneurship, they have done so under a tight rein that enables them to maintain the status quo. This is what Evan Osnos calls in *Age of Ambition: Chasing Fortune, Truth, and Faith in the New China* "a collision of two forces: aspiration and authoritarianism."

Lei Jun, a computer engineer and the founder of the smartphone company Xiaomi, is making a concerted effort to avoid a collision of any kind. Through his multibillion-dollar and widely watched company, Jun is encouraging his Chinese compatriots to think, imagine, and innovate. His approach offers China's leaders a powerful solution to an increasingly growing problem in China: *How does the country continue to grow?* Lei Jun seeks to benefit and strengthen the country—a goal that the Chinese Communist Party itself is in pursuit of. That is what he suggested during Premier Li's meeting at Zhongnanhai in January 2014.

China, Jun recognizes, has come a long way from being a "third world" backwater. Yet to truly solidify its place in the first, the country needs to embrace not only economic change but also political and social change. The country's success depends on the participation of its people.

"I suggest the government this year should keep an eye on the entrepreneurial environment," Jun said, in obvious deference to China's second-in-command. Yet he did go farther than anyone else in the room by outlining *how* the Chinese government should keep an eye on the entrepreneurial environment. Jun suggested that the government afford startup founders more flexibility. The state cannot dictate innovation. Instead, it must make room for those who can innovate. While this may disturb the status quo, flexibility—rather than an authoritarian grip—is what will unleash Chinese innovation and solidify China's place as a global economic powerhouse.

• • •

EVERY WEEKDAY morning, thousands of scrappy young people clutching smartphones and sporting backpacks file past the large orange letters "MI" into Xiaomi's expansive offices in Qinghe, in Beijing's far northern Haidan district. Most of Beijing's startups call Zhongguancun, the pricey tech district between Tsinghua University and Beijing University in the city's northwest corner, home. Xiaomi sits next to a shopping mall in a shiny building beyond what is called the "seventh ring road"—the farthest from the center. The closest subway stop is more than a fifteen-minute walk away. It's so far from the center of town that it cannot be found on a map of Beijing proper. Perhaps that's not accidental. Xiaomi is not only physically at the edges of China's tech scene, but metaphorically as well. Unlike other Chinese companies, focused on churning out the latest tech gadgets or software products, Xiaomi is determined to unleash Chinese innovation—and with it the "next big thing." It is determined to empower ordinary Chinese citizens to dream, experiment, and take chances.

Xiaomi's bright and open space contains what you'd find at any typical tech startup: foosball tables, beanbag chairs, large plants, Bose noise-canceling headphones; there is even a dog and a doghouse. There is also a large slide in the lobby that extends through several floors above. However, it is what happens and how it happens on the floors above and, interestingly, outside the building itself that make Xiaomi of interest. This is something that most Chinese companies have shied away from: encouraging people to think big and take action on their ideas.

Xiaomi develops and manufactures tech devices, the most notable being an iPhone-like, Android-operated smartphone. It isn't "merely another phone that has been 'made in China' but a remarkable technological achievement that has been conceived, designed, and delivered in China," as journalist Brad Stone wrote in *Businessweek*. Xiaomi's MI phones run on Chinese engineering and are put together with foreign components. They are high-quality components, including a high-quality display from LG and Qualcomm processors. Yet MI phones are not expensive. Unlike most phone manufacturers, Xiaomi sells low, in a deliberate strategy designed to pull in revenues not from hardware, but from sales of its software offerings. Xiaomi's software offerings are made up of an operating system, a cloud service, a mobile payment platform, and an array of apps. Like Amazon's e-book reader, the Kindle, Xiaomi sells its phones at cost in order to push out its virtual services.

Virtual services are what inspired Lei Jun to launch Xiaomi in 2010. While Jun is eager to sell high-quality smartphones that people yearn to own, his true focus is dominating the software and various applications that make a smartphone "smart." Interestingly enough, his strategy for doing so is to rely less on himself and the thousands of developers and programmers he has hired at Xiaomi and more on complete strangers. Though Lei Jun is a savvy computer engineer with years of experience in the software industry, he has turned to open source technology, a coding system open for anyone to access, alter, and utilize. Xiaomi's MIUI (pronounced Me-You-I) Firmware operates on open source technology. It depends on public input and engagement, particularly on community contributions, to improve the company's offerings, make suggestions for new ones, and troubleshoot bugs. For Xiaomi, the consumer is a participant and content creator.

Appealing to the public for input and engagement is new in China, once known as the Middle Kingdom. For millennia, the Chinese took orders from above, a legacy perhaps of Confucianism, a philosophical system based on the teachings of Confucius that emphasizes hierarchy and order. When the Communists came to power in 1949, the situation worsened. China's "red" leaders determined where people could live, what jobs they could have, where they could travel, and what they could own. The majority of property and resources lay in the hands of China's Communist Party. An ordinary citizen could do very little without obtaining permission from a government official or member of the party. While such restrictions have been rolled back in recent years, the Chinese government has remained wary of "community contributions" or anything that encourages public engagement. For Lei Jun, the latter approach will only strengthen China.

In adopting open source technology for Xiaomi, Jun has won huge "fans," the name the company has given to users of its products and services. They are not original products and services. They are, however, products and services adapted to Chinese behaviors and habits. Xiaomi phones sell in batches of 100,000 directly to consumers online; the company does not offer its products at retail stores. These batches online sell out in a matter of seconds. "It's the technology equivalent of Air Jordans," *Businessweek*'s Brad Stone has written. In four years, Xiaomi has sold over five hundred million handsets and has eighty-five million active MIUI users. In 2014 Xiaomi recorded $11.97 billion in sales. This has allowed the company to overtake Samsung to become the largest smartphone vendor in China and the third largest smartphone maker in the world.

This is a considerable accomplishment for a company that went from zero to several billion in sales in just four years. Xiaomi launched in 2010.

All of this has made Xiaomi one of China's most exciting companies and Lei Jun one of the country's most popular entrepreneurs—on a par with Steve Jobs. In fact, given that Jun also manufactures smartphones, curiously dresses in the same dress-down black T-shirt and jeans, and hosts Apple-like launch events for his Xiaomi products, he has been called, not surprisingly, the "Steve Jobs of China," and his company has been compared to Apple. It is a comparison he flatly rejects, perhaps too vehemently—as if it is part of a deliberate "us versus them" marketing strategy, a strategy similar to the one that played out between Coke and Pepsi or Hershey and Mars, fueling the "cola" and "chocolate" wars, respectively.

"They [Apple] don't really care about what the users want," Jun responded to a question in 2013 about whether Xiaomi was China's Apple. "They imagine what the users want." Xiaomi, he has noted, works with users to make the best possible product—an ironic swipe at Apple's top-down and secretive practices. "Xiaomi's priority is not revenue, not profit, nor market share. . . . We focus on making the product that makes users scream"; that is, a product that users feel they have been a part of producing.

eBay, the Silicon Valley auction website launched in 1995, enabled millions to become virtual shop owners and sales-people—not quite "entrepreneurs," but people who could made extra money or even earn a living. Hundreds of others have followed suit, including China's own e-commerce giant Alibaba. In fact, Jack Ma cites "China's potential" as a reason for launching Alibaba. "Chinese brains are just as good as theirs," he once said, the "theirs" referring to Silicon Valley techies. Xiaomi has pushed that notion to prove Chinese innovation. Lei Jun is paving the way for the ordinary Chinese person to experiment, take risk, and innovate. It is an approach intended to shake up China's private sector, to get it to think beyond "copycatting" and thinking about innovation as something inherently Chinese.

Experimentation and risk are at the heart of innovation. In theory, they should be in entrepreneurship as well. But as noted in chapter 3 on Pakistan, innovation and entrepreneurship aren't always the same thing. That is no less true in and about China—the world's second-largest economy after the United States and the world's largest goods trader. In 2013 China imported and exported $4.16 trillion worth of goods, a significantly greater amount than the United States, which traded $3.57 trillion. In 2014 China overtook the United States in the number of patent applications filed. In 2014 Alibaba listed on the New York Stock Exchange in the world's biggest initial public offering, at $25 billion.

Yet the more I learned about Chinese startups and China's entrepreneurial landscape, the more I found that these dazzling numbers and statistics do not equal innovation. The former Google head in China, Kai Fu Lee, has noted as much. "China is a state where entrepreneurs' major desire is to gain influence and wealth," Lee has remarked. As a result, China "is not likely to come up with the next world-changing product. Innovation is likely to come from taking products that are already known and applying them in another context."

Most startups in China, in fact, are not innovative. Rather, they are "copycats"—replicating an existing idea or brand adapted to local conditions. Copycatting goods of known brands, generally Western and luxury, is what helped jumpstart China's gangbuster growth over the past decade and a half. Think Gucci and Louis Vuitton.

With the advent of the Internet and the rise of Silicon Valley tech companies such as Facebook, Google, and YouTube, the Chinese rolled out local versions of those platforms, with different features and ways of monetization. These are not flat-out "copycats" but adaptations nonetheless. They are what longtime China venture capitalist and the founder of the venture capital firm Qiming Venture Partners Gary Rieschel calls "in China, for China." That is, the majority of Chinese startups aren't focused on the "next big thing."

A number of factors contribute to this. First, China doesn't have a long history of capitalism, let alone entrepreneurship. Second, education in China is outdated. It is focused on rote learning rather than creativity and critical thinking. And third, rigid laws enforced by an even more rigid regime bent on maintaining the status quo discourage many in China from undertaking risk. Rather, they are content to profit from China's thriving export market and, more relevantly, the country's billion plus population, 1.35 billion to be exact—the largest in the world.

To all appearances, Lei Jun is testing not only the "in China, for China" model, but also the hierarchical and static economic structure that perpetuates it. He has set up Xiaomi to defy the very notion that wealth creation is a matter for the state. Original, innovative ideas, he knows, spring from the ground up. In fact, they must do so in order to sustain China's growth. Entrepreneurs are job and wealth creators. Through Xiaomi Jun is not only encouraging everyday Chinese citizens to move away from the assembly line toward job and wealth creation, but is also encouraging them to create value. He is encouraging them to "think big": to find solutions to existing challenges, inject Chinese entrepreneurship with innovation, and change business as usual in China—transforming it into business with and, more importantly *for*, the world. If he succeeds, he very well might change the sociopolitical dynamic in China.

• • •

LEI JUN IS simultaneously outspoken and visible but also private and elusive. While he is ready to appear on television or speak at a conference, Jun keeps his personal life closely guarded. This dichotomy, along with the meteoric rise of his company, Xiaomi, is what intrigued me about him. How Jun developed and then honed a vision to build a company that would go up against established giants—Apple and Samsung on the one hand and the Chinese government on the other—amazed me.

Jun is not a social activist, nor is he political. Unlike many entrepreneurs in China, who depend on connections, especially with those influential in the Communist Party, he did not grow up rubbing shoulders with party members or socializing in circles with government insiders.

Lei Jun was born in 1969 in a midsize city in the central Chinese province of Hubei, which is quite literally China's "Midwest." In the 1990s he attended university in Hubei's capital Wuhan, an industrial center called "China's Chicago," where the smokestacks of factories crowd the gunmetal skyline. Most of the city's residents worked in these factories. Jun, however, wanted more. Even in the early 1990s, when China was still struggling economically, Lei Jun believed, as many did and still do, in his country's potential to become a great power once again.

In blog posts and in interviews, Lei Jun has said that it was a book he read as a college student at Wuhan University that spurred that belief. That book was *Fire in the Valley: The Making of the Personal Computer*, written by Michael Swaine and Paul Freiberger in 1984. Swaine and Freiberger traced the history of the computer industry, telling the stories of the individuals behind the microchip, the processor, and the first personal computers. In particular, the book tells the story of the Homebrew Computer Club, a gathering of self-described sci-fi geeks and tech enthusiasts who lived in and around what eventually became known as Silicon Valley, which began in 1975. Steve Jobs was one of its members.

The Homebrewers, as one reviewer of the book noted, "believed computers could usher in an age of human empowerment, perhaps even a utopia." After reading about them, Jun, an average-built man with a mop of hair, started to believe so as well. He had instinctively gravitated toward computer engineering, in which he majored at school. But it was upon reading *Fire in the Valley* that Jun began to grasp the magnitude of what computers and technology in general could actually do.

"Business technology can also be implemented to serve the country," he has said. And that prompted him to dive into the world of tech. He, along with a few college buddies, tooled around with code. They developed antivirus software and experimented with starting their own tech company. But since they lacked any business experience, the company never took off.

Lei Jun moved to Beijing in 1992 and applied for a job at Kingsoft, a software firm that is China's version of Microsoft. He worked his way up the company's hierarchy, playing a pivotal role in securing the Chinese government as Kingsoft's main client. All of the several hundred million computers used in Chinese government offices switched from Microsoft to Kingsoft. This coup earned Jun the title of CEO in 1998.

At Kingsoft's helm, Jun pushed for the company to migrate onto the Web. The West, he had seen on several trips abroad, had already started leveraging the Internet and adding value to business, particularly through the World Wide Web and the cloud, a network that analyzes, enables, moves, and stores information—and makes it available whenever and wherever users want it. Your e-mail is part of the cloud. Dropbox, Instagram, and many Google services such as Google Drive are examples of cloud-based operations. These offerings have made it easier for others, particularly small businesses or individuals eager to launch a startup idea, to access resources for limited cost and without the need to install software.

Jun recognized the cloud as a phenomenon that would become huge. People turned to technology for ease of use. The ability to access information wherever and whenever—rather than having to haul around disks or files—was something that would appeal to everyone, everywhere. Jun, recognizing the opportunity, did not want to continue selling software through disks and retailers. He wanted Kingsoft, following Microsoft's precedent, to make its software products available online. He wanted Kingsoft to be just as aggressive and innovative as the Seattle-based giant. Moving online and into the cloud was, Jun believed, what Kingsoft needed to do in order to become globally competitive.

For Jun, it wasn't enough to be big in China. Convinced of his country's capabilities and talent, he wanted a Chinese company to be globally recognized. Jun wanted Kingsoft to compete on the same level as Microsoft and other Western tech companies. At the time that he was Kingsoft's CEO, however, he had not yet hit upon the revelation that in order to do so he had to "think different," as the erstwhile Apple slogan suggested. He had to focus on ideas, experimentation, risk taking, and disrupting the status quo. Instead, Jun was operating on 1960s-era management theories that embraced hierarchy, rigid structures, and linear thinking. This is why he pursued an initial public offering (IPO) on the Hong Kong stock exchange in 2007 rather than challenging the staff at Kingsoft to take initiative and come up with the "next big thing." As a result, Jun got his IPO and along with it a handsome windfall of money; Kingsoft raised $99 million. But what he didn't get was the excitement and growth that had befallen a handful of other Chinese tech startups—the BATSS: Baidu, Alibaba, Tencent, Sina, and Sohu.

Baidu had become China's Google; Alibaba had become China's eBay/Amazon; Tencent is China's online entertainment platform; Sina put itself on the map with the Chinese version of Twitter, Weibo; and Sohu had become China's second most popular search engine. That Jun had failed to get Kingsoft counted among these rising startup stars troubled him. Soon after Kingsoft listed on the Hong Kong stock exchange, Jun took some time off—the first and only time in his life that he has done so. Taking a career break is not normal in the tightly wound, hard-working world of China. It was even more abnormal for Lei Jun, who as his friends have noted, is extremely hard working. But according to various accounts, Jun was fed up.

"[Lei] was financially secure, but he didn't feel reputationally secure," Robin Chan told *Businessweek*. "He wasn't being considered in the same breath as Jack Ma [Alibaba] and Pony Ma [Tencent], which is where he is now. It drove him."

. . .

During his "time off," Lei Jun thought hard about how to capitalize on China's startup craze, quite literally. Entrepreneurship, he recognized, was a movement that required more than just codes and engineers. It required capital, which has always been difficult to access in China. "Venture capitalists are the entrepreneurs' helpers behind the scenes," he has said. "Investment clearly can help entrepreneurs conduct better business."

Investments in Chinese startups had reached the billions—still quite short of the figures in Silicon Valley, but significant nonetheless. China ranks third worldwide in terms of venture capital activity in funds raised and invested. The United States and Europe are first and second, respectively. There are over one thousand Chinese venture capital funds, divesting billions in hundreds of deals. In 2013 Chinese funds managed over $150 billion and backed nearly 120 deals valued in the hundreds of millions.

With admittedly little understanding or experience, Lei Jun tried his hand at investing. He became an angel investor, placing his own money at risk in a startup for a percentage of equity. "I became an angel investor to share the joy of entrepreneurship," Jun said. "New ideas make me happy."

Entrepreneurship, Jun concluded, had to cease being a lone-man or lone-woman endeavor in China. It had to be a movement that encouraged people not only to take a chance on their ideas but also to share and exchange them. Sharing and exchanging ideas was difficult in China. The government created a climate of fear. As a result, the culture that pervaded the country was cutthroat, not collaborative. In the face of rigid laws, weak intellectual property laws, and the prospect of punishment—as had happened to Yana Yakovleva in Russia—few Chinese entrepreneurs are willing to experiment or undertake true risk. Original, innovative ideas are copied, not protected. They are inevitably co-opted in order to be replicated, not to fulfill their potential.

Investments in China also suffer from similar short-sighted thinking. "Few investors think about what value they bring the entrepreneur," Rui Ma, an investor with the startup accelerator and seed stage fund 500 Startups, told me. "They [investors] continue to put the onus on the entrepreneur who doesn't understand the importance of what money brings—contacts, experience, and guidance." This is actually a common problem in many emerging market countries. Investors in these places fail to provide entrepreneurs with guidance. Worse, they seize far too much equity, leaving the entrepreneur with little control over his or her company. This "predatory" investing has been responsible for the failure of startups in emerging markets such as China to scale up and succeed.

Lei Jun wanted to bring contacts, experience, and guidance to China's entrepreneurs as an angel investor. Angel investing of any kind was a completely radical idea in China at the time. The Chinese government put heavy restrictions on investments. But Jun's China-first approach at Kingsoft and his inherent pride in China's potential, which he expresses at every opportunity, had won the confidence of several members of the country's Communist Party. That confidence provided Jun the leeway to put into practice the decades-old Silicon Valley practice of backing companies.

That, Jun said, enabled him to work with people he otherwise would not have had the opportunity to work with—and to meet the people who eventually would help him build Xiaomi.

Jun backed companies such as Joyo, a business to customer (B2C) e-commerce site. In 2004 Amazon acquired Joyo for $75 million, giving Jun a comfortable return. He also backed a top online retailer as well as a leading mobile Internet company, UC Web. Mobile phones, Jun recognized, had proliferated rapidly in China—as they had throughout much of the developing world. Globally 990 million mobile phones were sold in 2006. A year later, according to Gartner, a research analysis firm, that number went up to 1.15 billion. The country's technology future—as well as that of the world—lay in reaching those mobile users in the same way Web companies reached personal computer (PC) users in the West.

In fact mobile, Jun thought, could be a way for China to make its mark. Mobile was still new. As in the early days of the Internet, its capabilities and potential had yet to be proven.

"I think in a year's time the mobile Internet will become one of the hottest in decades; it will exceed the current size of the Internet business," Lei Jun wrote in a blog post in October 2008. That, he explained, was a result of first rapidly advancing technology and second accessibility. Whereas a PC was out of reach both in price and practicality—lack of broadband or even dial-up—for most people in the world, a mobile phone was not. Mobile would be even bigger than the PC ever was.

With that in mind, Jun made plans to get into the mobile phone business. He carried, as *Businessweek*'s Brad Stone points out, "two dozen phones in his backpack which he meticulously studied . . . he talked obsessively about the software that ran on smartphones and how it could be improved for China's massive population of mobile phone users, which was about to surpass 1 billion."

Lei Jun focused on software. Specifically, he planned to launch a startup that would transform the mobile Internet. "The Internet is an idea!" Jun declared. It is an idea that leads to other ideas—and solutions, which is what really excited him. Amid China's hierarchical system, solutions rarely came from the bottom-up. If China was going to compete globally or stand a chance of resurrecting innovation—as it had in the fifth century BC when the Chinese invented paper—that needed to change. Lei Jun may or may not be the next Steve Jobs, but the next Steve Jobs most certainly lives in China today. In order for him or her to emerge, Jun has recognized, it is necessary to enable ground-up innovation.

Also necessary are flexibility, openness to uncertainty, and the embrace of disruption. Interestingly, this is not so far-fetched for China's leaders. Since the 1980s China's leaders have shown willingness to reform in the name of progress.

• • •

DENG XIAOPING, China's reformist leader in the 1980s, initiated his country's economic opening and eased the Communist Party into not only accepting it, but driving it forward. At the time Deng ascended to power in the late

1970s, China was suffering from severe underdevelopment. Having spent time abroad in France and Russia, Deng understood that China had a disadvantaged position in the world. It was not only poor but backward. While other countries pushed forward with space exploration and technology, China subsisted on agriculture. That, he believed, posed a threat to the Communist Party. Deng famously rationalized that "poverty is not socialism."

Deng believed that the party couldn't merely embrace ideology. It had to deliver results. Through his *gaige kaifang*, reform and opening up, Deng opened China to investors and encouraged imports and exports. He relaxed rules about where farmers could sell produce, allowing them to travel into the major cities and set up shop. Deng made it easier for individuals to own property.

Notably, he created special economic zones in 1980. One of the first was in Shenzhen, just across the harbor from Hong Kong in the Guangdong province. Located near a key port, it was far from Beijing, so that, as longtime China correspondent James Fallows noted, if the experiment failed, the government could shrug it off. Deng's government invited foreigners, particularly those from the West, to set up factories in Shenzhen, luring them with preferential economic incentives. They came. In just a few years Shenzhen went from "sleepy fishing village" to bustling urban center, in which local Chinese started taking up the startup mantle. By the 1990s Chinese entrepreneurs were running their own factories, mass-producing Western products or imitations of them. These factories pulled hundreds of thousands of Chinese out of poverty and into the middle class.

According to Helen Wang, author of *The Chinese Dream: The Rise of the World's Largest Middle Class and What It Means to You*, 25 percent of China's 1.35 billion people, between 330 and 400 million, are in the middle class. The majority of them live in cities, and 600 million Chinese continue to live below the poverty line, mainly in the rural countryside. Author Evan Osnos points out that "the difference in life expectancy and income between China's wealthiest cities and its poorest is the difference between New York and Ghana."

China's leaders are determined to narrow that gap and keep economic growth moving forward so that it eventually reaches a majority of their population. They are doing so in a Catch-22 of enormous size. Technology, innovation, and entrepreneurship, China's Communist Party has begrudgingly come to recognize, are key to the country's continued advancement and, ironically, their own political survival.

Technology, innovation, and entrepreneurship do indeed risk empowering individuals. Yet they are also necessary to help sustain current levels of prosperity as China's leaders grapple to find ways to raise the standard of living of those dwelling in the impoverished countryside and provide jobs for those rural migrants flooding into China's cities. The Chinese economy is struggling not only to create employment for the unskilled labor market but also to keep up with the number of skilled college graduates. In 2014, 7.27 million people graduated from college in China. A G-20 report on China notes that high-end job creation in the tech sector is not able to "keep pace with the graduates' growth. Vacant posts suitable to graduates are in short supply." As a result of this dearth of jobs, Chinese college grads are naturally gravitating toward entrepreneurship, creating their own employment. Most of these efforts are in the tech sector, particularly focused on the Internet.

China's leaders have taken measures to control the Internet and thereby speech and thought, through the "Great Firewall," a real-life Orwellian mechanism that employs millions of monitors, engineers, and developers to watch cyberspace and functions as a filtering mechanism. These hired guns scan blogs and other public social media for words or phrases with bad or potentially bad associations and any reference to the government. "Tiananmen," "Tibet," "Falun Gong," and "Arab Spring" are just a few terms that are blacklisted. "Censorship" is another. Mentioning the name of any senior government official, especially the president or the premier, is forbidden. Chinese censors delete anything they deem inappropriate or shut down sites that they deem threatening. And they do so in minutes.

Thousands of sites have been blocked, particularly those that originate abroad, such as Google, Facebook, and Twitter. In fact, Chinese leaders have made it difficult, if not outright impossible, for the majority of Silicon Valley tech startups to operate in their country.

Not willing to defy Chinese authorities, Lei Jun, like most Chinese Internet entrepreneurs, complies with the government's censorship rules. "There are a thousand roads to success," he has said. And while he believes that public participation is a key avenue to get there, he has also shown deference, if not loyalty, to the Chinese Communist Party. (Jun, like most Chinese entrepreneurs, outwardly supports the Communist Party and in fact is a party member.) This may be a viable, if ironic, approach to moving China's leaders to embrace disruption and flexibility—and ultimately to unleash Chinese innovation.

. . .

AT THE SAME time that Jun has appealed to strangers and the Chinese public to contribute to Xiaomi's MIUI Firmware, he has also imbued the company with Chinese pride. China's "red star" is Xiaomi's symbol. Originally Jun had named his company Red Star. But after careful consideration, according to a number of press reports, he and his team decided on a name that "would stand out." They settled on "little rice," *Xiaomi*. Rice is a staple in the Chinese kitchen, a food accessible to all. Beyond that, Xiaomi is also the fusion of the words "xiao," which comes from the Buddhist concept that great things start small and simple, and "MI," which Jun used as an acronym for both "mobile Internet" and "Mission Impossible"—a clever branding feat.

Cleverness has been a part of Lei Jun's mode of operation. 500 Startups' Rui Ma told me that Xiaomi was a "concerted" effort by Jun and his investors "to execute a different smartphone." Rather than "move fast and break things," as some in Silicon Valley circles do, Jun spent two years plotting out the company that has become Xiaomi. First, he lured away top talent from tech firms such as Google.

Next he approached investors. Gary Rieschel, the founder of the China-based Qiming Venture Partners, told me that software was Jun's primary interest, not hardware.

Rieschel, an ebullient, white-haired American who has spent the last two decades in China, met Lei Jun when both invested in UC Web, a mobile Internet company. Jun came to Rieschel and Rieschel's former partner Hans Tung (who is now an investor at GGV Capital) to raise capital.

Jun wanted Xiaomi to be a software company that would create an iTunes or Amazon-like interface across multiple hardware platforms. "Part of our input on this was that we felt Xiaomi needed to have its own phone to drive the success of its software," Rieschel told me. "Several months after our discussion on this topic, Xiaomi came to us with their plans for a fully integrated device and a set of services." And that's when Rieschel and Tung decided to back Jun. But because Jun had decided to manufacture and market a hardware device, he needed a substantial infusion of cash. While Qiming had the money, they, in the same mold as most Silicon Valley venture firms, wanted others to get in on the deal; they wanted others not only to add value to Xiaomi, but also to share the burden of the risk.

Entrepreneurs in China have had a harder time raising capital than those elsewhere. China's leadership holds a firm hand over capital, monitoring its formation and allocation. It is part of a phenomenon that has come to be known as "state capitalism," the antithesis of Adam Smith's "invisible hand." Under state capitalism, the government is the market: wealth of, by, and for the state.

The state creates part of this wealth through state-owned enterprises (SOEs). The majority of large enterprises in China are SOEs. It is not surprising that the Chinese government has assured that the majority of capital is allocated for its SOEs and is not readily available for individual start-ups. Banks, along with much of the economy, are state con-trolled. Until recently there have been few other sources of finance. Private firms, relative to their state-owned counter-parts, cannot easily access capital from banks. Data from China's central bank show that for much of the past decade only 20 percent of working capital loans went into private hands.

As a result, entrepreneurs in China have had to raise capital through friends and family or government funding sources. Truly daring individuals have opted for persuad-ing a panel of judges on *Shark Tank*–like reality television programs such as *Win in China*. Having experimented with angel investing, Lei Jun wanted venture capital money, not because of any rosy-eyed notions about venture capi-tal, but because he sees it as an important way of helping China move away from its factory-based economy toward one driven by new capital creators, innovators rather than manufacturers.

Capital is power—for an individual, a company, and a country. For an entrepreneur, it is the key to igniting an idea, without which a startup cannot get off the ground.

So Jun reached out to Temasek, a Singaporean invest-ment firm; IDG Capital, a China-based venture capital fund; and Morningside Ventures, a US-based venture firm—all of which signed on as investors. Altogether, along with Qim-ing, they invested $41 million in Xiaomi. That proved to be valuable beyond the capital. According to Rieschel, among the challenges Jun and his cofounders faced was execution, in what he described as a "very competitive business." Jun not only wanted to dominate the smartphone market, he wanted to do so by unleashing Chinese innovation.

As Jun had predicted in 2008, smartphones exploded. According to Benedict Evans, an analyst at the venture firm Andreessen Horowitz focused on the mobile industry, there will be two to three times more smartphones than PCs by 2020. Smartphones will make up almost all phone sales— perhaps four hundred or five hundred million a quarter worldwide—five hundred million per quarter!

Mobile is the defining element driving the tech space today. At its helm, as Evans points out, are Apple and Google. "Apple now sells around 10 percent of all the 1.8 billion (and growing) phones sold on Earth each year and Android the next 50 percent split roughly between say two-thirds Google Android outside China and one-third non-Google Android inside China," Evans has written. Because of Google's troubles with the Chinese government, its competitors, such as South Korea's Samsung and a series of Chinese-based firms, are vying to dominate China's market share. Xiaomi is but one of a handful of mobile phone manufacturers in China trying to win over customers. As Benedict Evans points out, it has been among the few, however, working to rebuild and redesign the Android front end, "the whole UI from the launcher and notification panel down to the preference panels—to make it simpler and cleaner." More important, it has focused on building services that rely on outsourcing and public input. Phones, Jun has noted, change quickly. "It's helpful to incorporate customer commentary into product planning; to listen to the views of users." That, Jun believes, is the root of innovation.

"I believe in the masses, rely on the masses, from the masses to the masses!" Jun, in a hat tip to Mao and the Chinese Communist Party, has said.

• • •

CONTROL WORKED wonderfully to transform China from a backwater into a world power. The Chinese Communist Party's monopoly on power, Fareed Zakaria notes in *The Post-American World*, "allowed it to make massive reforms quickly. It could direct people and resources where needed." Amid a burgeoning entrepreneurial scene, one focused on the Internet and technology, that is becoming increasingly more difficult to do. One approach, one methodology, or one process, like one size, doesn't fit all. Economic advancement reshapes the socioeconomic landscape. It empowers individuals and redistributes wealth and the hold on resources.

As Chinese citizens have moved and continue to move into the middle class, their wants and struggles have and do change. Survival is no longer defined by hand-to-mouth existence. While struggles continue, daily life is more predictable. People have access to education and health care. They have more time for recreation. There is time for social awareness and political engagement. There is time for experimentation.

China's leaders want to micromanage this experimentation or, as Anne-Marie Slaughter, the president of the New America Foundation, noted in an article in *Foreign Affairs*, "The Chinese government is determined to develop innovation as if were developing a fancy variety of soybeans, relying on industrial parks that mix equal parts technology, education, research, and recreation in self-described 'talent highlands.'"

Indeed, Chinese leaders have poured significant investments and incentives into the tech sector through a dedicated government agency, the Ministry of Science and Technology. These incentives include tax breaks, grants, seed funding, technology incubators, and science and technology programs.

Starting in the mid-1980s China's leaders have supported programs such as the 863 Program, the 973 Program, the Torch Initiative, and the Spark Program. They are, in one form or another, designed to enable and support research in a multitude of disciplines—agriculture, biotech, energy, medicine, and technology—and then help bring products and services to market. Some of these initiatives, such as the Torch Initiative, establish high-tech industrial zones around China. Zhongguancun, in northwestern Beijing, is one such example, with more than ninety others around the country.

China's leaders have also made research and development (R&D) a priority. According to the Organisation for Economic Co-operation and Development (OECD), the country spends 1.98 percent of its GDP on R&D. In 2013 that totaled $284 billion. (The United States spent $465 billion.) China plans to raise the amount it invests in R&D to 2.5 percent of GDP by 2020. When it does it will outspend the United States, which allocates less than 1.5 percent to R&D.

China's leaders would like innovation to happen under their control—under their terms and guidance. The things about innovation is that it can't be controlled, imposed, or orchestrated. Innovation happens at the edges and in the unlikeliest of places. It is part of a process, one that renews like the changing seasons. More important, it belongs to no one person. Anyone with an idea and the will to see it through can innovate, even amid the most difficult obstacles.

Lei Jun is one such individual. His company, Xiaomi, is producing cutting-edge and coveted smartphones along with sought-after mobile services built through open source efforts. They are efforts that have excited China's tech scene and have turned Xiaomi into one of the country's most valuable companies. In 2014 Xiaomi raised $1.1 billion in venture capital. The investment helped boost the company's valuation to $45 billion—larger than Uber or any other venture-backed startup in the United States. Xiaomi has become a serious player on the Chinese and global startup scenes. The company is branching out into other areas. Like Bülent Çelebi in Turkey, he is producing set top boxes to stream television. He is diving into the mobile payment space with a platform similar to Paga Tech in Nigeria.

More than that, however, Xiaomi has poised itself to become a possible partner for China's leaders in sustaining and pushing forward the country's growth. Both China's leaders and Lei Jun, along with other Chinese businesspeople, have a vested common interest in maintaining progress and prosperity. China's leaders must recognize that they lack the capacity to single-handedly do that on their own. Indeed, all leaders must recognize this.

In *Disruptive Power: The Crisis of the State in the Digital Age*, Taylor Owen notes that "disruptive innovators" are "chipping away" at the institutions that defined international affairs in the twentieth century—foreign ministries and armed forces, for example. "Hierarchical organizations," he says "built on an industrial model in an era of command-and-control governance and economic activity" are not capable of serving the twenty-first century. "They must adapt."

The economy of the twenty-first century, whether "globalized," "new," or "shared," is unprecedented. No longer are the twentieth-century models that made the assembly line and Fortune 500 companies thrive relevant. Today's digital and dynamic economy is not beholden to top-down corporate structures. Instead, it is contingent upon ideas and self-initiative. It is an economy being fueled and powered by entrepreneurs.

Today's startups are largely a result of the breakthroughs that came about a decade earlier: the personal computer, the laptop, and the smartphone are just a few examples. Each has enabled someone to solve a problem or simply test out an idea. That is something that needs to be encouraged, not held back or suffocated by regulation, regulators, or government. What may have worked in the twentieth century doesn't work in the one we're living in now. Governments, like people, must adapt.

Lei Jun has taken the first step that will shake up China's status quo. He has become the role model who has dared. He has done what the likes of Steve Jobs, Bill Gates, and Larry Page and Sergey Brin did to turn Silicon Valley into the mecca of innovation and what Bülent Çelebi in Turkey, Tayo Oviosu in Nigeria, Monis Rahman in Pakistan,

Enrique Junco Gomez in Mexico, Shaffi Mather in India, and Yana Yakovleva in Russia are doing in their respective countries. The status quo changes with initiative, commitment, persistence, and vision. It changes through entrepreneurs. And entrepreneurs are no longer found only in Silicon Valley, but the world over.

Epilogue

It is not down in any map; true places never are.
—HERMAN MELVILLE, *MOBY DICK*

Silicon Valley

My journey to learn about the world's entrepreneurs began with a simple question: *What were entrepreneurs outside of the United States doing, and how were they doing it?* What I knew about business in many places in Africa, Asia, Latin America, and the Middle East was that it was difficult, if not impossible, to do. Too many obstacles stood in the way: lack of skilled talent, poor infrastructure, insecurity, lack of collaborating space, monopolies, corruption, and the status quo.

After visiting Turkey, Nigeria, Pakistan, Mexico, India, Russia, and China—emerging market countries with large, significant economies—I realized that while these obstacles have not been entirely eliminated, they no longer hold back individuals abroad. Global entrepreneurs have emerged and are on the rise, especially in the world's largest markets.

That rise has prompted analogies and comparisons to the Bay Area region. Indeed, a number of places have come to be dubbed "Silicon something"; Silicon Alley in New York, Silicon Cape in South Africa, Silicon Dragon in China, Silicon Savannah in eastern Africa (Kenya, Tanzania), and Silicon Wadi in the Middle East are just a few. None, however, is the next Silicon Valley. Nor do any of the entrepreneurs in this book believe it will be or want it to be.

While Silicon Valley may be the mecca of tech startups, it alone does not define or represent entrepreneurship. Progress does.

Entrepreneurship is much more than a tech startup, a business, a product, or a service. Inherently, entrepreneurship is change and renewal, a reset button of sorts. Each of the entrepreneurs here has hit that button.

In Turkey, Bülent Çelebi used culture, the organizational values and principles of a company, to overcome the country's lack of skilled talent. In adopting "culture" for his company, AirTies, Bülent outlined a roadmap that didn't miraculously improve Turkish talent overnight but did help him maintain perspective; it kept him focused on customers and excellence. Perspective and focus are what eventually cracked open a new door on doing business in Turkey and started to attract the type of talent that has made AirTies, along with other tech startups, thrive.

In Nigeria, Paga Tech, the mobile payment system Tayo Oviosu built, is leading to improvements in Nigeria. Through Paga Tech, Tayo is contributing, quite literally, through his own investments in fiber optic lines, to the slow improvement of his country's infrastructure. More than that, however, his mobile payment platform is building the "pipelines" to provide all Nigerians with financial services. "We're doing something that's greater than any one of us," he told me.

In Pakistan, Monis Rahman has used the Internet to overcome the lack of collaborative space. He has encouraged Pakistanis to convene, create, and in some instances collaborate, initially online, but also in person. Those efforts has given rise to a vibrant tech scene, one that has begun to offer the country and the world a narrative about Pakistan anchored in ideas rather than insecurity.

In Mexico, Enrique Junco Gomez identified a niche where he alone could build a business and circumvent the roadblocks Mexico's monopolies have used to discourage competition. In zeroing in on energy efficiency, Enrique has become one of Mexico's top entrepreneurs and has helped fan the flames of entrepreneurship and competition throughout the country.

In India, Shaffi Mather realized that as long as corruption in India persisted, the country would continue to lack efficient and effective public services. In building 1298, a for-profit ambulance company, Shaffi has bolstered a growing chorus of voices that had already been calling for increased accountability, ethics, and transparency in India's governance.

In Russia, Yana Yakovleva refused to admit guilt to false charges. Instead, she fought for and continues to fight for justice: for an environment that allows Russians to dream and innovate without fear. Under Putin's leadership that has been difficult, though not impossible. Yana's efforts, particularly through Business Solidarity, have resulted in laws and policies that protect Russian entrepreneurs. It is unfortunately difficult to say how long those protections will last.

In China, Lei Jun is encouraging his fellow Chinese compatriots to not just copy Silicon Valley, but to think, imagine, and innovate on their own. He built Xiaomi, his technology company, around the concept of open source technology, a system that encourages public participation. Jun very much wants Xiaomi to be a global tech titan, on a par with Facebook, Google, and his direct competitor, Apple. He knows that to get there it is not enough for him to gain customers, scale up, and drive in revenues. Xiaomi must innovate. But a company, like a country, cannot will that. Innovation happens organically, in places open to change. China embraced change to drive economic growth and prosperity. If it can continue to embrace reform and disrupt political obstinacy, loosening the Communist Party's authoritarian grip, China not only will solidify its place as a global economic powerhouse, but will stand as a worthy rival to Silicon Valley.

As noted at the outset, entrepreneurship is a process of "creative destruction," the elimination of old processes and the birth of new approaches and, therein, possibilities. More than just putting up a storefront or rolling out new technologies, entrepreneurs—in going up against all sorts of odds—introduce new behaviors, systems, and ways of thinking. Entrepreneurs force a transformation.

Just as early entrepreneurs of Silicon Valley shattered established corporate models and sparked waves of innovation, intrepid individuals in countries that were once delicately, if not dismissively, called "developing" started to replicate ideas conceived of in Silicon Valley. They built moneymaking enterprises. They started delivering *globally* competitive products and services that are now attracting international praise and, more important, investment. This has started to destroy the status quo and has brought more to people in the places I visited for this book—Turkey, Nigeria, Pakistan, Mexico, India, Russia, and China—than has any international organization, nongovernmental organization (NGO), or nonprofit assistance program I had seen in the past.

Development is no longer confined to government. Similarly, I found throughout my travels for this book that wealth creation is no longer exclusive to a small elite or a small group of countries. It has moved out of shiny office towers and into the hands of men and women with visions that extend beyond a stand-alone mom-and-pop shop or ketchup factory.

Whether in Lahore or Lagos, Monterrey, or Mumbai, people across the world are using entrepreneurship to solve the problems that have plagued them for so long and to revolutionize the systems that have denied them progress. They are doing what Silicon Valley did to corporate America in the 1960s: changing what is possible economically in their own lands. Their efforts have thrown open the limits of what is possible anywhere. They have made prosperity multilingual.

And their stories are just beginning.

Somewhere in the world, someone is working on something that will be the next Apple, eBay, Facebook, Google, Hewlett-Packard, or Intel. The next great innovator—the next Steve Jobs—won't be from Silicon Valley, but will come from Mexico, Nigeria, Pakistan, or even Turkey. Indeed, the next Steve Jobs lives in one of those places today.

Acknowledgments

My maternal grandmother, Rüveyde Çakır, was illiterate. My great grandparents didn't see the point of educating a girl. An educated girl, they believed, is "dangerous." She would only be focused on writing love letters to boys. Grandma Rüvede saw beyond that. An education empowered and freed a woman. That's what she wanted for her daughters, my mother, Nesrin, and my aunt, Nermin. My mother in turn made sure not only that I received an education but also that I, as she once told me, "never depend on a man."

While I have embraced independence, I have also come to recognize the importance of friends—of community. In writing this book I have depended on many: family, friends, teachers, and mentors. There are many of you to thank, for reading through chapters, for giving me valuable insights, but most especially for holding me up as I wrote: Demmy Adesina, Carrie Agnoff, Barış Aksoy, Philip Auerswald, Tara Ayacağak, Christine Bader, Neil Bahtiya, Mostafa el-Baradei, Kim Barker, Allison Berliner, Matthew Bishop, Andrew Blackwell, Lauren Bohn, Eva Burgess, Denise

Burrell-Stinson, Elena Ciprietti, Bene Cipolla, Aengus Collins, Tyler Cowen, Dilek Dayınları, Tom Downey, Masha Drukova, Amanda Dugan, Tess Eisenhart, Adam Ellick, Robin Epstein, Venky Ganesean, Pamir Gelenbe, Fadi Ghandour, Grace Gold, Lisa Goldman, Michael Green, Zvika Haas, Lynda Hammes, Stephanie Hanson, Craig Heit, Mark Hessen, Robin Hessmen. Ömer Hızıroğlu, Catherine Hochman, Kelly Hoey, Clare Hutchinson, Shakir Hussein, Andrew Huszar, Josh Jackson, Jalak Jobanputra, Mohanjit Jolly, Caroline Krzakowski. Ali Karabey, Valerie Kelly, Joshua Kendell, Stephen Kinzer, Mark Lambert, Josh LaPorte, Marvin Liao, Rui Ma, Lucy Marcus, Charles Masson, Suketu Mehta, Kate Mahoney, Kate Maloff, Eyrique Miller, Sarah Murray, Numan Numan, Charlie O'Donnell, Shannon O'Neil, Siobhan Oat-Judge, Krista Parris, Michelle Portman, Paul Prettitore, Shaifali Puri, Amy Resnick, Riva Richmond, Andrew Rosen, Laura Seay, Cem Sertoğlu, Emrys Schoemaker, Adam Sexton, Izak Shay, Lawrence Scott Sheets, Lina Srivastava, Laura Stone, Allen Taylor, Vijay Vaitheeswaran, Laura Weidinger, Dennis Whittle, Josh Woodward, Michele Wucker, Lina Xu, Geoff Yang, and Mosharraf Zaidi.

My writing group partners Brooke Shaffner and Julia Miller cheered me on and provided me with tremendous guidance.

Kimberly Braswell introduced me to Linda Rottenberg and Endeavor; I am particularly grateful to Linda and to Peter Kellner, who founded what is hands down the greatest nonprofit.

The Turkish Philanthropy Funds provided tremendous support for this project. I'm grateful to Haldun Taşman, Özlenen Kavlav, and most especially, Şenay Ataselim.

Thank-you Laura Villalobos and Mario Diab for taking care of me as I traveled the world.

Cindy Ko introduced me to yoga, a practice without which this book could not have been completed. Jennifer Kazenstein made me love the practice and taught me the most important lesson of all: "progress, not perfection." Sara Morgan, Dina Ivas, and most especially, Jennifer Guarneri, helped carry my yoga practice forward—and miraculously upside down. (I just had to put my head to it!)

Gillian MacKenzie believed in me and this project and cheered both of us on even during my absurdist moments. I'm grateful to John Mahaney for helping to shape it into the manuscript that it is and pushing me to be a better writer. Thank-you, John. And thank-you to the team at PublicAffairs.

A heartfelt, special thanks to what can only be called the jackpot of friends: Kim Barker, Lauren Bohn, Adam Ellick, Robin Epstein, Michael Green, Stephanie Hanson, Ömer Hızıroğlu, Kelly Hoey, Joshua Kendall, Stephen Kinzer, Shaifali Puri, and Lina Srivastava, who always paused in their tracks to listen to me, make me laugh, and—best of all—hand me a glass (or two) of wine and whiskey—and in some instances, both.

My family provided unbelievable support, even if they didn't always know or understand what it is they were supporting. They have always been my biggest champions—#TeamElmira from day one: my mother Nesrin, father Rasim, brother Er-cüment, sister-in-law Lisa, beautiful niece Rina, and amazing sister Elif. My sister is a light in my life. She is beautiful, generous, grounded, kind, smart, and talented—the woman I can only dream of being.

Book writing is not fun or easy. Thankfully traveling the world and meeting the entrepreneurs in this book most definitely was. I'm grateful to all those who carved out time from their busy schedules to allow me to follow them around and pepper them with what may have seemed like endless and, perhaps, pointless questions. Each was gracious beyond measure. I'm also grateful to the numerous caring and kind people I met along the way, people who stopped to help me when they didn't have to—with directions, language, or simply to share a story or smile. World, you are incredibly beautiful.

This book changed my life, as did the person who encouraged me to write it and cheered me along to the near end. *Allah'a bin şükür.*

Notes

Introduction

7   **Jack Ma rolled out Alibaba:** The account of Alibaba is drawn from the documentary *Crocodile in the Yangtze* (Porter Erisman, 2012).

11   **what distinguishes techies in Silicon Valley:** Ranil Dissanayake, "On Entrepreneurs, Capitalism and History," *AidThoughts*, November 23, 2010.

Chapter 1: The Green Light

23   **Mesh was used in Haiti:** Primavera de Filippi, "It's Time to Take Mesh Networks Seriously," *Wired*, January 2, 2014.

23   **launched the Open Mesh Project:** Primavera de Filippi, "It's Time to Take Mesh Networks Seriously," *Wired*, January 2, 2014.

23   **mesh networks are keeping a community . . . connected:** Noam Cohen, "Red Hook's Cutting-Edge Wireless Network," *New York Times*, August 22, 2014.

38   **fewer than 13 percent of Americans:** José Ernesto Amorós and Niels Bosma, "Global Entrepreneurship Monitor Report 2013," http://www.gemconsortium.org/docs/download/3106.

41   **a little over 300 million television sets:** Digital TV Research, "Massive Boom Forecast for Connected TV," October 9, 2013, http://www.digitaltvresearch.com/press-releases?id=69; Mark Hoelzel, "The Number of Internet-Connected TVs in Use Worldwide Will Double by 2018," *Business Insider*, March 25, 2014, http://www

.businessinsider.com/the-number-of-internet-connected-tvs
-in-use-worldwide-will-double-by-2018-2014-3.

41   **expected to increase to 759 million:** Mark Hoelzel, "The Connected TV Landscape: Why Smart TVs and Streaming Gadgets
Are Conquering the Living Room," *Business Insider*, August 13,
2014.

44   **"What Microloans Miss":** James Surowiecki, "What Microloans Miss," *New Yorker*, March 17, 2008.

45   **Sir Roger . . . broke a record:** Fadi Ghandour, comments at
White House Entrepreneurship Summit, April 27, 2010.

Chapter 2: Moving Money

49   **80 percent—do not have access to a bank:** Michael King,
"Services in Nigeria," World Bank, January 28, 2013, http://
blogs.worldbank.org/allaboutfinance/the-unbanked-four-fifths-in
formality-and-barriers-to-financial-services-in-nigeria-michael
-king-janu; "Africa Banking Industry Customer Satisfaction Survey," KPMG, April 2013; EFInA, "Access to Financial Services in
Nigeria Survey," n.d., http://www.efina.org.ng/our-work/research
/access-to-financial-services-in-nigeria-survey.

50   **Some bypass this risky system:** Author interviews in Nigeria,
June 6–12, 2013; "I Was Just Trying to Help," *This American Life*,
August 16, 2013.

50   **put their money in notoriously unreliable:** Author interviews;
DAI Partner Zone, "Benefits of Bringing Mobile Banking to the
Unbanked," *The Guardian*, n.d., http://www.theguardian.com
/global-development-professionals-network/dai-partner
-zone/benefits-of-bringing-mobile-banking-to-the-unbanked;
WBEZ, Episode 503: "I Was Just Trying to Help," *This American Life*, August 16, 2013, http://www.thisamericanlife.org/radio
-archives/episode/503/transcript; Motoko Rich, "The World's Unbanked Poor," *New York Times*, April 30, 2012.

50   **Moving money over a mobile phone:** Philip Auerswald, "Mo-
bilizing the Masses," in *The Coming Prosperity* (New York: Oxford
University Press, 2012), 75.

51   **nearly half of Kenya's population uses M-Pesa:** Vodafone, "M-Pesa," http://www.vodafone.com/content/index/about/about -us/money_transfer.html; Daniel Thomas, "Vodafone to Expand M-Pesa Transfers," *Financial Times*, October 22, 2012; Daniel Thomas, "Africa's Digital Money Heads to Europe," *Financial Times*, March 30, 2014.

51–52 **Nigeria's leaders required mobile money providers:** Interview with Tayo Oviosu, Central Bank of Nigeria, June 10, 2013; Simone di Castri, "What Could We Learn from Nigeria Barring MNOs from Participating in the Mobile Money Market?" GSMA, April 29, 2013, www.gsma.com; Emma Elebeke, "Why We Refused Telcos Mobile Money Licences," *Vanguard*, February 22, 2012, www.vanguardngr.com; Festus Akanbi, "Mobile Money: CBN Defends Restrictions on Telecom Firms," *This Day Live*, May 5, 2013, http://www.thisdaylive.com/articles/mobile-money -cbn-defends-restrictions-on-telecom-firms/146739/; "Why CBN Picked Banks for Mobile Money Operation," *The Nation*, March 21, 2013, http://thenationonlineng.net/new/why-cbn-picked -banks-for-mobile-money-operation/.

52   **"419 scams":** Dayo Olopade, *The Bright Continent* (Boston: Houghton Mifflin Harcourt, 2014), 19.

54   **Alipay recorded more than 100 million users:** Juro Osawa, "Alipay Wallet Hits 190 Million Active Users," *Wall Street Journal*, October 15, 2014; Laura He, "Sorry PayPal: China's Alipay Is World's No. 1," *Marketwatch*, February 10, 2014, http://blogs .marketwatch.com/thetell/2014/02/10/sorry-paypal-chinas -alipay-is-worlds-no-1/.

54   **"We're going from 1.5 billion PCs":** Benedict Evans, "In Mobile, Everything Is Still Wide Open," April 7, 2014, http://ben -evans.com/benedictevans/2014/4/7/in-mobile-everything-is-still- wide-open.

54   **mobile payment market will grow to $721 billion:** "Gartner Says Worldwide Mobile Payment Transaction Value to Surpass $235 Billion in 2013," Gartner press release, June 4, 2013, http ://www.gartner.com/newsroom/id/2504915.

54   **mobile payments are forecast to be $160 million:** "Gartner Says Worldwide Mobile Payment Transaction Value to Surpass $235 Billion in 2013," Gartner press release, June 4, 2013, http://www.gartner.com/newsroom/id/2504915.

56   **United States ranks twenty-fifth in infrastructure quality:** Klaus Schwab, "The Global Competitiveness Report 2012-2013," World Economic Forum, http://reports.weforum.org/global-competitiveness-report-2012-2013.

56   **10 percent increase in infrastructure investments:** World Bank Brief, October 8, 2014, www.worldbank.org.

56   **China's growth over the past two decades:** Yougang Chen, Stefan Matzinger, and Jonathan Woetzel, "Chinese infrastructure: The Big Picture," *McKinsey Quarterly* (June 2013); KPMG, "Infrastructure in China: Sustaining Quality Growth," 2013, https://www.kpmg.com/CN/en/IssuesAndInsights/ArticlesPublications/documents/Infrastructure-in-China-201302.pdf.

57   **Nigeria overtook South Africa:** Daniel Magnowski, "Nigerian Economy Overtakes South Africa's on Rebased GDP," *Bloomberg*, April 7, 2014.

57   **About 14 percent of that GDP:** "Step Change," *Economist*, April 10, 2014; Acha Leke, Reinaldo Fiorini, Richard Dobbs, Fraser Thompson, Aliyu Suleiman, and David Wright, "Nigeria's Renewal: Delivering Inclusive Growth," McKinsey Global Institute, July 2014; "Countries: Nigeria—Analysis," U.S. Energy Information Administration, February 27, 2015, http://www.eia.gov/countries/cab.cfm?fips=ni.

57   **fourth-largest oil producer:** "Countries: Nigeria—Analysis," U.S. Energy Information Administration, February 27, 2015, http://www.eia.gov/countries/cab.cfm?fips=ni.

57   **60 percent of Nigerians:** Central Intelligence Agency, *The World Factbook*, n.d., https://www.cia.gov/library/publications/the-world-factbook/fields/2046.html; Daniel Magnowski, "Nigeria Overtaking South Africa Mask Poverty Trap: Economy," *Bloomberg*, March 18, 2014.

57   **Nigeria's potential as a lucrative consumer market:** Robyn Curnow, "Consumer Giant Targets Africa's Billion Potential

Shoppers," CNN, April 3, 2013; Paul Collier and Acha Leke, "The Other Nigeria," Project Syndicate, July 17, 2014.

61   **AirTel . . . one of the top three mobile . . . providers:** Nigerian Communications Commission, www.ncc.gov.ng.

64   **representative from Domino's Pizza:** Drew Hinshaw and Patrick McGroarty, "Nigeria's Economy Surpasses South Africa's in Size," *Wall Street Journal*, April 6, 2014.

64   **representative from the South African chain Shoprite:** Drew Hinshaw and Patrick McGroarty, "Nigeria's Economy Surpasses South Africa's in Size," *Wall Street Journal*, April 6, 2014.

66   **number of handsets . . . has grown fortyfold:** Christopher Mims, "Africa Now Has More Mobile Subscribers Than the US or EU," *Quartz*, December 20, 2012.

66   **80 percent penetration rate:** Natasha Lomas, "ABI: Africa's Mobile Market to Pass 80% Subscriber Penetration in Q1 Next Year," Techcrunch, November 28, 2012.

66   **growing at 4.2 percent annually:** Lomas, "ABI."

66   **Africa's mobile phone market:** Christopher Mims, "Africa Now Has More Mobile Subscribers Than the US or EU," *Quartz*, December 20, 2012.

66   **one billion mobile phone subscribers . . . by 2016:** Jon Russell, "Mobile Tipped to Grow 60% in Africa Passing 1 Billion Subscriptions by 2016," The Next Web, November, 7, 2011.

66   **number of Internet-enabled smartphones:** James Manyika, Armando Cabral, Lohini Moodley, Suraj Moraje, Safroadu Yeboah-Amankwah, Michael Chui, and Jerry Anthonyrajah, "Lions Go Digital: The Internet's Transformative Potential in Africa," McKinsey Global Institute, November 2013.

67   **a birth certificate:** UNICEF Information Sheet, July 2007, http://www.unicef.org/wcaro/WCARO_Nigeria_Factsheets_Birth Registration.pdf.

67   **a way to be identified:** "A Toolkit for Making Everyone Count in Sub-Saharan Africa," World Bank, October 9, 2014, http://www.worldbank.org/en/news/feature/2014/10/09/a-toolkit-for-making-everyone-count-in-sub-saharan-africa.

67 **Key people at major development agencies:** World Bank, www.worldbank.org; African Development Bank, www.afdb.org; International Finance Corporation, www.ifc.org; International Telecommunications Union, www.itu.int; Jeffrey D. Sachs, *The End of Poverty: Economic Possibilities for Our Time* (London: Penguin Press, 2005); Liz Ford, "Mobile Phones Have Been a Gift for Development, Says Jeffry Sachs," *Guardian*, September 23, 2013.

68 **110 million active mobile subscribers in Nigeria:** "Nigeria Records 110.3 Million Active Subscribers as Number of Inactive Lines Soar," *Ventures*, January 30, 2013, http://www.ventures -africa.com/2013/01/nigeria-records-110-3-million-active-subscrib ers-as-number-of-inactive-lines-soar/.

68 **majority of mobile connections . . . are over 2G:** Natasha Lomas, "ABI."

68 **20,000 BTS points throughout Nigeria:** The Immigration and Refugee Board of Canada, "Nigeria: Situation of the Communications Infrastructure in Nigeria," November 6, 2012, www .refworld.org/docid/50b4c7a02.html.

69 **average revenue per user:** "The Internet's Impact on Aspiring Countries," McKinsey & Company, January 2012, http://www .mckinsey.com/client_service/high_tech/latest_thinking/impact _of_the_internet_on_aspiring_countries.

69 **fining four mobile service providers:** Immigration and Refugee Board of Canada, "Nigeria"; Akin Oyebode, "Mobile Money Operators Must Be Willing to Lose Significant Revenues," proudlyekiti, October 15, 2013, https://proudlyekiti.wordpress .com/2013/10/15/much-ado-about-m-pesa/.

73 **" . . . be willing to lose significant revenues to drive growth":** Akin Oyebode, October 13, 2013, "Much Ado About M-Pesa," https://proudlyekiti.wordpress.com/2013/10/15/much-ado-about -m-pesa/.

73 **accounting firm Ernst & Young:** "Mobile Money—the Next Wave of Growth," March 2014, http://www.ey.com/Publication /vwLUAssets/EY_-_Mobile_money_-_the_next_wave_of_ growth_in_telecoms/$FILE/EY-mobile-money-the-next-wave .pdf.

73   **the McKinsey report reads:** Beth Cobert, Brigit Helms, and
      Doug Parker, "Mobile Money: Getting to Scale in Emerging Mar-
      kets," McKinsey, May 2012, http://www.mckinsey.com/insights
      /social_sector/mobile_money_getting_to_scale_in_emerging
      _markets.

76   **"A truly mobile wallet":** Jenna Wortham, "I'm Still Waiting for
      My Phone to Become My Wallet," *New York Times*, July 27, 2013.

78   **"tip" an idea . . . into the mainstream:** Malcolm Gladwell, *The
      Tipping Point* (New York: Little, Brown, 2000).

79   **grown between 5 and 7 percent annually:** The World Bank,
      "GDP Growth (Annual %)," http://data.worldbank.org/indicator
      /NY.GDP.MKTP.KD.ZG; Joshua Robinson, "The 20 Fastest
      -Growing Economies This Year," *Bloomberg*, February 25, 2015.

79   **50 percent of Nigeria's GDP:** "Africa Overview," The World
      Bank, October 10, 2014; International Monetary Fund, "IMF
      Executive Board Concludes 2014 Article IV Consultation with
      Nigeria," March 4, 2015, http://www.imf.org/external/np/sec/pr
      /2015/pr1591.htm; Trading Economics, "Nigeria GDP Growth
      Rate 2013–2015," http://www.tradingeconomics.com/nigeria/gdp
      -growth.

79   **"Africa strategies of consumer-goods firms":** "Africa's Test-
      ing Ground," *Economist*, August 21, 2014.

79   **Nollywood, Nigeria's film industry:** "Global Cinema Survey,"
      United Nations Educational, Scientific and Cultural Organiza-
      tion (UNESCO), May 5, 2009.

80   **a $48.5 million food processing plant:** "Dangote Subsidiary
      to Build Africa's Largest Food Processing Plant," *Ventures Afri-
      ca*, September 25, 2013, http://www.ventures-africa.com/2013/09
      /dangote-subsidiary-build-africas-largest-food-processing-plant/.

Chapter 3: Steve Jobs Lives in Pakistan

80   " . . . **multifaceted outlet for human energy and expres-
      sion":** Jared Cohen and Eric Schmidt, *The New Digital Age* (New
      York: Knopf, 2013).

86 **Samaa ... produced a reality show:** "Karachi Maya Khan Catching Dating Couples—Live on Samaa TV," YouTube video, January 24, 2012, https://www.youtube.com/watch?v=J2OWh5YMqvI.

87 **small and medium-sized enterprises ... on the rise:** "Financial System Stability Assessment," International Monetary Fund, July 22, 2014, https://www.imf.org/external/np/fsap/fssa.aspx.

87 **geographic, ethnic, and tribal lines:** Anatol Lieven, *Pakistan: A Hard Country* (New York: PublicAffairs, 2011).

88 **criticized as "solutionism":** Evgeny Morozov, *To Save Everything, Click Here* (New York: PublicAffairs, 2013).

89 **prime minister Nawaz Sharif, reported:** Sabrina Tavernise, "Pakistan's Elite Pay Few Taxes, Widening Gap," *New York Times*, July 18, 2010.

91 **a "child's chemistry experiment":** Michael Lewis, *The New New Thing: A Silicon Valley Story* (New York: W. W. Norton, 1999).

93 **an average 7 percent annually:** Wendy J. Chamberlin, "Dignified Exit for Musharraf," *Real Clear Politics*, August 14, 2008; Riaz Haq, "Musharraf's Economic Legacy," *Haq's Musings*, August 19, 2008, http://www.riazhaq.com/2008/08/musharrafs-economic -legacy.html.

93 **Close to seventy million Pakistanis, 40 percent of the population moved into the middle class:** Naween A. Mangi, "Pakistan: Land of Entrepreneurs," *Bloomberg Business*, November 29, 2012.

96 **Dov Frohman ... had adopted:** Dan Senor and Saul Singer, *Start-Up Nation* (New York: Twelve, 2009).

97 **Frohman and his team developed and designed smarter chips:** Senor and Singer, *Start-Up Nation*.

98 **venture capital funds operating *in* Israel:** Sarah Lacy, *Brilliant, Crazy, Cocky: How the Top 1% of Entrepreneurs Profit from Global Chaos* (New York: Wiley, 2011).

99 **"Moving to the city is the first step":** Mohsin Hamid, *How to Get Filthy Rich in Rising Asia* (New York: Riverhead, 2013).

99 **90 percent of all enterprises in Pakistan:** International Finance Corporation, "IFC and HBL Supporting Job Creation in Pakistan," *IFC Knowledge Series in MENA*, no. 4 (February 2014), http://www.ifc.org/wps/wcm/connect/faacc9004333f68394b

9fc384c61d9f7/Jobs+Study+-+Pakistan+issue+4+final.pdf? MOD=AJPERES; "The State of Pakistan's Economy," *SME Financial Review* (2nd quarter 2010), http://www.sbp.org.pk/reports /quarterly/fy10/Second/SpecialSection.pdf; Small and Medium Enterprises Department, State Bank of Pakistan.

99   **nearly 60 percent of Pakistan's GDP:** Pakistan Ministry of Finance, "Pakistan Economic Survey 2013–2014," http://www .finance.gov.pk/publications/FPS_2013_14.pdf.

100   **Fortune 500 companies . . . got off the ground:** Alec Lynch, "10 Reasons the Best Time to Start a Business Is During a Downturn," *Forbes*, July 24, 2013; "5 Businesses That Started During a Recession," *Investopedia*, http://www.investopedia.com/slide -show/recession-businesses/.

101   **"There's still something tangible":** David Gilboa, "It's Boom Times for Pop-Up Shops as Mobile Shopping Clicks," *NPR All Things Considered*, July 28, 2014.

111   **key to growing an entrepreneurial ecosystem:** Brad Feld, *Startup Communities: Building an Entrepreneurial Ecosystem in Your City* (New York: Wiley, 2012).

113   **Detroit-born patrons are helping:** Stacy Cowley, "Hanging a Single in Detroit," *New York Times*, April 17, 2014; Jennifer Conlin, "Detroit Pushes Back with Young Muscles," *New York Times*, July 3, 2011; Monica Davey, "A Private Boom Amid Detroit's Public Blight," *New York Times*, March 5, 2013.

113   **"both a rescue mission and a business venture:** David Segal, "A Missionary's Quest to Remake Motor City," *New York Times*, April 13, 2013, http://www.nytimes.com/2013/04/14/business/dan -gilberts-quest-to-remake-downtown-detroit.html.

Chapter 4: Goliath-n-David

117   **Eduardo Garcia . . . suspected that was wrong:** Tim Padgett, "Carlos Slim's Embarrassment of Riches," *Time*, July 11, 2007; Eduardo Garcia, interview with author, November 27, 2013.

118   **monopolists are powerful . . . in politics as well:** Ruchir Sharma, *Breakout Nations: In Pursuit of the Next Economic Miracles* (New York: W. W. Norton, 2012).

119   **"us versus them":** Lawrence Weiner, "How Mexico Became So
       Corrupt," *Atlantic*, June 25, 2013.

119   "... **30 percent higher than international averages":** Shar-
       ma, *Breakout Nations*, 76.

120   "... **institutions that made Carlos Slim who he is":** Daron
       Acemoglu and James Robinson, *Why Nations Fail: The Origins of
       Power, Prosperity, and Poverty* (Crown Business, 2012), 40.

127   **$507 billion worth of goods:** Office of the United States Trade
       Representative, Mexico, www.ustr.gov/countries-regions/americas
       /mexico.

127   **top consumer of Coca-Cola per capita:** Roberto A. Ferdman
       and Matt Phillips, "The World's Fattest Major Country Consumes
       an Astounding Amount of Coca-Cola Products," *Quartz*, Novem-
       ber 5, 2013; "Coca-Cola to Launch in Mexico Amid Increased Soft
       Drink Scrutiny," Nasdaq, September 3, 2014.

128   **"If the United States and Mexico are working together":**
       "President Obama Speaks to the People of Mexico," May 3,
       2013, The White House, https://www.whitehouse.gov/photos-and
       -video/video/2013/05/03/president-obama-speaks-people-mexico
       #transcript.

130   **CFE ... charges businesses ... 25 and 60 percent more:** Ari
       Phillips, "Mexico Building Latin America's Largest Solar Farm to
       Replace Old, Dirty Oil-Power Plant," *Think Progress*, February 25,
       2014.

130   **electricity is produced using oil reserves:** "Energy Produc-
       tion," World Bank, www.data.worldbank.org/indicator/EG.EGY.
       PROD.KT.OE; Trading Economics, http://www.tradingecon
       omics.com/mexico/electricity-production-from-oil-gas-and-coal
       -sources-percent-of-total-wb-data.html.

132   **allow private companies to generate their own electric-
       ity:** "Countries: Mexico—Analysis" and "Countries: Mexico—
       Overview/Data," U.S. Energy Information Administration, April
       24, 2014, http://www.eia.gov/countries/country-data.cfm?fips=MX
       and http://www.eia.gov/countries/cab.cfm?fips=MX.

135   **Monterrey Tech tries to be to Mexico:** Dean of Technológico
       de Monterrey, interview with author, April 10, 2013.

136 **whether General Electric . . . would survive:** www.ge.com /about-us/history.

136 **a story about climate change:** "Another Ice Age?," *Time,* June 24, 1974.

137 **a major study on global warming:** National Academy of Sciences, United States Committee for the Global Atmospheric Research Program, National Research Council, *Understanding Climate Change: A Program for Action* (Washington, DC: National Academy of Sciences, 1975), available at http://archive.org/stream /understandingclioounit/understandingclioounit_djvu.txt.

138 **high costs of producing electricity through solar panels:** John Aziz, "Are We on the Cusp of a Solar Energy Boom?," *The Week,* May 21, 2013.

139 **tourism is one of Mexico's largest industries:** Jose Arrioja, "Tourism Seen Jumping to No. 3 Mexico Cash Source by 2018," *Bloomberg,* June 25, 2013.

141 **nearly $200 billion industry:** Advanced Energy Now, 2015 Market Report, www.info.aee.net/aen-2015-market-report.

141 **90 percent of the total increase in greenhouse gases:** 153 Cong. Rec. 2001 (June 18–26, 2007); DEG (Deutsche Investitions und Entwicklungsgesellschaft mbH), "Addressing Climate Risk: Financial Institutions and Emerging Markets," September 2009, https://www.deginvest.de/DEG-Englische-Dokumente/PDFs -Download-Center/AddressingClimateRisk.pdf.

141 **global temperatures have risen nearly 1.5 degrees:** Intergovernmental Panel on Climate Change (IPCC), "Climate Change 2007: Synthesis Report," https://www.ipcc.ch/publications_and _data/ar4/syr/en/spms3.html and https://www.ipcc.ch/pdf/assessment-report/ar4/syr/ar4_syr_spm.pdf; United Nations Framework Convention on Climate Change, "Feeling the Heat: Climate Science and the Basis of the Convention," https://unfccc.int/essential _background/the_science/items/6064txt.php.

141–142 **$108 billion in damage . . . $50 billion in damage:** National Hurricane Center, "Tropical Cyclone Report: Hurricane Sandy, October 22– 29, 2012," February 12, 2013, http://www.nhc.noaa .gov/data/tcr/AL182012_Sandy.pdf; "2013 National Hurricane

Center Forecast Verification Report," April 23, 2014, http://www .nhc.noaa.gov/verification/pdfs/Verification_2013.pdf.

142 **defaulting on a $535 million government-issued loan:** Jeff Brady, "After Solyndra Loss, U.S. Energy Loan Program Turning a Profit," *NPR*, November 13, 2014, http://www.npr. org/2014/11/13/363572151/after-solyndra-loss-u-s-energy-loan -program-turning-a-profit; U.S. Department of Energy, "Key Facts: Solyndra Solar," n.d., http://energy.gov/key-facts-solyndra-solar and "Testimony of Jonathan Silver, Executive Director Loan Programs Office, U.S. Department of Energy Before the Subcommittee on Oversight and Investigations Committee on Energy and Commerce U.S. House of Representatives," September 14, 2011, http://energy.gov/articles/testimony-jonathan-silver-executive -director-loan-programs-office-us-department-energy; U.S. Department of Treasury, Office of Inspector General, "Audit Report," April 3, 2012, http://www.treasury.gov/about/organizational-struc ture/ig/Agency%20Documents/OIG%20Audit%20Report%20 %20-%20Consultation%20on%20Solyndra%20Loan%20Guaran tee%20Was%20Rushed.pdf.

142 **" . . . 'biggest economic opportunity of the twenty-first century'":** John Doerr, *Salvation (and Profit) in Greentech* (video), TED [Technology, Entertainment, Design], March 2007, http:// www.ted.com/talks/john_doerr_sees_salvation_and_profit_in _greentech.

143 **Energy is an emotional issue for Mexicans:** Randal C. Archibold and Elisabeth Malkin, "Mexico's Pride, Oil, May Be Opened to Outsiders," *New York Times*, December 12, 2013.

144 **Unable to compete with low costs:** John Audley, Demetrios G. Papademetriou, Sandra Polanski, and Scott Vaughan, "NAFTA's Promise and Reality: Lessons from Mexico for the Hemisphere," Carnegie Endowment for International Peace, 2004.

144 **NAFTA increased foreign direct investment in Mexico:** Alfredo Cuevas, Miguel Messmacher, and Alejandro Werner, "Foreign Direct Investment in Mexico since the Approval of NAFTA," *World Bank Economic Review* 19, no. 3 (December 2005).

145 **Mexico became Latin America's largest exporter:** "Pacific Pumas," *Economist*, November 15, 2014.

145 **export multiplier effect . . . is much lower in Mexico:** Shannon O'Neil, *Two Nations Indivisible: Mexico, the United States, and the Road Ahead* (New York: Oxford University Press, 2013).

146 **mecca for the rich and famous:** Aric Chen, "In Acapulco, a Return to Glamour," *New York Times*, March 2, 2008.

147 **serious overdevelopment . . . hijacked the city's haloed status:** Nathaniel Parish Flannery, "Can Acapulco Bounce Back?" *Forbes*, December 30, 2014; Nicholas Casey and Alexandra Berzon, "Mexico Tourism Feels Chill of Ongoing Drug Violence," *Wall Street Journal*, June 8, 2011.

150 **" . . . a positive development impact":** Overseas Private Investment Corps, "Section I: Non-Confidential Project Information," n.d., https://www.opic.gov/sites/default/files/files/optima-energia -info-summary-2013.pdf.

150 **startups in "disruptive" sectors . . . need expert guidance:** True North Venture Partners, "Michael J. Ahearn," n.d., http:// www.truenorthvp.com/our-team/michael-j-ahearn/.

152 **"Competition unleashes investment and innovation":** "President Peña Nieto Submits Telecommunications Reform Bill to Congress," March 11, 2013, http://en.presidencia.gob.mx /articles-press/president-pena-nieto-submits-telecommunica tions-reform-bill-to-congress/; Anthony Harrup and Nicholas Casey, "Mexico Goes After Its Monopolies," *Wall Street Journal*, March 11, 2013, http://www.wsj.com/articles/SB1000142412788732 40964045783545439176740444.

152 **Latin American Venture Capital Association . . . "scorecard":** Latin American Private Equity & Venture Capital Association, "Mexico, Colombia and Peru Post Gains for Private Equity & Venture Capital Investors in 2013 LAVCA Scorecard," April 18, 2013, http://lavca.org/2013/04/18/mexico-colombia -and-peru-post-gains-for-private-equity-venture-capital-investors -in-2013-lavca-scorecard/.

154 **on its scale of ease of doing business:** World Bank Group, "Ease of Doing Business in Mexico," *Doing Business*, n.d., http://www

.doingbusiness.org/data/exploreeconomies/mexico; World Bank Group, "Doing Business in Mexico 2014," *Doing Business*, May 29, 2014, http://www.doingbusiness.org/Reports/Subnational-Reports/Mexico.

155 **"I now have the answer: Mexico":** Thomas Friedman, "How Mexico Got Back in the Game," *New York Times*, February 23, 2013, http://www.nytimes.com/2013/02/24/opinion/sunday/friedman-how-mexico-got-back-in-the-game.html.

155 **"Progress . . . crawls on its belly like a guerilla":** Michael Lewis, *The New New Thing: A Silicon Valley Story* (New York: W.W. Norton, 1999), 16.

Chapter 5: "A Little Bit of Extra . . . "

163 **" . . . nothing moves . . . unless the palm . . . is greased":** Amartya Sen, *An Uncertain Glory: India and Its Contradictions* (Princeton, NJ: Princeton University Press, 2013), 95.

163 **scandal involving a Swedish arms company, Bofors:** "Bofors Scandal," n.d., *Wikipedia*, http://en.wikipedia.org/wiki/Bofors_scandal.

164 **ranked India at the bottom of an annual index:** Transparency International, "Corruption Perceptions Index 2007," http://www.transparency.org/research/cpi/cpi_2007; "Corruption Perceptions Index 2009," http://www.transparency.org/research/cpi/cpi_2009/0/; "Corruption Perceptions Index 2011," http://www.transparency.org/cpi2011.

164 **"a shift toward grand corruption":** Milan Vaishnav, quoted in Beina Xu, "Governance in India: Corruption and Bribery," Council on Foreign Relations Backgrounder, September 4, 2014, www.cfr.org/corruption-and-bribery/governance-india-corruption.

164 **pocketed as much as $18.42 billion:** Laveesh Bhandari and Bibek Debroy, *Corruption in India: The DNA and RNA* (New Delhi/Seattle: Konark Publishers, 2011).

165 **it produces "bad decisions":** "A Bad Boom: Fighting Corruption in India," *Economist*, March 13, 2014.

165 **Murthy . . . launched Infosys:** Infosys, "30Years of Infosys: Annual Report 2010–11," http://www.infosys.com/investors

/reports-filings/annual-report/annual/Documents/AR-2011/pdf
/Infosys-AR-11.pdf.

169 **India occupied considerable space on that landscape:**
Thomas Friedman, *The World Is Flat: A Brief History of the Twenty-First Century* (New York: Farrar, Straus and Giroux, 2007).

170 **Indian government allocates . . . between 1 to 4 percent of
the country's GDP:** Aditya Kalra, "India PM Modi Likely to Keep
Tight Rein on Health Spending," Reuters, February 25, 2015, http
://www.reuters.com/article/2015/02/25/india-budget-health
-idUSL4N0VZ3A220150225; Aditya Kalra, "India's Universal
Healthcare Rollout to Cost $26 billion" Reuters, October 30, 2014,
http://in.reuters.com/article/2014/10/30/uk-india-health-idINKB
N0IJoVN20141030.

170 **Private health care in India:** India Brand Equity Foundation, www.ibef.org; Invest India, http://www.investindia.gov.in
/healthcare-sector/.

170 **only 15 percent . . . has access to private . . . coverage:** "India
Tries to Break Cycle of Health-Care Debt," *World Health Organization* 88, no. 7 (July 2010).

171 **More than 80 percent . . . don't get . . . care:** Nasr ul-Hadi,
"India's Emergency Medical Care System in Tatters," *Associated
Press*, September 5, 2012; Manage India, http://www.pmi.org.in
/manageindia/volume5/issue09/cover.story.html.

172 **Heart attacks kill 25 percent:** American Association of
Physicians of Indian Origin, July 24, 2013, http://aapiusa.org
/Media/News-and-Announcements/ArticleID/248/Heart
-Disease-Emerges-As-Top-Killer-Among-Asian-Indians-AA
PI-Focuses-on-Cardiovascular-Diabetes-Stroke.

172 **60 percent of heart disease patients worldwide:** CNN, "Heart
Disease on the Rise in India," *Vital Signs*, April 3, 2009, http://
www.cnn.com/2009/HEALTH/04/02/india.heart.disease/index
.html?iref=24hours; "Heart Disease No. 1 Killer of Indians," DNA
[India], July 28, 2013, http://www.dnaindia.com/health/report-
heart-disease-no1-killer-of-indians-1866673; Andrew Giambrone,
"The Global Geography of Heart Disease," *The Atlantic*, August
23, 2014, http://www.theatlantic.com/health/archive/2014/08/the
-countries-losing-the-fight-against-heart-disease/379021/; American

Association of Physicians of Indian Origin, "Heart Disease Emerges As Top Killer Among Asian Indians, AAPI Focuses on Cardiovascular, Diabetes, & Stroke," *News and Announcements*, July 24, 2013, http://aapiusa.org/Media/News-and-Announcements/ArticleID/248/Heart-Disease-Emerges-As-Top-Killer-Among-Asian-Indians-AAPI-Focuses-on-Cardiovascular-Diabetes-Stroke.

172   **a "high-context" society:** Edward Hall, *Beyond Culture* (New York: Peter Smith, 1992).

173   **Mumbai . . . had become . . . "the Maximum City":** Suketu Mehta, *Maximum City: Bombay Lost and Found* (New York: Knopf, 2004).

179   **Aravind Hospitals operate on hundreds of thousands:** Tina Rosenberg, "A Hospital Network with a Vision," *New York Times*, January 16, 2013.

182   **" . . . choices and opportunity for themselves":** Francis Fukuyama, "The Middle-Class Revolution," *Wall Street Journal*, June 28, 2013.

183   **Indian health care is a $65 billion:** Arpan Sheth and Sriwatsan Krishnan, "India Private Equity Report 2013," Bain, http://www.bain.com/Images/BAIN_REPORT_India_Private_Equity_Report_2013.pdf; India Private Equity Report 2013, Bain; http://www.slideshare.net/harithirumal/report-on-indian-healthcare-industry.

184   **chairman of the technology company Satyam:** Heather Timmons, "Satyam Chief Is Accused of Falsifying Size of Work Force, Then Stealing Payroll," *New York Times*, January 22, 2009.

184   **bids for the Commonwealth Games in 2010:** Jim Yardley, "As Games Begin, India Hopes to Save Its Pride," *New York Times*, October 2, 2010; "India's Commonwealth Games Bill Still Not Paid," *BBC*, October 13, 2011.

184   **telecom ministry had undersold licenses:** Jason Burke, "India's Rulers Lose £22bn in Massive Mobile Phone Scam," *Guardian*, November 16, 2010.

184   **passage of the Lokpal Bill:** Samanth Subramanian, "The Agitator: India's Anti-corruption Crusader Enters Politics," *New Yorker*, September 2, 2013.

184 **to increase transparency and end corruption:** "Tough Steps Against Corruption Soon, Modi Says," *Times of India*, August 19, 2014.

185 **how a good company becomes a great one:** Jim Collins, *Good to Great: Why Some Companies Make the Leap . . . and Others Don't* (New York: HarperBusiness, 2001).

188 **". . . hold leaders accountable":** "Corruption and Development: Not What You Think?" Chrisblattman.com, November 5, 2012.

Chapter 6: Order in the Court

192 **More than 100,000 entrepreneurs and businesspeople:** Joshua Yaffa, "Signs of a Russian Thaw (Toward Business)," *New York Times*, December 28, 2013, http://www.nytimes.com/2013/12/29/business/international/signs-of-a-russian-thaw-toward-business.html; William Pomeranz, "How Russia Puts Business Behind Bars," Reuters, July 5, 2013, http://articles.chicagotribune.com/2013-07-05/news/sns-rt-pomeranz-russia-column-20130705_1_amnesty-russian-entrepreneurs-russian-economy.

192 **". . . social group persecuted on such a large scale":** Rebecca Kesby, "Why Russia Locks Up So Many Entrepreneurs," *BBC World Service*, July 5, 2012.

195 **"two days and two nights":** Julia Ioffe, "Roulette Russian," *New Yorker*, May 17, 2010.

195 **Russia would not "sit on the sidelines":** Dmitry Medvedev, comments at "Open Innovations" conference, Moscow, October 31, 2012.

196 **". . . permeated by a sense of inevitability":** Joshua Yaffa, "Signs of a Russian Thaw (Toward Business)," *New York Times*, December 28, 2013.

197 **only 5.8 percent . . . were . . . entrepreneurs:** Olga Verkhovskaya and Maria Dorokhina, "GEM Russia 2013 Report," GEM: Global Entrepreneurship Monitor, 2013 (can be accessed in Russian from http://www.gemconsortium.org/docs/3769/gem-russia-2013-report).

197 **". . . only a quarter of Russian employment":** "Russia's Economy: Tipping the Scales," *Economist*, May 3, 2014.

197 **over $60 billion in capital and assets:** Andrey Ostroukh, "Russia's Capital Outflows at a Whopping $63 billion in 2013," *Wall Street Journal*, January 17, 2014, http://blogs.wsj.com/emerging europe/2014/01/17/russias-capital-outflows-at-whopping-63 -billion-in-2013/; Anna Kuchna, "Russia Is Facing Record Capital and Investment Outflow," Russia Direct, January 29, 2015, http:// www.russia-direct.org/russian-media/russia-facing-record-capital- -and-investment-outflow; "Net Capital Outflow from Russia to Exceed $150 Billion in 2014," Tass Russian News Agency, January 16, 2015, http://tass.ru/en/economy/771670.

202 **a new leader, Vladimir Vladimirovich Putin:** Masha Gessen, *The Man Without a Face: The Unlikely Rise of Vladimir Putin* (New York: Riverhead Books, 2012).

204 **She was referring to Mikhail Khodorkovsky:** *Khodorkovsky* (video), Kino Lorber Films, 2011.

208 **the most vocal critic:** Evgeny Morozov, *To Save Everything, Click Here* (New York: PublicAffairs, 2013).

209 **Morozov extends his digital critique:** Evgeny Morozov, "Facebook's Gateway Drug," *New York Times*, August 2, 2014.

209 **Gladwell . . . noted in a critique:** Malcolm Gladwell, "Small Change: Why the Revolution Will Not Be Tweeted," *New Yorker*, October 4, 2010.

212 **Alexei Navalny . . . is the most prominent:** Julia Ioffe, "Net Impact: One Man's Cyber-crusade Against Russian Corruption," *New Yorker*, April 4, 2011.

214 **" . . . some elements are having a measure of success":** Gregory L. White, "Once-Jailed Russian Executive Pushes Law Changes," *Wall Street Journal*, December 30, 2009.

214 **World Bank's annual *Doing Business* ranking:** World Bank Group, "Ease of Doing business in Russian Federation," *Doing Business*, n.d., http://www.doingbusiness.org/data/exploreeconomies/russia; World Bank Group, "Doing Business in Russia 2012," *Doing Business*, June 21, 2012, http://www.doingbusiness.org /reports/subnational-reports/russia; World Bank Group, "Economy Rankings," *Doing Business*, n.d., http://www.doingbusiness .org/rankings.

214 " . . . money managers were excited about Russia": Jen Wieczner, "Time to Invest in Russia?," *Fortune*, March 31, 2014.

214 diverted more than $60 billion . . . out of Russia: Andrey Ostroukh, "Russia's Capital Outflows at Whopping $63 Billion in 2013," *Wall Street Journal*, January 17, 2014; Kenneth Rapoza, "Russia Warns of Capital Flight, Market Considers Capital Control," *Forbes*, March 2, 2015.

214 cut its growth forecast . . . from 1.3 to .2 percent: Anna Andrianova, "IMF Cuts Russian Economic Growth Forecast to 0.5% for Next Year," *Bloomberg*, October 1, 2014.

Chapter 7: At the Edges

217 "speak out—directly, without using euphemisms": Taylor Owen, *Disruptive Power: The Crisis of the State in the Digital Age* (Oxford; New York: Oxford University Press, 2015).

220 " . . . where progress is the servant of our needs": Lyndon B. Johnson, "The Great Society" (speech presented at the University of Michigan, Ann Arbor, May 22, 1964) (the text is available at http://www.umich.edu/~bhlumrec/c/commence/1964-Johnson .pdf).

222 "a collision of two forces": Evan Osnos, *Age of Ambition: Chasing Fortune, Truth, and Faith in New China* (New York: Farrar, Straus and Giroux, 2014), 7.

222 meeting at Zhongnanhai in January 2014: "Report on the Work of the Government," http://www.xinhuanet.com/english/2014lh/, http://en.people.cn/102775/209231/index.html; "Lei Jun," http://www.china.org.cn/business/2014-07/29/content_33084378_5. htm; "Keeping Tab on China's Favorites," Frank Talk blog, January 22, 2014, http://www.usfunds.com/investor-library/frank-talk/keeping-tabs-on-chinas-favorites/#.VWY-_FxViko.

224 "a remarkable technological achievement": Brad Stone, "Xiaomi's Phones Have Conquered China: Now It's Aiming for the Rest of the World," *Businessweek*, June 4, 2014.

226 "the technology equivalent of Air Jordans": Brad Stone, "Xiaomi's Phones Have Conquered China," *Bloomsberg Business*,

June 4, 2014, http://www.bloomberg.com/bw/articles/2014-06-04/chinas-xiaomi-the-worlds-fastest-growing-phone-maker.

226 **Xiaomi recorded $11.97 billion in sales:** Gillian Wong, "Xiaomi Says It Sold 61.1 Million Smartphones in 2014," *Wall Street Journal*, January 3, 2015, http://www.wsj.com/articles/xiaomi-says-it-sold-61-1-million-smartphones-in-2014-1420343590; Associated Press, "Smartphone Maker Xiaomi Says 2014 Sales Doubled," *New York Times*, January 4, 2015, http://www.nytimes.com/aponline/2015/01/04/business/ap-as-china-xiaomi.html.

226 **Jun responded to a question in 2013:** "Xiaomi CEO tired of Steve Jobs Comparison," Interview, *CNN Money*, September 12, 2013.

227 **"Chinese brains are just as good as theirs":** *Crocodile in the Yangtze* (video), Taluswood Films, 2012 (can be accessed at http://www.crocodileintheyangtze.com).

227 **China imported and exported $4.16 trillion:** "China Trades Up," *Economist*, January 13, 2014.

227 **China overtook the United States in . . . patent applications filed:** World Intellectual Property Organization, "Global Intellectual Property Filings Up in 2013, China Drives Patent Application Growth," press release, Geneva, December 16, 2014, http://www.wipo.int/pressroom/en/articles/2014/article_0018.html.

228 **China "is not likely to come up with the next world-changing product":** "Q&A: Where Will China's Innovator's Come From?" [interview with Kai-Fu Lee], *BBC News*, October 30, 2012, http://www.bbc.com/news/world-asia-20041320.

228 **"in China, for China":** Gary Rieschel, interview with author, May 13, 2013.

230 **traced the history of the computer industry:** Paul Freiberger and Michael Swaine, *Fire in the Valley: The Making of the Personal Computer* (New York: McGraw-Hill, 1999).

231 **"Business technology can also be implemented":** "Lei Jun: Entrepreneurship," July 31, 2013, Financial Network, http://news.itxinwen.com/2013/0731/515328.shtml.

231 **Lei Jun . . . applied for a job at Kingsoft:** Laura He, "Chinese Billionaire Lei Jun's Long, Twisting Road at Kingsoft," *Forbes*, July

19, 2012, http://www.forbes.com/sites/laurahe/2012/07/19/chinese
-billionaire-lei-juns-long-twisting-road-at-kingsoft/; David Barbo-
za, "In China, an Empire Built by Aping Apple," *New York Times*,
June 4, 2013, http://www.nytimes.com/2013/06/05/business/global
/in-china-an-empire-built-by-aping-apple.html; Brad Stone, "Xiaomi's Phones Have Conquered China: Now It's Aiming for the Rest
of the World," *Businessweek*, June 4, 2014.

233 **"He wasn't being considered in the same breath":** Stone,
"Xiaomi's Phones Have Conquered China."

236 **that number went up to 1.15 billion:** Gartner, "Gartner Says
Worldwide Mobile Phone Sales on Pace to Grow 11 Per Cent
in 2008," press release, August 5, 2008, http://www.gartner.com
/newsroom/id/736913.

237 **two dozen phones in his backpack:** Stone, "Xiaomi's Phones
Have Conquered China."

237 **Deng Xiaoping . . . initiated . . . economic opening:** Osnos,
Age of Ambition; Orville Schell and John Delury, *Wealth and Pow-
er: China's Long March to the Twenty-First Century* (New York:
Random House, 2013).

238 **the government could shrug it off:** James Fallows, "China
Makes, the World Takes," *The Atlantic*, July 1, 2007, http://www
.theatlantic.com/magazine/archive/2007/07/china-makes-the
-world-takes/305987/?single_page=true.

239 **between 330 and 400 million, are in the middle class:** Helen
Wang, "The Chinese Middle Class View of the Leadership Transition," *Forbes*, November 9, 2012, http://www.forbes.com/sites
/helenwang/2012/11/09/the-chinese-middle-class-view-of-the
-leadership-transition/; Tami Luhby, "China's Growing Middle Class," *CNN Money*, April 26, 2012, http://money.cnn
.com/2012/04/25/news/economy/china-middle-class/.

239 **" . . . the difference between New York and Ghana":** Evan
Osnos, Prologue to *Age of Ambition: Chasing Fortune, Truth, and
Faith in New China* (New York: Farrar, Straus and Giroux, 2014).

239 **" . . . posts suitable to graduates are in short supply":** "Employment Plan 2014: China," https://g20.org/wp-content/uploads
/2014/12/g20_employment_plan_china.pdf.

240 **"Great Firewall," a real-life Orwellian mechanism:** "China and the Internet: A Special Report," *Economist*, April 6, 2013.

244 **three times more smartphones than PCs by 2020:** Benedict Evans, "What Does Mobile Scale Mean?" December 18, 2013, http://ben-evans.com/benedictevans/2013/12/18/what-does-mobile-scale-mean?rq=smartphones%20pc.

244 **" . . . to make it simpler and cleaner":** Benedict Evans, "New Questions in Mobile," December 3, 2014, http://ben-evans.com/benedictevans/2014/11/20/time-for-new-questions-in-mobile?rq=smartphones%20pc.

245 **" . . . people and resources where needed":** Fareed Zakaria, "The Challenger," in *The Post American World* (New York: W. W. Norton, 2011), 112.

246 **" . . . self-described 'talent highlands'":** Anne-Marie Slaughter, "America's Edge," *Foreign Affairs* (January/February 2009).

246 **country spends 1.98 percent of its GDP on R&D:** Organisation for Economic Co-operation and Development (OECD), "OECD Estimates of R&D Expenditure Growth in 2012," January 17, 2014, http://www.oecd.org/sti/inno/Note_MSTI2013_2.pdf.

248 **"They must adapt":** Taylor Owen, "Disruptive Power," in *Disruptive Power: The Crisis of the State in the Digital Age* (New York: Oxford University Press, 2015), 22–36.

Index

JASON GARDNER

Elmira Bayrasli works on global development, entrepreneurship, and foreign policy. She is the cofounder of Foreign Policy Interrupted, a lecturer at New York University, and a fellow at the New America Foundation. She began her career at the State Department as an assistant to Madeleine K. Albright. From 2002 to 2005 Elmira lived in Sarajevo, Bosnia-Herzegovina, where she was the chief spokesperson for the OSCE Mission. In 2006 she joined Endeavor, a New York–based organization that supports global entrepreneurs. In 2011 Elmira founded the World Policy Institute's Global Entrepreneurial Project. Her work has appeared in *Forbes, Foreign Affairs,* Techcrunch, VentureBeat, Reuters, the *Wall Street Journal,* and the *New York Times.*

PublicAffairs is a publishing house founded in 1997. It is a tribute to the standards, values, and flair of three persons who have served as mentors to countless reporters, writers, editors, and book people of all kinds, including me.

I. F. STONE, proprietor of *I. F. Stone's Weekly*, combined a commitment to the First Amendment with entrepreneurial zeal and reporting skill and became one of the great independent journalists in American history. At the age of eighty, Izzy published *The Trial of Socrates*, which was a national bestseller. He wrote the book after he taught himself ancient Greek.

BENJAMIN C. BRADLEE was for nearly thirty years the charismatic editorial leader of *The Washington Post*. It was Ben who gave the *Post* the range and courage to pursue such historic issues as Watergate. He supported his reporters with a tenacity that made them fearless and it is no accident that so many became authors of influential, best-selling books.

ROBERT L. BERNSTEIN, the chief executive of Random House for more than a quarter century, guided one of the nation's premier publishing houses. Bob was personally responsible for many books of political dissent and argument that challenged tyranny around the globe. He is also the founder and longtime chair of Human Rights Watch, one of the most respected human rights organizations in the world.

· · ·

For fifty years, the banner of Public Affairs Press was carried by its owner Morris B. Schnapper, who published Gandhi, Nasser, Toynbee, Truman, and about 1,500 other authors. In 1983, Schnapper was described by *The Washington Post* as "a redoubtable gadfly." His legacy will endure in the books to come.

Peter Osnos, *Founder and Editor-at-Large*

MORRIS AUTOMATED INFORMATION NETWORK

0 1804 0307487 3

DATE DUE

JAN - - 2016

WITHDRAWN